THE WARDEN OF ENGLISH

The Life of H. W. Fowler ✿

THE WARDEN OF ENGLISH

The Life of H. W. Fowler

Jenny McMorris

OXFORD
UNIVERSITY PRESS

OXFORD

UNIVERSITY PRESS

Great Clarendon Street, Oxford OX2 6DP

Oxford University Press is a department of the University of Oxford.
It furthers the University's objective of excellence in research, scholarship, and education
by publishing worldwide in

Oxford New York

Athens Auckland Bangkok Bogotá Buenos Aires Cape Town Chennai
Dar es Salaam Delhi Florence Hong Kong Istanbul Karachi
Kolkata Kuala Lumpur Madrid Melbourne Mexico City Mumbai
Nairobi Paris São Paulo Singapore Taipei Tokyo Toronto Warsaw
with associated companies in Berlin Ibadan

Oxford is a registered trade mark of Oxford University Press
in the UK and in certain other countries

British Library Cataloguing in Publication Data
Data available

Library of Congress Cataloging in Publication Data
Data available

ISBN 0-19-866254-8

1 3 5 7 9 10 8 6 4 2

Typeset by Alliance Phototypesetters
Printed in Great Britain by
T. J. International Ltd
Padstow, Cornwall

To my beloved sons,
Ewan *and* Kester McMorris,
*who have constantly supported
and encouraged me*

✧

Contents

List of Plates

Plate 1: Henry watching the Ten Mile race at Sedbergh in 1899.
Reproduced by kind permission of the Headmaster of Sedbergh School.

Plate 2: Henry relaxing on the deck of an unidentified ship. Photograph taken from a lantern slide.
Reproduced by kind permission of the Headmaster of Sedbergh School.

Plate 3: Studio portrait of Henry probably taken in St Peter Port at about the time of his marriage.
Reproduced by kind permission of Mrs M. E. Pippin.

Plate 4: Jessie Fowler. A studio portrait probably taken before her marriage to Henry in St Peter Port.
Reproduced by kind permission of Mrs M. E. Pippin.

Plate 5: Henry's Cottage at Les Reveaux.
Reproduced by kind permission of the Secretary to the Delegates of Oxford University Press.

Plate 6: Moulin de Haut in the early twentieth century.
Reproduced by kind permission of Guernsey Evening Press.

Plate 7: Henry and Raven.
Reproduced by kind permission of the Secretary to the Delegates of Oxford University Press.

Plate 8: Henry and Jessie, taken in the garden of Le Moulin de Haut in 1924.
Reproduced by kind permission of the Secretary to the Delegates of Oxford University Press.

Plate 9: Henry in sporting attire.
Reproduced by kind permission of the Secretary to the Delegates of Oxford University Press.

Plate 10: Florence Shayler, the devoted nurse to the elderly Fowlers.
Reproduced by kind permission of the States of Guernsey.

Introduction

On a snowy morning in the winter of 1985 I first encountered the archives of the *Oxford English Dictionary* and its 'children' stored in an annexe behind the dictionary offices in 37a St Giles, Oxford. In a large collection of cardboard boxes I found the working papers and correspondence of a distinguished group of editors and their assistants. Among their complaints and demands and the graphic descriptions of ill health which Victorian academics sent to their correspondents, it was refreshing to find many letters from Henry Watson Fowler, a man whose quiet courage and gentle humour made him stand out from the rest. Henry's lengthy correspondence with the University Press covered his work, at first with a younger brother, Frank, on several books, including a first success with *The King's English*, followed by the first edition of the *Concise Oxford Dictionary*. After Frank's death Henry worked on alone finishing the Pocket dictionary, which they had begun together, and then producing the work for which he is still remembered, *Modern English Usage*.

At our first meeting Henry's attractive personality appealed to me, and my search for the background to the life and work of this remarkable man began. Unfortunately, research proved rather difficult: no cache of family papers has survived and no survivors remain to be questioned, leaving me to piece together the details of the Fowlers' lives. With this lame excuse I apologize for any errors in this story, and emphasize that no faults can be attributed to those who helped me and whose kindness I am anxious to acknowledge here while apologizing to any omitted from my expressions of gratitude.

I quickly discovered that Henry showed the most remarkable taste, or good fortune, in choosing places to live and work; I was able to spend time in most delightful locations while investigating his life. During two very enjoyable visits to Guernsey and in response to many enquiries on other occasions, the island archivist, Dr Darryl Ogier, gave me invaluable help with local matters, particularly with the complications of the legal system. Marie de Garis, a most distinguished expert on the Guernsey language, talked to me about her memories of the passing athlete, and

Alfred Lainé passed on his father's experiences of life at the Moulin de Haut. I was helped also by the Librarian and staff at the excellent Priaulx Library. Mary Riggs from Wantage came with me on both my island visits, ably supporting my researches and explorations.

In Cumbria I visited Sedbergh School, where the archivist, Elspeth Griffiths, showed me the archives and photograph collection and kindly answered my enquiries on later occasions too as I attempted to unravel Henry's teaching career. The staff of the County Record Office in Kendal dealt also most patiently with my enquiries.

On two visits to Devon I spent much time in the Record Office in Exeter, where the staff were also most helpful, and I made use of the excellent facilities provided by the Westcountry Studies Library. In Buckfastleigh I was helped by Sandra Coleman, whose vast local knowledge was invaluable, and by Mary Maguire, who kindly allowed me to see the deeds of the London Inn.

In Hinton St George, Rosemary and Graham Tout generously allowed me to visit Henry and Jessie's last home and showed me other places of interest in the area connected with them. Captain and Mrs T.G.F. Hardy allowed me to see the pools in their garden where Henry swam during his time in the village. Mrs Betty Ireland described her memories of Henry and Jessie stopping at the family farm for tea on their way back from town, and Mrs Mavis Pippin talked to me of life in the Fowler household as seen through the eyes of a visiting child and allowed me to reproduce the two fine studio portraits seen here.

Many other local history centres proved useful, particularly the libraries at Eastbourne, Tunbridge Wells, and Oxford, the Oxfordshire Record Office and the Centre for Kentish Studies, Maidstone. In London I was helped at the Greater London Record Office, Westminster City Archives, Southwark Archives, Hammersmith and Fulham Archives, and the local history library at Kensington and Chelsea Central Library.

School and college archivists at St Paul's School, Marlborough College, and Rugby School, and at Corpus Christi and Balliol Colleges in Oxford and Christ's College and Peterhouse in Cambridge, dealt kindly with my enquiries. Jonathan Harrison, Special Collections Librarian at St John's College, Cambridge, gave me particular assistance with understanding the complications of Robert Fowler's academic career, and also helped with my access to the Fowler war letters kept there. Extracts from these letters are reproduced by permission of the Master and Fellows of St John's College, Cambridge.

At Oxford University Press Susie Dent first gave me the chance to pursue this dream, for which I shall always be grateful. Alysoun Owen guided me expertly through many problems and Elizabeth Knowles and Helen Cox helped me during the final stages. Many others provided support, encouragement, and advice: Peter Foden, Susan Lloyd, Martin Maw, Helen Rozier, Penny Silva, John Simpson, Edmund Weiner, and Drs Sara Kirkham and Ewan McMorris on medical matters. Many read all or part of the manuscript and helped me with their comments; Lynda Mugglestone, Philip Durkin, Marie de Garis, Elspeth Griffiths, Susan Lloyd, Kester McMorris, Darryl Ogier, and Michael Riggs.

Juliet Field most patiently supported me with daily encouragement, read the manuscript as it first appeared, and coped with my frequent bouts of self-doubt. Simon Winchester, visiting the archives at Oxford, encouraged me and set an admirable example of drive and determination. My sons too were always encouraging, and persuaded me to begin turning my researches into something more substantial. To all I offer my heartfelt thanks.

Jenny McMorris

Abbreviations and Symbols

b.	born
BBM	H. W. Fowler, *Between Boy and Man* (Watts, 1908)
BL	British Library
BLib.	Bodleian Library, Oxford
CL	Letters of G. G. Coulton deposited in the Library of St John's College, Cambridge
COD	*Concise Oxford Dictionary*
d.	died
DNB	*Dictionary of National Biography*
DtoJ	H. W. Fowler, *Rhymes of Darby to Joan* (J. M. Dent, 1931)
GGC	G. G. Coulton, *H. W. Fowler* (SPE 43, Clarendon Press, 1934).
HSM	H.S. Milford
KE	F. G. Fowler, and H. W. *The King's English* (Clarendon Press, 1906)
Lucian	H. W. and F. G. Fowler, trans., *The Works of Lucian* (Clarendon Press, 1905)
m.	married
MEU	H. W. Fowler, *A Dictionary of Modern English Usage* (Clarendon Press, 1926)
MPF	H. W. Fowler *More Popular Fallacies* (London, 1905)
OED	*Oxford English Dictionary*
OEDA	Oxford English Dictionary Archives
OUPA	Oxford University Press Archives
PRO	Public Record Office, Kew
SA	H. W. Fowler, *Sentence Analysis* (Clarendon Press, 1906)
SCV	H. W. Fowler, *Some Comparative Values* (Blackwell, 1929)
SL	Sedbergh Letters: letters between H. G. Hart and H. W. Fowler, deposited by G. G. Coulton in the Library of St John's College, Cambridge
SM	H. W. Fowler, *Si Mihi!.* (Brown, Langham, and Co., London, 1907)
SPE	Society for Pure English
TAG	Diaries of T.Anstey Guthrie deposited in the British Library
TLS	*Times Literary Supplement*
WL	H. W. Fowler's letters written to his wife, Jessie, during his war service, deposited in the Library of St John's College, Cambridge
WWH	H. W. Fowler, *If Wishes Were Horses* (George Allen & Unwin, 1929)

Family Tree

Henry *m* Sarah
(1785–1868)   (1791–1845)

Robert *m* Caroline Watson
(1823–1879)   (1831–1895)

John Townsend *m* Adelaide
(1830–1912)

6 others

Harry de Galle Lewis *m* Madeline
(d. 1927)

Henry Watson
(1858–1933)
m
Jesse
Marian
Wills
(1861–1930)

Charles
Robert
(1859–1929)

Alexander
Wilson
(1861–1879)

Edward
Seymour
(1864–1886)

Edith
Caroline
(1865–1914)

Arthur
John
(1868–1939)
m
Ada
Lemarchand
(1863–1925)

Francis
George
(1870–1918)
m
Una Jane
Mary Maud
Godfrey
(1889–1936)

Herbert
Samuel
(1873–1905)

Foreword

From time to time letters of inquiry, admiration, or amiable dispute still arrive at the University Press in Oxford, addressed to Henry Watson Fowler, though it is now nearly seventy years since his death. The older inhabitants of the pretty little Somerset village of Hinton St George still just remember him—the slightly terrifying 'HW', sitting at his desk in his cool limestone house, immersed in patient scholarship. And the book that all his thinkings and ponderings created, and which prompts the continuing light drizzle of optimistic letters to the Press—the blue volume known formally as *A Dictionary of Modern English Usage*, but which we all call simply 'Fowler'— remains with us, as fresh and stern as though the author were still alive, advising and cajoling all of us to write and speak more fluently and properly.

The book, 'the general vade-mecum of English writing' as its author once described it, advises and cajoles in such a school-masterly way that we can still just hear the voice, quavering with age and infirmity perhaps, but somehow still clear enough to allow us to suppose indeed that Henry Fowler might be here amongst us still, offering his kindly counsel whenever we are lexically challenged, verbally stumped, or simply know not what to say.

There seems to have been more than a little of old Mr Chips about this curious, eccentric, decent, and very English man. Few can be the households that have not been touched in some way by his rather tweedy, tobacco-scented, bespectacled teachings. The schoolboy who wonders at the difference between a semi-colon and its cousin; the secretary who needs to know if it is better to write *alright* or *all right*; the noisy uncle who wants to settle 'once and for all' the vexing argumentation over the split infinitive— all of such people, and all of us, turn to Fowler with equal and familiar ease. I sometimes think it is as if we are picking up the telephone, hearing it ring on the polished mahogany side table in the far-away, flag-stoned Somerset hall, and asking questions of the kindly old gent who answers, certain he will set us right.

Henry Fowler was an unusual man, it is true. We might have ragged him, with his strange shyness and his eccentric dress, his passions for early morning runs and all those swims, those endless swims, in water as cold as could be borne. I cherish one image, not a scholarly one at all: it is of Henry Fowler in what looks today like an absurdly old-fashioned swimming costume, all zebra stripes and inconveniently sited lumps, just back from his morning dip in the waters off the island of Guernsey, where he and brother Frank then lived, ready for a day of lexicographical toils. Yet whatever the degree of mild amusement such memories trigger, we are—just as the schoolboys were with Mr Chips—inexpressibly fond of the old man too, and we perhaps worried there might come a time when he was no longer around to dispense his wisdom and his cool authority—after which, we fretted, to whom would we turn in our distress? But of course there was never a need to fret: 'Fowler' seems always to be there, the book if not the man, reprinted again and again, a constant comfort.

All his doings seem to have been imbued with decency, goodness, principle, and propriety. He believed in etiquette, but was not a pedant. He was correct, but not too stuffy. He was careless of money, sometimes sending back to Oxford sums the Press insisted on paying him for his works. He seemed in manner neither to have been pompous nor pretentious. He just seemed to know what was right, he taught it, and he lived as he taught. Despite his crippling shyness he managed to project always a comfortable intimacy—an image so very different from the aloofness of most dictionary men, and one that has endeared him to us down the years.

And he was wonderfully kind, as one instance powerfully suggests. Though he cared not one whit for the teachings of the church, he knew that his abundant wife Jessie had loved them, and had particularly loved the peals of the broken bells of Hinton St George. Once she had died he arranged, quite anonymously, that they should be repaired and re-hung once again so that she could hear them ring perfectly from her place of rest.

It saddened him that young Frank, who until his death from consumption after the Great War was his co-editor on earlier dictionaries, could never share in the pleasure he won for himself from the reception of his *Modern English Usage*, and so he dedicated it to his memory. 'I think of it as it should have been,' he wrote, 'with its prolixities docked, its dullnesses enlivened, its fads eliminated, its truths multiplied. He had a nimbler wit, a better sense of proportion, and a more open mind, than his twelve-year-older partner'.

A sense of goodness and decency to the end seems to have infused this strange, unsocial, learned, and endearingly funny-peculiar figure. Read about both him and his unforgettable books in the pages that follow, and know that thanks to a remarkable intellectual partnership forged over the years between the late Henry Watson Fowler and his wonderfully enthusiastic admirer Jenny McMorris, all grammar, syntax, and style will be impeccable, and the story poignant, impossible to forget, and exceeding well told.

Simon Winchester

1

Beginnings

❧

T he young man reading a newspaper in a corner seat on the train into Paddington is travelling from Oxford on his way home to Tunbridge Wells, that epitome of genteelness. He is just twenty-one, dark-haired with blue eyes; although small, about 5 feet 6 inches tall,[1] he is sturdy and clearly fit, with the physique of an athlete and swimmer. He sits quietly reading and, being extremely shy, if approached will only respond with a brief, nervous smile; his closest friends alone experience his gentle humour and ready wit. This is Henry Watson Fowler, an Oxford student with a scholarship at Balliol College, although at present, in May 1879, he is not making his mark academically despite a promising beginning at school.

This reserved youth will endure years of drudgery in the classroom before casting aside his chosen career and setting out fearlessly, a middle-aged man, to make a new life as a writer. His accumulated experience and natural flair, joining with his stoical application to his work, will eventually bring his name to a book which will capture the imagination of the English-speaking world in an area where professionals have difficulty in sustaining interest: the study of the use and misuse of the English language. His dictionaries too, patiently constructed with the assistance of a much-loved younger brother, will be found in countless school satchels and on bookshelves in homes, schools, libraries, and offices; they will be taken down and pored over by students both at home and overseas, by anxious crossword lovers and challenged Scrabble players, and by curious readers and perplexed writers. Years of trial lie before Henry as the train carries him towards the capital, but this quiet Englishman will live his life with charming eccentricity and considerable natural courage. His present worries occupy him now, however, for he is travelling home to the bedside of his dying father, Robert, and to offer his support to his distressed mother, Caroline.

✤ ✤ ✤

Earlier Fowler journeys may have come back into Henry's mind as he journeyed home, memories of childhood, with mounds of luggage and a troop of dishevelled small boys. The Fowlers would have gone back to their roots, for both Caroline and Robert had been born in Devon, and their families still lived there when Henry was a child. Arriving with their growing brood the Fowler parents would perhaps have chosen first to visit Plymouth, and Grandfather Henry Fowler, for whom the eldest of their boys had been named; an ageing widower, he was a lodger with distant family members in Cambridge Street, but did also visit his son's home in Tunbridge Wells. When Henry senior died in 1868, when his eldest grandson was ten, a codicil to his will declared that all books in his house had been borrowed from his son Robert and should be returned to him.

Robert Fowler and his father, Henry, were remarkable men, and had worked hard in very different fields, Henry as a builder in a Devon village and Robert as an academic and later a schoolmaster. Henry and his wife, Sarah, were living in Buckfastleigh[2] when Robert, their elder son, was born in 1823; a younger brother, John Townsend Fowler, arrived seven years later. Henry Fowler was not a local man, but came originally from the village of Yealmpton, about 16 miles away in the direction of Plymouth. He had settled in Buckfastleigh with his wife before the two boys were born, and worked as a builder after beginning his career as a carpenter. Henry had clearly considerable entrepreneurial flair, for in 1833 he bought for £610 a long lease on the London Inn,[3] a property in Fore Street, Buckfastleigh. He made many changes and additions to the building; when he finally sold on the lease, it had been converted into fourteen dwellings, workshops, and shops, the occupiers including Boarder, a shoemaker, Searle, a bookseller, and Crannaford, a thatcher. The family may have lived in the building, but when the boys were older and Sarah had died of tuberculosis, Grandfather Henry, left alone, moved into Plymouth. He kept his interest in the property for a time, but eventually sold up, perhaps in need of money as he grew older.

Although no trace remains of where Henry's two boys, Robert and John,[4] were at school, they were certainly exceptional young men, and both became schoolmasters. When the new Diocesan Training College[5] opened in Cathedral Close in Exeter in January 1840, one of the first four students was seventeen-year-old Robert[6] who spent eighteen months training as a teacher there, a course for which his father would have paid £20 a year. Robert's first post as a schoolmaster was at a private school in Vicarage Street, Barnstaple, run by a Mr Snow, who later praised his assistant in a report to the Training College, regretting his loss when he moved on to a similar post in Plymouth. After this Robert left his home county and taught in Staffordshire and London, before, still in his early twenties, he was appointed as Vice-Master of the Royal Military Asylum for Children of Soldiers of the Regular Army[7] in Chelsea, a post obtained against stiff competition from graduate schoolmasters; perhaps it was this experience which persuaded him that he should try for similar qualifications himself, and he was soon off to become a student again.

In 1849 Robert went up to Cambridge and was admitted as a sizar to St John's College, facing once more tough competition; sizars had at one time been required to perform some menial duties in return for financial assistance during their time as students, but these duties had ceased in the late eighteenth century and only the monetary advantages remained. Robert stayed for five terms at St John's, doing well in the college exams and winning book prizes for his successes as a mathematician. He then moved to Christ's College as a pensioner, a student without financial support from his college, but did eventually gain a scholarship which would have brought him both status and some financial support. At Christ's also he performed well, being placed first in his year in 1852 and second in the following year, again winning valuable book prizes and other awards for his work and finally graduating with a first-class degree; mathematicians placed in this class were termed 'wranglers' and Robert was sixteenth wrangler in his year. After all this academic success he was ordained,[8] and with this necessary clerical qualification was elected Finch and Baines Fellow at Christ's and later Lady Margaret Fellow. At the end of 1856, however, he returned to Devon and married, by which act he vacated his fellowship.

Rummaging through his memories behind his newspaper in the London train, Henry might have turned from Grandfather Henry and the excitements of Plymouth, the ships and the sea, and remembered country holidays with the Watsons, his mother's family. Leaving the train at Totnes, the family would have travelled the short distance to Dartington to be met by a surviving grandmother, Harriett; Caroline's father, Humphry Watson, had died not long before her marriage. He had for many years been the tenant[9] of the farm at Dartington Hall, and after his death his eldest son, Henry Harris Watson, continued farming there.

Caroline and Robert were married in the parish church at Dartington in December 1856; as the church was almost in the farmyard, the marriage party would have had a very short walk to the ceremony.[10] Robert must have known Caroline since childhood, for Dartington is only 5 miles from Buckfastleigh, and although she was seven years younger, she had older brothers with whom he might have been at school.

✧ ✧ ✧

After this Devon wedding the young couple set out for Kent, where Robert had secured a post as mathematics master at Tonbridge School. Here their first two sons were born, Henry Watson Fowler, the young man on the London train, on 10 March 1858 and Charles Robert seventeen months later. Robert remained only briefly at Tonbridge School before moving the short distance to Tunbridge Wells, where the family lived at 3 Lion Terrace and where in 1861 a third son, Alexander Wilson Fowler, was born.

During these years Robert published three mathematics textbooks, the first two on algebra[11] during his time at Tonbridge and, after the move to Tunbridge Wells, a small volume of answers to the questions set for the admission examinations at the Royal Military Academy, Woolwich. This tied in with his new post as assistant to a local headmaster, Robert Jones, at Clyde House in Garden Road; here the pupils were young men in their late teenage years who were being prepared for careers in the army and entrance to the military academies such as Woolwich.

By the time a fourth boy arrived in 1864, Edward Seymour Fowler, always known as Seymour, the family had moved again, to Grosvenor House in the town, and here Robert began his own school, on similar lines presumably to Robert Jones's establishment, preparing youths for military examinations. The house, demolished long ago, must have been large, for in 1871[12] there were, in addition to the family, twelve pupils living in, with a cook, nurse, four maids, and a young curate, William Thompson, who assisted with the teaching; in later years Henry was to show a preference for a quiet, self-sufficient home life, perhaps fuelled by distaste for this bustling household. The school was clearly a great success, and Robert, a 'burly bearded clergyman-coach',[13] as a family friend later described him, must have been a notable figure in the town. As the school expanded so too did the Fowler family: Edith Caroline arrived in 1865, Arthur John in 1868, Francis George in 1870, and finally Herbert Samuel in 1873.

It was to this family that Henry was returning on his melancholy train journey, to his parents, Caroline and Robert, his six brothers, and his small sister. Charles was by that time at Christ's College Cambridge, his father's old college, and Seymour was away at school at Marlborough, but perhaps they too were making their way home to their father's bedside.

✤ ✤ ✤

Tunbridge Wells was a very fashionable town, providing facilities for visitors who came to take the celebrated waters for their health. Chalybeate springs had been discovered in the seventeenth century and at first the site, popularized by royal patrons such as Charles II visiting with his court, was just a resort for summer visitors, who drank the waters but stayed six miles away in Tonbridge. In the nineteenth century it grew to be a sizeable and flourishing town with 29,000 inhabitants, and was no longer deserted in winter; there were the many private schools which filled all fashionable watering places, both seaside and spa towns such as this, and hotels and boarding houses for the water-drinkers. These visitors to the springs were met by 'dippers', women who kept clean the granite basins into which the water trickled and handed over glasses to the visitors, giving them sage leaves afterwards to clean their teeth.

It seems perhaps odd to a modern observer that in a town which depended on its water and would naturally take great care of its supply, Robert Fowler should die of typhoid fever, a water-borne disease, but it was of course still quite common at that time; Prince Albert, the prince consort, had died from it some years before. Robert became ill on about 4 May and at first appeared to be fighting the disease; but a week before his death chest problems complicated the course of the illness and he died on 31 May 1879, aged only fifty-six. His eldest son, Henry, who had been with him, registered the death and began to help his mother sort out the family's affairs.

❧ ❧ ❧

Caroline Fowler is rather a shadowy figure in her eldest son's story, for he mentions her only once, recounting a rather foolish tale of his own snobbery as a schoolboy. He was embarrassed by her habit of trimming lamps and polishing glass in the house each morning, and felt that she did this because there were not enough servants to allow her to leave these things alone as, he believed, a lady should; she had explained to him that servants rarely did these small tasks satisfactorily. Only later did he understand the financial burden of educating eight children and that his mother needed to do some small jobs around the house. Although the boys were sent to schools where they won scholarships to help with the fees, their education was still an expensive business.

With Caroline and her eldest brother, Henry Harris Watson of Dartington, Henry was appointed an executor of his father's will and a trustee of the remaining funds. Caroline was guardian to the other seven children who were still minors, ranging from Charles, who was nineteen, down to Sam, aged only five. Henry nevertheless took his duties as the eldest son very seriously. Sixty years later Arthur, one of the younger children, was to confide in a friend that, left 'in loco parentis' at this early age, Henry had ruled the family 'with a rod of iron' and that 'they all stood in wholesome awe of him';[14] some were to be more successful in resisting this steely older brother than others.

Robert had left provision in his will for any son or group of sons who might be interested to take over his school, but as they were all so young this course was clearly impossible. Caroline also needed to raise money by the sale of the school as a going concern to keep and to continue educating her family. So the death of her husband was followed by the loss of her home, and further tragedy was to come.

Alexander Fowler, the third child of the family, seems never to have been well, and was not fit enough to be sent away to school with the other boys. He had suffered from kidney disease for some time, but despite this the decision was made to send him, an unfit eighteen-year-old, on the long and arduous journey to Australia, where two uncles had settled some time before. The children of one of these uncles visited England years later and an 'invasion of hitherto unknown Australian cousins' was described by Arthur Fowler. The uncles had left home with very little money and, Arthur explained, 'one made £70,000, the other a slightly smaller number of children'.[15] The uncle responsible for Alexander was George Harris Watson, another of Caroline's brothers, who had settled at Malmsbury[16] in Victoria; the largest nearby town was Bendigo,[17] the centre of an extensive gold mining area, perhaps the reason for the two adventurers leaving England. Alexander arrived there in October 1879 and survived only for six weeks, dying on 21 November. A witness, with George Watson, to Alexander's burial[18] in the cemetery at Malmsbury, was Walter Watson Hannaford, a son of one of Caroline's older sisters, Anne, and perhaps Alexander's companion on the journey out from England.

After the loss of her own home Caroline moved between two of her sisters; all her children were soon at boarding school or university and must have spent their holidays with sympathetic family members during this troubled period. Caroline stayed at times with Sarah, her youngest sister, who was also a widow and lived in central London, keeping a boarding house in St George's Street, near Oxford Circus. At other times she stayed with Maria, one of her older sisters, who had married well and was a prosperous Devon grocer's wife, living near Newton Abbot. A friend of Henry's, writing much later, asserted that after their father's death 'the boys had absolutely no settled home but met wherever their mother was in the holidays',[19] and this was certainly true for the first two years. This critical remark does, however, reveal a considerable lack of sensitivity to Caroline's problems. It would inevitably have been some time before Robert Fowler's will and the accompanying problems were sorted out and Caroline could dispose of the school, but in late 1881 or early 1882 she was able to take a house in London, where she could make a home for her family.

✿ ✿ ✿

With all as far as possible settled, Henry was able to return to Balliol and his disrupted education. This had begun long before, when he was sent to a private boarding school in Germany some time before 1870—perhaps rather a surprising decision, as he would have been aged at most eleven. Henry only mentioned this school once in a story, where he described receiving pots of jam in a hamper from home which he intended eating 'on bread like a Christian'. His companions would have none of this politeness; '"*Wie kindisch!*"—*what a baby trick!*—they cried, and with one consent dipped their spoons into it for direct transference to their mouths'.[20] This early experience of studying in German could well have prompted Henry's lifelong interest in language. He certainly often used German phrases when writing, although perhaps not as often as Latin and Greek; on receiving proofs of a new book, for instance, he wrote back to the publishers with delight about the 'ten clean sheets on sumptuous paper', adding the comment 'herrliche Pracht' ('glorious luxury').[21] In this same book, *The King's English*, he did warn against using German phrases in writing as few then understood the language; modern languages were taught in very few schools at that time, although Henry, who went on to Rugby School, was able to continue with German there.

Henry entered Rugby in January 1871, a nervous small boy of twelve. Life at Rugby would have been hard for such a shy youngster, although his natural wit seems to have helped him through this very tough world. The older boys disciplined the younger ones and organized the sport, and at that time fagging was still part of school life. Henry rarely mentioned his time at school, but described one scene suggesting a life of Dickensian grimness. On Saturday evenings the boys in his house met in a large room for boxing, all standing round in a ring to watch the spectacle. After the older boys had finished their own bouts they selected for their amusement younger ones to fight each other. It was usually the nervous and apprehensive who were chosen, for 'boxing was recognized to be especially good for the reluctant'.[22] Henry quickly realized that by standing at the front and looking enthusiastic he was far less likely to be chosen than if he tried to escape notice by hiding at the back of the crowd.

Henry had entered the school at a very difficult time in its long history, although as a smaller boy he probably would not at first have been aware of it. A new headmaster, Henry Hayman, had been appointed in 1870 and the school's fortunes rapidly declined during his time. His appointment had not been popular, and many of his decisions as headmaster led to disputes with masters, parents, and the older boys; Henry's tutor in School House, E. A. Scott, had been involved in numerous disagreements and would have been dismissed had it been possible for Hayman to do so. Discipline suffered during this unsettled time and there was a decline in the number of boys in the school, leading inevitably to the dismissal of some staff. After this disastrous period the situation was retrieved by the appointment in 1874 of a new head, a former pupil, Thomas William Jex-Blake, who quickly restored the fortunes of the school.

Sport, of course, was very important in all boys' schools, and particularly at the home of rugby football. Henry took little interest in the game at school, although later as a schoolmaster he did play and referee with enthusiasm. Teams had in earlier times included as many as three hundred boys, but were by this time down to twenty a side, although at Rugby some matches still continued with great numbers of players and Henry would perhaps have been involved in these; the first match of the season, for instance, was a great spectacle in which the sixth form, the top two years, played the rest of the school. Running, on the other hand, was always to be important to Henry, and cross-country running had been organized at Rugby since the eighteenth century, with twelve named runs described and mapped out. The school magazine, *The Meteor*, recorded Henry's successes; on a miserable autumn afternoon in 1876, for example, he came third in the Barby Hill run, taking just over 48 minutes, in dreadful conditions, as the ground was very wet and it was impossible to run over some ploughed fields on the course. Swimming too was to be an enthusiasm for Henry throughout his life and this also began at Rugby, for a new pool was opened soon after Jex-Blake became headmaster, as his gift to the school.

On the academic side Henry was a great success, studying Latin and Greek as his principal subjects and excelling in Greek; this was at a time when the importance of classics in a public-school education was beginning to decline and its place in the curriculum was a matter for discussion; in the school debating society, of which Henry was for a time secretary, he spoke in a debate on classical education to oppose a motion 'that preposterous prominence is given in modern Public Schools to classical studies'. Rugby had been the first English school to teach science, but Henry chose French and German, which were the alternative. Prizes came his way for English and Greek, and in his final year he carried off Dr James's Prize for Greek Iambi with a translation into Greek verse of a piece from Shelley's *Prometheus*. This he read at the final Speeches of his school career, before a large audience in the assembly room of the town hall at Rugby, having first played the part of a Boeotian with birds and fish in an extract from the *Acharnians* of Aristophanes. Henry had had earlier experience of acting on such occasions, and at the previous year's Speeches had played Conrad in an extract from *Much Ado About Nothing* and Armande, a bluestocking, in Molière's *Les Femmes Savantes*; the local newspaper unfortunately condemned 'the ladies' in the last piece, reporting that they 'were so anxious to speak in true lady-like fashion that their remarks were almost inaudible'.[23]

The greatest influence on Henry during his time at Rugby came in the later years of his school career, when he joined the form known as 'the Twenty' and met its master, Robert Whitelaw,[24] who prepared boys for the work they would meet in their final school years and managed to impart his own great love of classics and English literature to those in his care. He was to teach this form for forty-three years and was remembered by many boys; some recalled his teaching, as Henry did, but many perhaps treasured other details such as his tricycle, with two saddles positioned side by side, on which amazing machine some boys were allowed to accompany him. More than fifty years later Henry remembered how, when he was ill in the sanatorium for three weeks during his final year, Whitelaw would come in and read to him 'lyrics of Browning in that impassioned voice & manner of his'.[25] Whitelaw died in 1917, but Henry had always kept in touch with the older man, even maintaining the correspondence when with the army in France.

At the end of his school career Henry became head of his house, School House, with all the duties involved. Some were serious, involving discipline and such matters, others rather less so. Lamb-singing, for instance, was inflicted on the 'lambs' or new boys in the house, who were required to stand on a bed in one of the dormitories and sing to the head of house and rugby captain sitting on another bed. If the boy's efforts were considered acceptable then he escaped punishment; if not, the assembled judges and audience would begin singing 'Rule Britannia', and the 'lamb' would be required to drink an appalling concoction of salt, mustard, tooth-powder, and other disgusting ingredients. Henry would have endured this as a small boy as well as presiding over it as head of house; his adult attitude to singing was perhaps coloured a little by this experience, for, although he could appreciate the efforts of others, he later revealed that he only sang a little Gilbert and Sullivan himself when sure that he was quite alone.

Three years after Henry's arrival at Rugby he was joined there by a young cousin, Harry de Galles Lewis Fowler, the eldest son of his father's brother John. Harry had been sent home from India for school and university and was under the care at first of his uncle Robert and, after his death, of Caroline; on the day of the 1881 census he was staying with her at her sister's house, making at least one extra child for her to provide a home for at this time. The arrival of this boy may have been irritating to Henry, whose world Rugby was until he appeared; in an uncharacteristically spiteful note which perhaps indicated Henry's resentment at this intrusion, he later referred to the seeming pretentiousness of the 'de Galles' in his cousin's name (which was only added because the child had been born on board a ship off the Pointe de Galles on the coast of Sri Lanka). Eventually Harry followed his cousin Henry to Balliol, perhaps fuelling his resentment even more; certainly there was no lasting friendship between the two.[26]

Henry had made a great success of his time at Rugby, managing despite his shyness to take part in drama and debating, doing well academically, and presiding over School House as its head. He won a scholarship to Balliol and left in 1877 with a reputation for brilliance and a glorious academic future in front of him.

✤ ✤ ✤

After being a most important young man at Rugby Henry moved to the glittering world of Oxford in the late 1870s, and his natural shyness prevented him from making a mark socially. He made few lasting friendships during these years, only one or two fellow students appearing in his story later. One young Irishman, Terence Woulfe Flanagan, did become a friend and was to play a very significant role in Henry's later life; he returned to Ireland after his Oxford degree to study medicine in Dublin, but worked in London later as a doctor in Chelsea, where he and Henry were able to meet again. Other Rugby boys went up to Balliol in Henry's year, but he was not particularly close to any of them. A later friend recounted lists of the distinguished men at college with Henry but he made no friendships among them, seeming only to have admired them from afar. They were also, it is said, 'impressed by his reserve and his refinement,'[27] but although he was respected he made few friends.

Henry took little part in Oxford sport, although he did row for Balliol in Torpids, the boat races held between the colleges every spring. He began, however, a habit which was to continue throughout his life, stopping only a few weeks before his death; a morning run was followed by a swim in the sea or some convenient pool or river; at Oxford he ran in the University Parks and swam at the bathing place for gentlemen on the river Cherwell, Parson's Pleasure.

Academically Henry failed to achieve the success which had been expected, with seconds in both Moderations and Literae Humaniores, but of course his father's death, coming as it did at the end of Henry's second year at Balliol, must have greatly disrupted his college career. He clearly felt unable to apply himself to his work, and later is said to have frequently confessed to feelings of envy for a fellow scholar who displayed 'the attractive pallor of a true student'; Henry wished that he could himself 'rise to the same intense expenditure of tissue over his books'.[28] Although he left Oxford in 1881, he was not finally awarded his degree until 1886 because he failed to pass the obligatory Divinity examination, a situation not unusual at that time.

At the end of Henry's Oxford years Benjamin Jowett,[29] then Master of Balliol, wrote a testimonial for him. Jowett had a 'very high opinion' of Henry, and spoke of the respect felt for him in the college, believing him to be 'quite a gentleman in manner and feeling' with 'good sense and good taste'. The final sentence of this document in fact set Henry upon the path followed by his father and uncle, for Jowett believed that as 'a very fair scholar' the young man had 'a natural aptitude for the profession of Schoolmaster'.[30]

✤ ✤ ✤

From Oxford Henry moved north to Edinburgh for a temporary situation for two terms teaching at Fettes, one of the great Scottish schools. A master from the school had visited Oxford to look for new staff and chose also another new Balliol graduate for a temporary post, Percy Matheson;[31] he found life as a schoolmaster rather difficult, but Henry's company helped him through this difficult time, and after his spell in Scotland he returned quickly to Oxford, where he pursued a long and distinguished academic career. The two young men kept in touch but never became great friends; their paths were to cross again, however, for, during later years when Henry was writing books for Oxford University Press, Matheson was a Delegate of the Press, a member of the board drawn from university academics to decide Press policy.

After Henry's brief stay in Edinburgh he moved south to Yorkshire to a permanent post as a master at Sedbergh; his success in obtaining this new appointment was perhaps helped by C. C. Cotterill, the second master at Fettes, an old friend of the new headmaster at the Yorkshire school, Henry Hart. Henry settled to teach at Sedbergh, developing his skills and working for many years to achieve success in this family profession to which he was eventually to discover that he was not really suited.

2

Dura Virum Nutrix

'Dura virum nutrix' was Sedbergh's motto, 'Stern nurse of men', and for Henry the school was certainly to play this role. Here he was to mature, growing from an unformed youth of twenty-four to a man of experience able to admit his failures and acknowledge his beliefs. Inspired by the example of Robert Whitelaw at Rugby, Henry arrived at his new school filled no doubt with hopes of a long and rewarding teaching career; when he left, seventeen years later, he had learnt much and his hopes had been shattered, but he had developed the inner resources to begin again. Sedbergh with its spartan life and tough discipline was to prepare him for his future.

✣ ✣ ✣

When Henry arrived in Sedbergh in the spring of 1882 he found a typical small northern market town set high in the fells, on the very western edge of the Yorkshire Dales but close to the eastern side of the Lake District. An attractive town with historic buildings, narrow streets, and cobbled yards, Sedbergh lies in an area of great beauty among the Howgill Fells, majestically impressive in summer sun but remote, bleak, and forbidding in winter. With even higher moors behind it, the great mass of Winder Fell rises behind the town and school to 1,500 feet; even now new boys are taken to climb to the summit soon after their arrival, many captivated by the open countryside for the rest of their lives.

A market town since the thirteenth century, Sedbergh has a long history, and its school also has ancient roots. It was first opened in Tudor times as a chantry school, attached to the local church, but some years later, after the religious upheavals of the mid-sixteenth century, it was refounded as a grammar school. Over the next three centuries its fortunes varied: some headmasters were excellent scholars, managing the school most efficiently, but there were bad times, and eventually school numbers fell to fifteen and amalgamation with a neighbouring school, Giggleswick, was proposed. The efforts of local people and old boys averted this danger, and the school was saved and put into a good state for a successful future by a new headmaster. By the time of Henry's arrival the numbers of boys and staff had been built up and, with new buildings and a properly constituted board of governors, the school was well established.

To a young man brought up in the traditions of Rugby School there must have been much about Sedbergh at that time which seemed familiar, for the headmaster, Henry Hart,[1] had been one of Henry's predecessors as head of School House at Rugby. Hart had gathered about him at Sedbergh a collection of talented masters, later given by him the title of 'the Old Gang', and Henry joined this group when he arrived in Sedbergh for this first permanent teaching post. A later photograph of the 'Old Gang' shows them all; Hart is sitting at the front, separated by a potted palm on a small table from Bernard Wilson, his second master. At the back between the French and music masters Henry stands, a slightly detached figure, leaning against a wall with his hands in his pockets and standing on a doorstep, which hides his lack of inches.

Hart had reported to the school governors that he had 'appointed Mr. H. W. Fowler, who was a scholar of Balliol College, Oxford, and considered at Rugby one of the best scholars they had known there'.[2] The appointment was also noted in the *Sedberghian*, the school magazine, and apparently the Balliol scholarship made an impression on Henry's charges, for years later one recalled how the words 'struck the imagination of the more thoughtful schoolboy'.[3]

✣ ✣ ✣

The new master received an annual salary of £200, rising after some years to £250, with his board and lodging also provided. He would have lived at first in rooms in the town; a masters' hostel was proposed but not built until long after Henry had become a house tutor, with the advantage of a room in school. He was in fact quickly to gain some experience of the duties involved in running a house when, during his first autumn term at Sedbergh, Bernard Wilson became seriously ill with typhoid fever, and Henry was asked to take over his house until he recovered. Stepping into his shoes was probably rather a daunting task for a shy new arrival, but Henry seems to have satisfied the headmaster, who reported to the governors that he had managed it most successfully.

Henry did need some help in the house, as Mrs Wilson was of course occupied with her sick husband, and so a great friend of the school came to the rescue, a Miss Sedgwick,[4] who lived nearby; she covered Mrs Wilson's duties and cared for the boys. For extra help Charles Fowler, the brother next in age to Henry, was taken on as a temporary master, possibly for only one term; fresh from Cambridge at the start of his career as a schoolmaster, he left for a post at Wimborne Grammar School. Despite Henry's efforts Charles always seemed very reluctant to be drawn into working with him; perhaps being so close in age made him more wary of Henry than the younger boys were.

Henry Hart believed that new masters, however distinguished their previous careers might have been, should begin teaching with the smallest boys, and so Henry began with the first form, teaching Latin, Greek, and English. He recounted later, in a series of published essays intended for much older boys, one tale of these early years, reflecting the very different attitude of the nineteenth-century schoolmaster to the plight of the bullied child:

> I remember one little wretch who used to be bullied. I once had a talk with him, and urged him, in the usual way, to give one in the eye to the next of his own or any smaller size who persecuted him . . . but he only dissolved in tears, poor little beast! And said, 'I can't, sir'.[5]

Certainly the small boys regarded Henry as uninspiring. 'A cold mechanical machine'[6] was the opinion of Sir Alexander Lawrence, when asked years later about him, and others must have felt similarly. At the time of Henry's death another former pupil, masquerading under the initials W. S.,[7] described him as 'a thorough and conscientious, if not . . . a very inspiring teacher . . . His manner was reserved, not to say cold. In the popular phrase, "he took some knowing".[8] Despite Henry's experience of small boys as the eldest of such a long family, he probably, being shy, found his new pupils rather daunting.

Henry quickly advanced to sixth-form work and taught Lawrence again. 'In those days I should have said he lacked humanity,' Lawrence recorded later, finding his feelings little changed; he felt that no one 'ever got through his shell to know him as a human being'. The causes of this remoteness the adult Lawrence saw quite clearly, ascribing Henry's problems as a schoolmaster to 'shyness, coupled with his great fastidiousness (moral and intellectual)'.

Nevertheless Lawrence did enjoy being taught by Henry and felt great respect for him, particularly valuing his teaching of English literature, with happy memories of being introduced to Elia and Pope, and of Henry's success when presenting Browning to an unpromising form. Lawrence did rather shamefacedly recount his own failure, and more frequently that of his fellow pupils, to appreciate efforts at innovations to catch their interest. Henry, for instance, always particularly enjoyed reading aloud, and began a new practice of reading brief verse or prose pieces to the boys before beginning his lessons. Inevitably most of his small charges 'only welcomed it as meaning that much less Latin or Greek'.[9]

Another innovation introduced at this time was probably greeted with even less enthusiasm by the boys, but suggested perhaps the gradual development of Henry's future interests during these years. He devised a system set out on cards for use with the standard textbook to help small boys unravel the intricacies of syntax. These cards, printed locally, were greatly valued by the staff and used for years at Sedbergh, long after his departure. Eventually Henry, urged on by his former colleagues, incorporated them into a small book for use in schools; but that was all in the future.

Despite his shortcomings as a teacher, the boys did feel affection for this rather remote figure. To them he was known as 'little Joe' or 'Joey Stinker', for he and his room always smelt strongly of tobacco. Another member of the 'Old Gang' portrayed him as 'the Joey', a small furry figure sitting on ice with skates for feet; skating was one of Henry's favourite pursuits in this northern retreat. This caricature, in a collection presented as a book of animals based on the staff, was drawn by Ralph St John Ainslie, the music master, a very talented artist who later made his living from this type of work. The feelings of the boys are best summed up by one anonymous commentator who showed after Henry's death some tardy appreciation of his abilities: 'No one could fail in the retrospect to love H. W. and to wish that somehow they could have got closer to the wonderful fineness of his mind and character.'[10]

🧦 🧦 🧦

Among the other drawings in Ainslie's collection is an anxious figure with sharp features and haunted eyes presented as 'the Arthajay' with the explanatory caption; 'This queer animal runs and sits down and strokes its hands and is sinnical.' This was Arthur Fowler, by then a master but formerly a pupil, having transferred from Rugby for his final eighteen months at school.

Arthur John Fowler was the sixth child of the family, following Edith, and therefore the fifth boy, born on 29 February 1868, the date proving an endless source of family amusement, and of delight in later years to his pupils; in 1920, aged fifty-two but celebrating only his twelfth birthday, he was given by his form a football as a suitable gift. He followed Henry to Rugby and then to Sedbergh in January 1886, becoming a prefect and leaving for Corpus Christi College, Oxford, with an exhibition. The two brothers had much in common, both studying classics and sharing a love of similar sports, especially running. Arthur at Oxford distinguished himself particularly as an athlete, winning a blue and representing the university as a three-miler and in cross-country, twice coming second in the Oxford and Cambridge race. After university he returned to Sedbergh, remaining as an assistant master and later a housemaster until his retirement forty years later.

Henry told long afterwards a little story about a brother who can be identified as Arthur from Henry's description of him as ten years his junior. This child was 'given to investigating' his adult brother's 'property without leave asked' and Henry, anxious to stop this behaviour, resorted to a small trick. Discovering some mouldy tobacco, he suggested to the child that its state was the result of 'his having neglected to screw down the jar-top after his last illicit pryings'.[11] The child was upset and the undesirable behaviour ceased, but Henry's point in repeating the tale was that he sank so far in his small brother's esteem when the subterfuge was discovered that the effort seemed hardly worthwhile. Arthur was by this time obviously a reformed character and had outgrown this irritating curiosity.

A year after Arthur's arrival another troublesome Fowler child, Herbert Samuel, known as Sam, arrived at Sedbergh; he was the baby of the family, aged only five when his father died. With Frank, who was next in age, Sam had been at a small school in Devon and later at St Paul's in London. There he was not a great success, and surviving school reports show his lack of progress; he was 'idle and troublesome' and described also as 'generally unsatisfactory', although a hopeful master considered him 'young enough to retrieve his character'. This unfortunately Sam failed to do, and he was eventually sent to his brother at Sedbergh. Undoubtedly it was thought he would benefit from being under Henry's wing and in the presence of the virtuous Arthur but this was not to be: Sam stayed for only one year and left, aged fourteen, for an uncertain future.

While the boys were both in school they caused space problems in Tower's house, where Henry had become a tutor. Sam, the last to arrive, made an extra boy in the house; to solve the problem, Henry gave up his room for his two young brothers, moving himself into a single room formerly occupied by another boy. Presumably he felt the sacrifice to be worthwhile, as he could help his mother by supervising one naughty boy and encouraging the other as he prepared for Oxford entrance.

᭞ ᭞ ᭞

Life at Sedbergh was hard for Henry in term-time, and later he confided to a friend that 'he worked for an average of ten hours a day … Sundays included'.[12] A colleague recorded that they saw more of one another during the holidays, as 'a stern and conscientious application to school-work' limited 'social intercourse in term-time'.[13] There were, on the other hand, compensations in the outdoor life, walking and climbing, for example, on the fells, sometimes with schoolmaster colleagues as companions. As in Oxford Henry exercised every morning, but here in a far more stirring landscape. He ran out from the town on the road to Kirkby Stephen and swam, even in the most icy winter weather, in a deep pool at Straight Bridge where the road crosses the river Rawthey, keeping 'a mat under a stone to stand on while he was drying himself'. One boy, allowed to accompany Henry in his last year at school, described the 6 o'clock start; fortified by a piece of sponge cake, they ran out for a mile or so to the bridge and, after the swim, 'ran or walked back to be in time for early 'prep' at a quarter past seven'.[14]

Swimming and running were also important in the boys' lives. They swam, as Henry did, in the nearby rivers, in pools called locally 'dubs'. Henry was on one occasion caught in a dramatic incident when supervising a group of boys in a pool by Jackdaw Bridge, where the railway crossed the Rawthey. A galloping horseman warned them 'of a cloudburst up in the fells which was bringing a heavy spate',[15] and Henry was just able to get his boys out before the rushing wall of water could sweep them away. Running held a more central place in school life: the annual Ten Mile race was, and still is, the most important event in the sporting year, with the record set when Henry was at Sedbergh remaining for nearly a century. It was run mostly on the fell, with only short distances at the beginning and end on the road, a very messy business in a wet year when the rivers were high; Henry, photographed as a spectator, must have remembered his own successes in the mud at Rugby.

As in all schools, team games were also important, although rugby football had only been introduced by Hart in 1880 and interest in it was still growing. Henry played his part, refereeing frequently for the boys' matches and even playing himself, sometimes for the Sedbergh Town side and often for the masters. He certainly scored tries for the masters' team and, one admirer recalled later, 'though light of build he was a marvellous first line forward'.[16] Games were often full of incident; the school magazine carried a description of a match when the ball was kicked 'into a passing waggonette, and was carried off, but quickly restored'.[17] For cricket, on the other hand, Henry cared very little, playing only occasionally in the masters' match and then rarely scoring any runs and often refusing to take part even when the French master, Paul Aubrey, had, most inappropriately, to be pressed into service.

Winter weather brought the most exciting sporting activities for those so inclined, including the Fowler brothers, although for some small boys the bitter cold and spartan life must have been a dreadful experience. Tobogganing was popular when the snow was suitable, School Hill[18] becoming like 'the ice runs at St Moritz'. On one occasion, when ordinary toboggans were banned as too dangerous as their occupants were crashing into the wall at the bottom of the slope, 'some genius . . . thought of sliding down on a small piece of wood.' This solved the problem; every old box in the school was broken up, and the hill soon became 'black with figures descending'.[19] Skating too was a favourite activity for both masters and boys and a walk of about four miles from the school along the Kendal road brought them to a small lake, Lilymere, which they were then allowed to use, playing there also bandy, a form of ice hockey. Skating was certainly a sport enjoyed greatly by the Fowler brothers and Ainslie's caricatures show both of them with skates. A colleague described Henry's anxiety to fit in skating between midday dinner and afternoon school; to achieve this he wore, instead of trousers, knickerbockers under his MA gown, an effect bordering 'on the ludicrous for anybody with less innate dignity'.[20]

✿ ✿ ✿

At Sedbergh Henry made friendships which were to last for the rest of his life. His rooms were 'a regular rendezvous' on Saturday evenings for staff members both young and old, and 'talk went on steadily till midnight'.[21] A colleague described how Henry 'suffered fools gladly': 'his deference to the opinions of others, in the light of his extraordinary omniscience, was a marvel of courtesy'.[22] In these situations the reserve which the boys had felt in the classroom disappeared and he entertained his guests with charming hospitality. Here many lasting friendships developed, with Ainslie, for instance, whom Henry was able to help in future difficulties, and F. P. Lemarchand,[23] who laid the foundations of the school's great success at rugby and was later Arthur's brother-in-law.

Soon after Henry's arrival he was made a tutor in the house run by Bernard Tower; 'my own oldest and best friend' Henry called him when writing his obituary just weeks before his own death. Tower[24] was slightly younger than Henry and had been at Pembroke College while Henry was at Balliol, although they never met in Oxford. The two men were very different; a junior master in the house noted that 'Tower's character was as expansive as Fowler's was shy and reserved'.[25] Bernard Tower's sporting feats were legendary both at rugby, 'barging happily along with the ball under his arm and two or three tacklers hanging round his waist' and at cricket, where his lobs were delivered with 'the confident air of infinite cunning'. On one occasion 'the strength of his forearm'[26] sent a ball through one of the parish church windows, causing great delight no doubt among the watching boys. The differences in their characters made the two an excellent team in the house and the friendship which grew there continued after Henry left to seek his fortune in London and Tower to take on a headmaster's post. They corresponded throughout the war, and were able to meet until the last months of their lives.

They were joined in the house in 1892 by a young schoolmaster, Gordon Coulton,[27] who was engaged for two terms as an assistant to help with the headmaster's work after an illness. Coulton had begun a career in the church but, not taking to the life, had started again as a schoolmaster. This was to be another long friendship and eventually Coulton became Henry's biographer, recording details of life in Tower's house. Coulton described Henry's protective manner, recording as an example how he made it clear to the new recruit that he must not allow the kindly housemaster to relieve him of any duties; his attitude to Tower, Coulton noted, was like 'an Airedale terrier quietly defending his master'. There are other glimpses of life in the house, of Henry reading aloud to the boys before bedtime, for instance. He was the 'guiding spirit' of Browning readings given by the staff, always believing that poetry should be read aloud, even when the reader was alone. Coulton described the exceptional beauty of Henry's reading voice, 'with complete absence of affectation and unerring justice of emphasis'.[28] Despite Coulton's short stay at Sedbergh the friendship begun there flourished and he was a frequent visitor to all Henry's later homes, eventually accompanied by his wife and small daughters; one of these little girls recalled being quizzed by Henry about words and completely defeated by a discussion about 'matinée hat', but by that time both men had moved on to quite different lives. Coulton was to the end a valued friend.

✤ ✤ ✤

Holidays were obviously important to Henry, a welcome relaxation after all the hard work of term, but only tantalizing glimpses of his summers remain. 'I made yearly expeditions to the Alps,' he wrote later, mentioning 'salmon-hued Dolomite sunrises' and 'virgin slopes of wind-carved snow'. It was, however, not for all these beauties, excellent as they were, that he went south; 'it was the climbing-pole I wanted,' he confessed, and certainly all his holidays seem to have been spent in the mountains, although visits to galleries in many major European cities are mentioned in passing: Paris, Rome, Florence, Berlin, Dresden just a few on the list.

Henry's friends also give snippets of detail about these summers in his more wealthy days, for as a young schoolmaster he was rather well paid and could afford foreign travel. Sadly these vignettes are used merely to demonstrate his concern about his appearance, his 'physical fastidiousness natural to a Rugby and Balliol man';[29] 'he was a stickler for etiquette,' one friend recalled, recounting a tale of a holiday in the Dolomites when, 'travel-stained and bearded', they met some acquaintances at the top of a mountain pass. Henry disappeared and, when the party entered Cortina some time later, a 'spick-and-span well-groomed figure'[30] met them, almost unrecognizable. Henry was always immaculate, wearing top hat and tailcoat for his Sunday tea with Paul Aubrey, the French master, and his wife.

Coulton spent one walking holiday with Henry tramping across Devon and part of South Wales, in the years after Sedbergh and before their marriages when they both had money difficulties. Unable to find rooms in an inn they spent a night on a haystack, which Henry found most uncomfortable, 'sitting bolt-upright and picking the particles fastidiously from his tweed jacket'. In the morning they found a village inn where he was able to take a room and repair the damage suffered during his rustic night, vowing never again to 'try a penurious holiday'.[31] Perhaps Henry's distaste seems more understandable to the modern reader than it did to Gordon Coulton, undoubtedly a scruffy traveller.

✤ ✤ ✤

Holidays would also have been a time for visits home to Caroline and the younger children, living in London at 39 Gratton Road in West Kensington, not too far from the delights and sights of the centre of the capital city. After moving around during the first unsettled years while she sorted out her finances and absorbed the shock of her husband's death and the loss of a much-loved son, Caroline had found this house in late 1881 or early 1882 and moved in with her family; she was able at last to provide the home they needed in the holidays, but the loss of another son was to cast a shadow again over her life.

Edward Seymour Fowler was born in 1864, the fourth son and the first born after the move to Grosvenor House. By the time of his father's death he was already at Marlborough, where he had followed Charles, both of them winning scholarships for sons of clergy. After leaving school Seymour, as he was known to his brothers, tried various occupations even beginning to train as a solicitor, but eventually he decided to apply for a post in the Ceylon Civil Service and was accepted as a cadet, setting out with two other young recruits on the steamer *Pekin* for Colombo. In January 1886, soon after his arrival, a notice in the Ceylon Government Gazette[32] recorded his appointment as an acting land surveyor in Customs at Colombo, but by June he was dead, aged only 22 years, like his father a victim of typhoid fever. Charles wrote for his mother to ascertain full details of Seymour's death,[33] but nothing remains of the official explanations and commiserations. He was buried in the general cemetery in Colombo and a stone erected there to his memory. Not a whisper remains in Henry's letters about Seymour, but years later Arthur described him to a friend in a recital of family history as 'a very handsome lad'.[34]

The family home remained in Gratton Road for some time after this further tragedy, but in 1889 or 1890 Caroline moved on to Eastbourne, then a very fashionable watering place and perhaps known already to Edith, who had been at school just along the coast, in St Leonards. By 1891 they were settled at 3 Hartfield Square, a narrow stuccoed house on five floors squashed in the middle of a short terrace in a smart square in Upperton, then considered the best area of the town. With a cook, Julia Cornford, and Elizabeth, the housemaid, Caroline and Edith would have been able to provide a pleasant base for the five remaining boys when they came home; Henry would have enjoyed his visits, finding the sea bathing in particular a great attraction. The Fowler ladies must have been financially secure but had Edith wanted to find a little work, perhaps teaching music, they were surrounded by schools for young ladies in the square; Eastbourne had at that time, it is said, a school for every day of the year.

This settled family home was not to last, for Caroline had become ill with stomach cancer some time after their arrival; her condition deteriorated and she died in February 1895. Henry, Charles, and Arthur would have been away at their teaching posts at the time, but Frank was at home to support Edith and sort out the necessary paperwork. Their mother's death inevitably had a great impact on all the children—on Edith in particular, who was left alone; perhaps it was also some small influence in the great change which Henry was to make in his life.

✤ ✤ ✤

'For a dozen years I carefully concealed from my friends that I was not a Christian,' Henry wrote in a later essay, explaining the cause of this reticence as his revulsion at the 'airs of intellectual superiority'[35] assumed by an agnostic friend. Similarly, he had earlier declared that never since leaving school had he made 'any statement from which any conclusion could be drawn' about his 'religious belief or want of it'.[36] The changes in his views over the years since his childhood 'in a clerical household'[37] were described some years later, when he set out plainly the alteration in his 'religious position': 'I can mark it off in decades clearly enough; thirty years ago I thought religious belief true; twenty years ago doubtful; ten years ago false; & now it is (for me, of course) merely absurd'.[38]

Gordon Coulton, writing after Henry's death, knew perfectly well his friend's feelings but described him as 'a Christian in all but actual faith',[39] a patronizing statement which would have annoyed Henry greatly; he had in fact condemned this smug approach to 'the unbeliever who is a credit to his unbelief', explaining that 'a confession of scepticism' would once have been accepted and believed, but had become a matter to be brushed aside by Christians with some glib remark such as 'essentially a religious man'. At Sedbergh Henry's feelings were not realized and, although something of his attitude might have been deduced from his behaviour, no clear discussion of his position and its implications took place. He was by nature reserved, but this secretive attitude to his strongly held beliefs contributed to misunderstandings which were greatly to influence his future, for, as he later explained, it was 'still now & then a temporal disadvantage not to be a Christian'.[40]

Henry must long have hoped for a post as a housemaster; he had assisted Tower for some years and knew the work involved, had even had some brief experience when deputizing for Wilson in his early days at Sedbergh. Yet in 1891, when a vacancy occurred and it was offered to him, he refused the post. Coulton recounted the whole story, but surprisingly there seems to have been at the time no clear reason given for this refusal. The house went to Ralph Ainslie, and Coulton and his other friends suspected that Henry had allowed the position to go to the younger man because he had family commitments with which the extra salary would help, a typically generous action to a man who was later to need Henry's help even more urgently.

In 1898 Ainslie left for a headmastership and the housemaster's post again became vacant. This time the position was given to another without any offer to Henry, for Hart assumed that he would refuse it if it were offered. The new man was felt by all to be clearly inferior to Henry, who protested to Hart, feeling that there should be some clear order arranged by which younger masters might be able to see when they could hope to secure a housemaster's position. He himself had believed for some years, 'a reasonable presumption', he thought, that he 'was next on the imaginary list of possible house masters'.[41] Hart's response was to explain with apologies that he had believed, after Henry's first refusal of the house, that he had no intention of ever taking one, thinking that a previous reluctance to prepare boys for confirmation was the reason for this.

Bernard Tower was an excellent candidate for a headmastership, and at this stage in the discussion Henry explained to Hart his concerns about his own position when Tower left the school. It would clearly be difficult for Henry to remain in the house with a younger and less experienced man in charge and both parties would certainly be unhappy with the situation. He did express some misgivings about his ability to begin in a new house, feeling doubtful about his 'capacity to get hold of boys', but of course in Tower's house, where he already knew everyone, this would be no problem; if the post were offered to him he would probably accept. On the confirmation matter, during these years nothing had changed; Henry could not prepare boys and never would be able to do so. He insisted to Hart that a housemaster who could not undertake this work might 'acquiesce just as a parent does in its being done by some one who is more competent than himself',[42] but Hart felt 'equally bound to inflexibility'.[43] The 'religious test', as Henry called it, was quite unacceptable and he wrote again to Hart resigning his post in view of this 'perfectly friendly, but irreconcilable difference of opinion'.

While Henry's decision was a great shock to the headmaster, it did not persuade him to relax his principles; he was anxious nevertheless to keep Henry at Sedbergh, and the correspondence continued with lengthy letters on both sides. Henry could only restate his position, confirming that he could not prepare boys for confirmation or 'co-operate from the religious point of view with any one who was preparing them'. He had believed that Sedbergh was non-denominational, and so felt that Hart's action was perhaps not legal as it would have been in a Church of England school; but even if Hart could convince him that it was, life there would no longer be tolerable.

Teaching had retained its interest for Henry while he felt able to make improvements in his techniques; at first, he readily admitted, he had been 'no great teacher', but after so many years he felt that he taught about as well as he was ever likely to, and had become 'stationary'. At Sedbergh teaching had become 'profoundly unsatisfactory', but there would have been compensations had he had a share in work outside the schoolroom. With that chance removed he had no enthusiasm for his remaining duties; 'to go on like this with no work of higher value to rise to is intolerable,' he told Hart. Phrases in Henry's letters reveal his unhappiness with the whole situation; 'intellectually stagnant', he called the atmosphere at Sedbergh, while confessing 'a certain reluctance to meddle with the insides of other people's minds'.[44] Years later he wrote of his attitude at the end of this time, 'I had become sceptical about the good of ramming logic into the heads of small boys'.[45]

With these complex feelings about his ability as a schoolmaster and his disappointed hopes of a housemaster's post, the wisest course for Henry was to leave. He once more submitted his resignation to Hart, who could do nothing but accept it, although he did eventually persuade Henry to remain for another year. Hart was himself about to retire, and was anxious that Henry should wait to meet his successor and perhaps benefit from a very different attitude to the situation which might give him a housemastership and the possibility of eventually applying for a headmaster's post elsewhere; but Henry would not be persuaded.

His friendship with Hart was not destroyed, as might have been expected, by this mammoth clash of principles and they continued to correspond and meet. On their retirement the Harts[46] moved south to Wimbledon, to a house which they renamed 'Sedbergh', and here Henry would have visited them while he was in London. Hart spent the war years reading newspapers and correspondence in the War Office, specializing in Norwegian which he had picked up during many holidays, at least one of which Henry shared; the two men remained correspondents until Hart's death in 1921.

A few brief lines in the school magazine in July 1899 recorded Henry's departure after seventeen years at Sedbergh. In later years these notices were to be far more effusive, but this restrained style would have seemed most suitable to him. He was in fact soon back at the school, returning to help out when needed during staff illnesses and to take occasional classes while he lived in London. Many friendships continued long after Henry's departure, and of course young Arthur was still a junior master. There is a chilling twist at the end of the tale of Henry's departure from Sedbergh; when Tower's house finally fell vacant three years later, on his appointment to the headmastership of Lancing, it was to Arthur Fowler that the new headmaster, Charles Lowry, turned when he came to appoint a housemaster. Had Henry remained he might have discovered that he was required to work as a subordinate of his much younger brother.

Henry was not forgotten at Sedbergh; after his death, his work was commemorated at the school, not with a chapel tablet as was normal at that time, but in the entrance of the Powell Hall, where beams were added to the ceiling and a fine lantern hung as a most fitting memorial. In the *Sedberghian* a much longer piece marked his passing, recalling the name he left at Sedbergh 'for Spartan discipline and omniscience'.[47]

✤ ✤ ✤

Henry may have been bred to be a schoolmaster but he was certainly not a born teacher. He had on the other hand developed at Sedbergh the ability to work hard and the patience to cope with uncongenial tasks, great assets in his future career. He had failed to touch the minds of his young charges but his wit and humour, hidden at Sedbergh by his overwhelming shyness, were with his fresh approach to bring him a devoted public away from the classroom. His immense reserve meant that those who met him face to face, as pupils, never felt they knew him; but those who encountered him later only on paper came to feel they knew him well.

So in the summer of 1899 Henry packed his bags and left Sedbergh and the northern fells where he might have whiled away his working life, and set off for the south to try earning his living in London with his pen, something he was in fact to do satisfactorily for the rest of his life.

3

The Hermit of Chelsea

⸎

Chelsea was to be Henry's London base when he arrived in 1899; it was probably an area already known to him, for the old family home in Gratton Road, with its memories of his mother and Seymour, was not far away in the neighbouring borough of Kensington. He found rooms in a lofty town house in Paulton's Square, just off the King's Road; a brief walk away, perhaps 200 yards down Danvers Street, was Cheyne Walk and the Chelsea Embankment, finished only twenty-five years earlier when this part of the river bank had been improved. From here Henry, out walking, would see the short stretch of the Thames between two bridges—Battersea, newly built to replace an old wooden bridge, and the Albert Bridge.

Number 14 Paulton's Square had been a very stylish house when newly built and in modern times is certainly a most handsome building in one of London's smartest areas, but when Henry arrived it was a boarding house and the square was at a low point in its fluctuating fortunes. One of Henry's friends, always fond of tramping London streets but at that time flat-hunting in the area, described it as 'a queer, rather grim place' with 'slatternly women looking out of upper windows' and glimpses of 'frowsy-looking interiors'.[1] The house had four floors and a basement; Henry took three unfurnished rooms, one on the first floor and two on the second, paying twelve shillings a week in rent.

The landlord was a Metropolitan police constable, Edmund Howe,[2] living also on the premises with his wife, Rosa Ann, and their only child, Edmund James. Although a countryman by birth Howe had been a London policeman for thirteen years, always stationed in Chelsea. When the Howes were first married they had lived in Seaton Street, a little further west, an area of poor houses in multiple occupation, demolished long ago. By 1899 they had moved to Paulton's Square, and it was there that Henry met them.

✤ ✤ ✤

Settled in London, Henry had to provide for metropolitan living. He had been well paid at Sedbergh but had saved nothing, so only his small inheritance of £120 a year remained, from which he had to find rent annually of about £32. He had always believed that a man should be able to live on £100 a year, but to survive in London he needed to supplement his income. This he did by writing, submitting articles to journals and newspapers and earning about £30 a year from this source.

Henry was never greedy and his tastes were certainly not expensive. In later years, when dealing with Oxford University Press, he was always surprised, perhaps even embarrassed, when sent annual bonuses, prompted by the excellent sales of his books; 'those sums of £50, £100, or £150, that come dropping upon me as the gentle rain from heaven about Christmas',[3] he called them. Remuneration for suggested projects was always his last consideration during discussions; 'All right; if you insist on making a millionaire of me, do so'[4] were his final words in one negotiation. He set out his attitude in an essay, published later but probably written during these London years, advising schoolboys on their choice of profession. They should not settle on an occupation which they would particularly enjoy, he told them, 'and then whine because the world does not see why it should pay you for choosing on that principle'. Henry's feelings about his own position were quite clear; work at Sedbergh, where he felt his lack of prospects, had become a form of drudgery;

> . . . if you are capable of deliberately preferring to starve (or something like it) over a congenial occupation, rather than drudge at a dull one to make a comfortable income, there is nothing, so far as I can see, to be said against it.[5]

So Henry wrote essays in his Chelsea room and sent them out, keeping 'a brief life-history of each',[6] now sadly lost. Of course there were many rejections, but there were also notable successes. Speaking later of the *Spectator* he remarked that he had been an occasional contributor, and this must have been one of his earliest triumphs, for an essay was published there soon after his arrival in London. 'Books We Think We Have Read' was the title of this piece, and in it Henry began with the suggestion that 'there are essentials of respectability which we all assume about our neighbours'. His readers would feel certain, for example, that they were not cowards, would feel 'no temptation to put their table-knives where Germans are supposed to put them', and most of all would feel that they were not ignorant of certain books. This last was, of course, the main point of the article, and the author went on to discuss the delusions which led his readers to believe that they had read 'all that decency requires of an educated man'. Books, for instance, which appeal to children and adults alike, 'nothing can save them, once stamped juvenile, from being taken as read'. If Homer had written in English, his work would have been classed as a boys' book; 'how he must hug himself for his happy thought of writing Greek.' He mentioned too the delusion, still current one hundred years later, about 'intimacy with Shakespeare' and the anger felt when this is challenged. From all this he passed on to discuss how to enjoy books which the reader believed he had read, perhaps 'with the half-reading of childhood', recommending that they should be slowly relished, 'no tossing off of ardent spirits, but the connoisseur's deliberate rolling in the mouth of some old vintage'.[7] This article was well received by readers and the editor of the *Spectator*, John St Loe Strachey,[8] known to Henry from Balliol days, passed on the comments of one who asked about the identity of 'the author of this charming essay, George Meredith or Augustine Birrell'. To be mistaken for these distinguished essayists must have been thrilling for Henry, but his friend Gordon Coulton recorded that his 'sense of humour stepped in here to temper his elation'.[9]

Henry's association with the *Spectator* seems to have ended with a disagreement and wounded pride on Henry's part. An article, accepted at first by Strachey, was eventually returned as there was finally not enough room for it. The editor sent a cheque in payment, feeling presumably that, as he had initially accepted the work, he should pay, but Henry was offended and, it is said, never again approached the *Spectator*. Naturally he could not accept money which, he believed, he had not earned; he often found it difficult to accept payments which he knew he had.

The *Anglo-Saxon Review*[10] also published an article. With its brief career almost matching Henry's stay in London, this was a handsome publication, finely and expensively bound, but sadly short-lived; at the cost of a guinea a volume it was doomed from the beginning to financial failure. Henry joined a distinguished assembly of contributors, a mixture of society ladies and men of letters—Henry James, Swinburne, Edmund Gosse, George Bernard Shaw heading a lengthy list.

Henry's article, with the title 'Outdoor London', celebrated life in the city streets, describing the fogs, sunrises, and sunsets of the capital, 'certain amethystine morning hues and evening smoky purples', and reserving special praise for the two distinctive city plants, the Virginia creeper and the plane tree which lines so many streets. 'She is rather a congerie of cities than a city,' he explained and went on to describe London by night: 'the coster's naphtha-flare, the butcher's perforated gas-pipe, the draper's and the publican's electricity, light the scene worthily.' The capital's people too were appreciated:

> What a welter of untold stories, in every fifty yards of crowded street, full of potentialities for emotion, diversion, instruction . . . speculation is fascinating, perhaps futile, perhaps inspiring.

The scenes he noticed still strike a chord—'a bicyclist in a tight place' giving the observer 'a momentary qualm', and the crowd springing 'out of the ground at the smallest street incident', while the reader is urged not to 'stalk in haughty indifference past'. Henry was clearly fond of his new home: 'render thanks to the city Genius for the contrasts of London,'[11] he wrote to end his piece.

All his unpublished essays Henry gathered into two typescript volumes, which have not, alas, survived the intervening century; and his plan was to publish them himself. Many years later, he described his intentions when he moved south: 'my ambition was to become a small essayist issuing occasional small volumes & paying their small expenses till such time as their small merits should be great enough to pay their own.'[12] After leaving London he was able to publish three books of essays, but unfortunately never achieved the success in this field that he hoped for.

✤ ✤ ✤

Newspapers provided from this time another source of income, tiny certainly but probably very rewarding. Competitions, in these years before the arrival of the crossword, were daunting to modern eyes. Translations of English verse into Latin or Greek were commonly set for cash prizes in the *Westminster Gazette*, always Henry's favourite newspaper; even as a soldier in France during the war his letters were sprinkled with comments to his wife about the failure of the 'WG' to reach him and his complaints sent to the office in London. He was a frequent winner, although the constant use of pseudonyms by contestants disguised his successes most effectively. Later his verses were on occasion published in the same newspaper, at least once as the result of a competition; prizes were offered for valentines in rondel form and Henry's submission was published.

> At the instigation, Dolly,
>   Of the *Westminster Gazette*
> I essay an ancient folly;
>   Did you know it lingered yet?
>   You I choose, not Sue or Bet,
> Madge, Euphemia, or Molly
>   (At the instigation, Dolly,
>   Of the *Westminster Gazette*).
>
> What, dear? 'Valentines are jolly
>   Tommy rot'? I know, my pet.
> 'Worse than mistletoe and holly'?
>   But we do it, you forget,
>   At the instigation, Dolly,
>   Of the *Westminster Gazette*.[13]

In Chelsea Henry began his days, as always, with a run, here through city streets to Hyde Park and a swim in the Serpentine. This was quite a short distance for a runner as experienced as Henry, but he must have been considered by his neighbours as eccentric here as he was elsewhere in later years. Perhaps young Edmund Howe watched his daily departure with wonder and amusement, as other children would after Henry left London. Tales were told of his swimming adventures; he apparently won once the traditional Christmas day race in the Serpentine but returned home injured; 'a thin crust of ice . . . had cut even his shaggy chest to pieces as he ploughed through it.'[14] In one of London's notable fogs he became lost and quite unable to reach the shore until, after a considerable spell in the chilly waters, he was rescued, completely exhausted, by a boatman.

There were other distractions from his working life; his brothers would presumably have been pleased to find somewhere to stay in London for holiday visits and there were also friends. His fellow student from Balliol, Terence Woulfe Flanagan, for instance, by that time a doctor, was practising in Chelsea and living in St Leonard's Terrace, not far from Paulton's Square, with his wife, Margaret, and their little daughter, Barbara. He was a frequent visitor to Henry's rooms and was to play a very important role in his later life.

Gordon Coulton also stayed often with Henry in Paulton's Square, and indeed visited all his later homes. Although a permanent position had been offered to Coulton after his two terms at Sedbergh, he had moved to Dulwich, tempted no doubt by the thought of London life; he spent only three years at the southern school, suffering a breakdown, brought on by overwork and a failed romance. After a suicide attempt and a long spell of convalescence overseas, he moved to Eastbourne and lived there, fully recovered, keeping a school with a friend. Henry certainly spent time there with Coulton, who told another swimming tale, of daring exploits on the pier this time. Henry liked to dive from the highest point, not for the faint-hearted and in modern times most definitely forbidden; one morning, when the tide was unusually low, he misjudged the height and dived into shallow water, flaying his chest and stomach. Luckily he survived, and became less reckless as he grew older.

Like Henry, Gordon Coulton was still single, but in 1903, on holiday in Switzerland, he met a much younger woman, Rose Ilbert,[15] to whom he became engaged. Rose was soon taken to Paulton's Square to meet her fiancé's best friend, 'the Bohemian H. W. Fowler',[16] as Coulton described him, explaining also that Henry was 'a strictly truthful man'.[17] Coulton eventually asked him to be best man at their wedding, although this was delayed for some time by poverty and the doubts of Rose's family.

As a frequent visitor, Coulton was able to paint a picture of Henry's life in Paulton's Square. The view from the back windows was described, where 'a whole grove of treetops stood out in the middle distance against the evening sky', and the breakfast arrangements after the morning swim, a boiled egg with toast, 'brought to an exact degree of crispness over the gas-ring'. Mrs Howe kept hens and supplied Henry with new-laid eggs at a penny each, a very generous price. Still anxious to depict his friend's fastidious behaviour, Coulton described these eggs, 'turned upside down every morning to guard the yolks from gravitating to the outer edge and so exposing themselves to decay'.[18]

Coulton naturally met some of Henry's other friends and visitors, and mentioned John Batten,[19] the artist and fairy-tale illustrator, who lived in the same area, in Margravine Gardens in Hammersmith, and called in when Coulton was staying to show Henry his illustrations to Dante. Flanagan also was seen several times by Coulton when he was visiting, but, despite all these encounters he painted a bleak view of Henry in his new home, calling him 'the Hermit of Chelsea'.[20] While describing him as 'too self-sufficient, in the best sense of that word, to feel really lonely', Coulton sketched a small incident to give an impression of isolation; at the end of a visit when Henry was taking leave of Coulton, 'there was a sudden gulp and choking in his throat which he himself resented; and he turned brusquely away'.[21] It is tempting to speculate that Henry might have been relieved at the departure of a tiresome guest, rather than upset at the parting; Coulton was later described as a 'controversialist', and his views, particularly in theological matters, were mostly quite different from his friend's, making his visits perhaps rather difficult for one who preferred to live quietly.

Henry was in fact making new friends in London, of whom Batten was just one. Soon after his arrival he had joined the Inns of Court Volunteers, and he was involved with them throughout his stay in the capital, even returning to camp with them after he left London. This involvement Coulton dismissed as only occasional, insisting that Henry joined 'mainly for the sake of healthy exercise and from old public-school habits'.[22] The Volunteers were in fact to play a very large part in Henry's London life, and amongst their ranks he found friends. He clearly enjoyed the camps and drills and took a full part in the duties involved. The years he spent in London were exciting times, both nationally and internationally, and his membership of the Volunteers allowed him to play a small part in these momentous events.

✤ ✤ ✤

Reports of British disasters in the South African war dominated the news in the autumn of 1899 and the following winter, and during the ensuing rush to enlist, driven by a wave of patriotic feeling, Henry and the men who were to become his companions for the next few years enrolled in the Volunteers. By good fortune one of these men was Thomas Anstey Guthrie,[23] the author, under the pseudonym 'F. Anstey', of *Vice Versa* and other successes; his detailed and entertaining diaries give an excellent description of life in the ranks and of Henry's involvement, for the two became friends during these years. Anstey Guthrie had joined the Volunteers in the winter of 1900, and described the initial training, the camps, and other duties which Henry would also have experienced.

After enrolment the new recruits were required for drills at headquarters in Lincoln's Inn twice on each weekday, in the morning and early evening; on Saturdays there was a morning drill only, and Sundays were free. For Anstey Guthrie this continued for two months from his enrolment in mid-February until the Volunteers went off to camp at Easter. After this there were fewer drills, but a weekly visit to the rifle range at Harrow was added. Henry must have begun his training at a similar time, for he was first mentioned by Anstey Guthrie in a group firing on the range on a stormy day in early June. From that time his name occurred frequently at parades, drills, and inspections until in high summer the Volunteers departed by train to camp for two weeks at Ludgershall on Salisbury Plain. Here they slept in tents and spent the time in drilling and in field days, when they set out to capture or defend ridges and other features in the local landscape. Henry and Anstey Guthrie spent a day working together in camp as tent orderlies, drawing rations, cleaning their area, and performing other domestic duties. At the end of the fortnight they all returned by train to London, arriving at Nine Elms and marching by the Embankment, Waterloo Bridge, and the Strand to Lincoln's Inn.

In late October 1900 the Volunteers turned out, Henry among them, for crowd control on the occasion of the return to London of the City Infantry Volunteers from South Africa. This must have been an exciting but terrifying day. After a warning from the colonel that they were not to join in the cheering, in fact were '"not to move an eyelash" as the procession passed',[24] they were marched out to take up their position in Fleet Street just under the clock of the Law Courts. Here they found a 'surging mob' which they struggled to control, only managing to hold their line by linking arms and using their 'backs, happily buttressed with rolled overcoats, as battering rams.'

Meanwhile the returning troops had arrived at Paddington in four trains from Southampton and were drawn up on the station platforms for their march across London, with no fewer than twelve accompanying bands. Their route took them past Hyde Park Corner, Marlborough House, where the Prince of Wales viewed the procession, and St James's Palace. They were greeted everywhere with tremendous enthusiasm, but after they reached Trafalgar Square the crowds were unexpectedly large; the struggle to march along the Strand and Fleet Street, where Henry and his companions were wrestling with the masses, meant that the troops arrived at St Paul's Cathedral two hours late, being forced at times to march through the crowds in single file. After the procession had passed a great surge broke the Volunteers' line completely; 'the human torrent' burst 'with a frantic yell through its guards'.[25]

The following morning there was much criticism in the newspapers about the failure of the authorities adequately to secure the route between Charing Cross and St Paul's. There had been some fatalities; a baby held in its mother's arms had died, for instance, in the dense crowd in the Strand, and there were many injuries, some extremely serious with more deaths expected. Nevertheless Henry must have felt some thrill at taking his part in these stirring events, so different from his struggles with schoolboys at Sedbergh.

There were great events at home also, with the death of the old queen in the following January. She had played, it seems, a small part in Henry's London life, featuring in a recurring dream in which he took tea with her; after her death she was joined in this bizarre situation by the new king but eventually disappeared from the tea-table, at which point the dream stopped.[26] The Volunteers were not required for funeral duties, but took part in the Coronation Review of troops the following year.

The weather seems to have been rather poor that summer; in London May had been cold with snow, and in June there had already been three inches of rain by the time the review was held on a very wet day in the middle of the month. Henry set out with the others on a Sunday afternoon and they spent the night in a pavilion at Bisley, sleeping little because of 'considerable giggling and snoring'.[27] At 4.15 they were woken and after breakfast set out to march, with a 'band playing abominably', to Laffan's Plain at Aldershot where 31,000 troops were to be reviewed by the new king. Here, having deposited their greatcoats and kit, they waited in the rain. Anstey Guthrie cadged 'half a pork pie' and some 'orange wine and water' and settled to enjoy the sights and sounds of the assembling army, 'glimpses of the dark green of the Cameronians, of the cock pheasant like colouring of the London Scottish, the feathers & white plumes of the Highland L.I. Militia'. Eventually their turn came; in 'faint sunlight just enough to throw shadows'[28] they set off to march past the royal carriage, where they were greatly surprised to see only Queen Alexandra to take the salute, with no sign of the king who was expected to review them. Shoulders and hands numb from holding their rifles at the slope for so long, they went back to their place beneath the pines and waited in more torrential rain until late afternoon, when they were marched to Aldershot. Here they were jeered by watching regular soldiers, rather hard to bear presumably after such a long wet day, and waited for two hours in the street and later in the station yard, until their train was ready. In London there had been no rain and the streets were dry; the newspaper posters reported the king's illness, with serious rumours and fears about complications. A few days later the grave nature of his indisposition was revealed with the cancellation of the Coronation after he underwent surgery for appendicitis, a malady which suddenly became rather fashionable.

These great events were just a small part of the Volunteers' schedule, with drills, rifle practice, one-day exercises, and camps filling their military timetable; the camps were held at least once a year, the regular Easter camp, and sometimes twice, with an August excursion added. At Easter 1903, for example, the Volunteers went to Bulford on Salisbury Plain for eight days; Anstey Guthrie described how they 'slouched to Nine Elms',[29] travelled by train to Amesbury, and then marched for three miles to the camp. The days began at 5.30 and consisted mainly of tactical exercises, drills, and parades, followed always in the evenings by singing, recitations, and other impromptu entertainments. Henry spent his free time with his friends Anstey Guthrie, Batten, and Guy Pollock,[30] a young freelance journalist whom he already knew; Henry went on occasions to dine with Pollock and his new wife, Edith, as did Anstey Guthrie, who knew him because they both wrote for *Punch*. On Easter Sunday the friends set out after lunch to walk to Stonehenge, visiting the Abbey at Amesbury on the way. They returned there for tea and, after a stroll along the river, had dinner at the George Hotel, walking back to camp eventually by moonlight. Heavy snow arrived the next day, followed by nights of hard frost and problems with the water supply. The friends would have been glad to retreat to their London homes.

Henry clearly enjoyed these camps, and despite his shyness seems to have taken a full part in everything, teasing Anstey Guthrie, for instance, about 'an organ-toned snore'[31] and getting up in the night during a storm to loosen the tent ropes. He returned at least once for an Easter camp, six months after leaving London, joining the Volunteers at Bisley. On this occasion he distinguished himself at shooting, becoming a marksman, and walked and talked in the evenings with Pollock and Anstey Guthrie. On the return journey he left the train at Woking and returned home; whether or not he saw his friends again is not known.

⚘ ⚘ ⚘

Of all the friendships Henry made through his membership of the Volunteers, that with Anstey Guthrie seems to have been the strongest; Batten, the artist, with his 'keen sense of humour & ready laugh',[32] was a frequent visitor in Paulton's Square, and Guy Pollock, although twenty years younger, was another whom Henry met socially. There were many acquaintances of course; William Archer,[33] for example, the theatre critic and journalist, was to come into Henry's life again after some years, when he expressed his opinions in print about *The King's English*. Nevertheless in Anstey Guthrie's diaries Henry is frequently to be found, as a travelling companion on journeys to and from Lincoln's Inn and Harrow, stopping off for tea at the rifle range, or occasionally invited up to his friend's rooms. Anstey Guthrie was immersed in theatrical business at that time, with West End plays in rehearsal, and he often gave Henry theatre tickets, for seats in the stalls which he could not normally afford. They often exchanged letters, including one from Henry in rhyme, and dined together, once at the Arts Club with Anstey Guthrie, of course, as the host.

Presumably the landlady, Rosa Howe, cooked when Henry entertained in Paulton's Square, as he had only an inadequate gas-ring. Guthrie came out to Chelsea on a snowy November night and enjoyed himself, describing the pleasant evening in his diary. He recorded many little stories, aids maybe for his lively imagination, and on this occasion noted down a sad tale of the landlady's family, whose fortunes had declined since Henry's arrival. Edmund Howe, the local police constable, had been 'afflicted with neurasthenia' and 'when asked to come & turn a man out of a public house he turned white and couldn't move';[34] he was reduced to a similar state, perhaps understandably, on seeing a horse fall down. This breakdown had obviously kept Howe from his work, but he recovered for a time and Henry meanwhile helped Rosa financially through this difficult period. This he did not confide to his fellow Volunteer, but his charitable act was uncovered by Coulton later.

Henry was able to enlist Guthrie's help in another small act of kindness at this time. Ralph Ainslie, whose delightful caricatures of his fellow staff members at Sedbergh had caused such amusement, had also fallen on hard times. He had left the school for a headmaster's post[35] but, incapacitated by epilepsy, had been forced to resign his post. He hoped instead to begin a new career as a professional artist, 'a black & white draughtsman',[36] and Henry asked Anstey Guthrie for advice, presumably about placing his work. Four months later a drawing by Ainslie appeared in *Punch*,[37] a charming and gently humorous piece with the title 'Sancta Simplicitas', showing a pretty little girl consulting her aunt about the boy sitting behind her in church who kept smiling at her. Ainslie was to make a good beginning with his new career, but his story soon ended sadly;[38] at his early death he left a widow and small children. Henry had been able to use this new friendship to help his old colleague but was unable to benefit from these relationships himself, as someone less reserved might have done.

✧ ✧ ✧

Henry was poised on the edge of the world in which these new friends, all talented and interesting men, lived and worked in literary London. Batten, Archer, and Pollock could, and perhaps did, introduce him to people who might help him establish a career as an essayist, publishing his work in journals and newspapers. Anstey Guthrie in particular knew all the best people in the social, political, and literary life of the capital, lunching and dining in a relentless round. His friendship with James Barrie, for instance, brought him valuable contacts, as did his position in the inner circle of *Punch* contributors. He was a man of great charm, much liked by all who met him; he clearly enjoyed Henry's company and could have helped him as he had Ainslie. Henry, with a little push, might have become part of this world; but he retreated and left London to live in a tiny cottage on Guernsey and collaborate with one of his younger brothers, Frank, who had been living and working there for some time. This seems an inexplicable withdrawal from a promising future, although eventually it turned out most satisfactorily in all aspects of Henry's life.

His fledgling career was actually beginning rather well and the annual total of £30 a year earned from it was quite a satisfactory sum, but maybe he was not making the progress he had hoped for and believed he never would. His shyness had perhaps seemed unimportant in the closed world of Sedbergh, where he had only occasionally to face the difficulty of coping with new acquaintances, but in London it made it impossible for him to make the advances necessary for success in his chosen field.

Henry enjoyed living in the capital but he also loved travel, certainly when his generous pay at Sedbergh permitted foreign holidays. Frank's life on Guernsey, with its mild climate, would have sounded tempting as another London winter approached with its cold and thick fogs. Family feeling also may have played some part, although Henry had always asserted that 'his family had a defective sense of clannishness . . . no two had ever cared to lodge together'.[39] Maybe the brothers had discussed collaborating on some piece of work which appealed to them both and Henry, after trying a solitary existence in London, decided to attempt island life and the company of his brother.

Whatever his reasons, Henry said farewell to his London friends, paid his rent for the last time to the Howes, and on 13 October 1903 landed at St Peter Port on the beautiful island of Guernsey.

4

An Island Home

‹. . . des morceaux de France tombés à la mer et ramassés par l'Angleterre . . .›
With these words Victor Hugo, once a Guernsey resident and a frequent
visitor after his return to France, described the Channel Islands, 'pieces of
France which have fallen into the sea and been picked up by England . . .'
Although the islands are tucked into the French coast in the Gulf of St
Malo, they have been possessions of the English Crown since their ruler,
William, Duke of Normandy, conquered England in 1066. Two hundred
years later King John lost his mainland French territories, but the Channel
Islands remained with England; they nevertheless resolutely kept their
independence and each of the main islands, with its own assembly, is still
self-governing. The Fowler brothers must have been intrigued, as modern
visitors are, by the lingering Gallic air, noticeable in many ways but
particularly in the very different legal systems and the languages based on
Norman French, still spoken by some native inhabitants.

Guernsey is the most westerly island, about 100 miles south of the
English coast. At that time it was noted for its knitting, particularly the
woollen sweaters, usually navy blue, known as guernseys, which were
much prized, as were Guernsey cattle, exported worldwide. It was,
however, the horticultural industry which first brought the Fowlers to the
island. The mild climate sustained by the Gulf Stream, which makes
Guernsey a paradise of wild flowers in spring, led to the growth of market
gardens whose produce, with the improvement of transport in the late
nineteenth century, could easily be shipped overseas. For the British market

grapes, flowers, and early potatoes and other vegetables were produced. Tomatoes, perhaps the most important crop, had been grown on Guernsey for about twenty-five years when Frank Fowler went out in 1899 to help a college friend grow them on his smallholding, known in Guernsey as a vinery.

✿ ✿ ✿

Francis George Fowler was the seventh child and sixth son of the family, born on 3 September 1870, and so aged eight when his father died. With his younger brother Sam he was sent away to a small school run by a Cornishwoman, Eliza Barnes, at Wolborough near Newton Abbot in Devon. It must have been comforting to Caroline, coping with the difficulties left after her husband's death, to know that her youngest children were safe in her home county, near her family. At Wolborough the boys were only two or three miles from their uncle and aunt, John and Maria Foss, who lived with their children at Castle Dyke House in High Week, a neighbouring village. Maria was another Watson sister, four years older than Caroline, and was comfortably settled, married to John Foss, a prosperous grocer and wine and spirit merchant in Newton Abbot. Caroline stayed with them at times until she found a home of her own, using their address when dealing with the older boys' schools. Edith too, although she was at school in St Leonards on the south coast, must have spent time in Devon during her holidays, for she became a friend of the Foss daughters, Annie Maria and Florence, even remembering them in her will many years later with bequests of jewellery and books.

From Wolborough the boys went on to St Paul's School in London, where they were much nearer home when Caroline took the house in Gratton Road, West Kensington. Frank entered the school in September 1882 and Sam two years later, but he soon left for Sedbergh after a brief and unsuccessful stay. Frank also began badly: 'thoroughly and desperately lazy' was the description given by the classics master reporting on his twelve-year-old pupil. He had been caned three times that term, but this had not helped; his performance was summed up as 'utterly unsatisfactory'. A final comment, 'but with plenty of ability', may have cheered Caroline, who must have been rather unhappy about the behaviour of her two youngest boys. At fourteen

Frank was little better, 'weak and indolent',[1] but gradually his work improved and he left school in 1889 with a scholarship to Peterhouse, Cambridge.

Like his brothers Frank excelled at long-distance running, and at university gained his Blue for cross-country and athletics, being particularly successful as a three-miler. Academically he initially did very well, with a First in the First Part of the Classical Tripos, but he came last of the ten in the Second Part. Perhaps this decline in his work at the end of his time in Cambridge was caused by unsuitable friendships, for he had made friends who were even less successful; among them, James Wilson[2] and Henry Rule Wetherall[3] both left Cambridge without degrees. Frank left with a Third in the final part of the Tripos and then stayed on in Cambridge for some years, living on his small income while taking private pupils; here Henry visited him at various times, perhaps making plans for working together in the future.

The brothers were certainly firm friends, despite the twelve-year difference in their ages, reflecting a pattern among the Fowlers. Charles, next in age to Henry, had a strong friendship with Arthur, eight years his junior, who, as an elderly man, named the stout schoolmaster as his favourite brother. Frank's character was described later as 'difficult'[4] and a school report had noted his 'reserved disposition',[5] but he clearly got on well with his eldest brother. Henry seems to have been the leader in the relationship, writing all the letters to Oxford, for instance, when they began to have dealings with the Clarendon Press. Although he referred to his brother and mentioned his opinions, he seems nonetheless to have controlled the enterprise; only when he was away did Frank write their business letters. Henry was the stronger of the two, both physically and mentally, and Frank followed him, often disastrously, certainly in their wartime adventures.

❦ ❦ ❦

Frank's friend James Wilson went out to Guernsey in early 1897 and bought a vinery in the parish of St Pierre du Bois with greenhouses and a windmill to pump water for crop irrigation; here he began his business as a tomato grower, but returned to England later in the year to marry, bringing his new wife, Mabel,[6] back to the island. In the summer of 1899 Frank went out to join them, at first as a working partner; he would have had little money to invest in the business at this time, but later the nature of the partnership changed when he had access to more funds. Arthur, a young schoolmaster at Sedbergh, described helping to make tomato crates during holiday visits to his brother, but there is no evidence that Henry visited before he moved out permanently. Married friends already living on the island, not named by Henry but undoubtedly the Wilsons, tried hard to persuade him that Guernsey was not for him, citing the lack of entertainment as one reason for staying in London; he, however, was quite determined, convinced that he would enjoy the 'rural isolation',[7] as he called it.

Henry Rule Wetherall also came out to Guernsey at about the same time to grow tomatoes, perhaps at first with James Wilson and Frank, or maybe arriving just two or three miles away quite by coincidence. He joined a group of young men setting up a horticultural business in the nearby parish of St Andrew, married, and spent his life on the island. The Fowlers must have known these fruit growers and may have been friendly with them, although the brothers settled down to a solitary life once Henry was established.

Frank had bought land adjoining the vinery at Les Reveaux and built a small granite cottage on sloping ground down the hill from the farmhouse where the Wilsons were living. When Henry arrived he built another about 50 yards away, lodging at a local farm while the work was done; the cottages, unfortunately destroyed some years ago, were reached by a track through the yard of this farm. Frank had built a three-room house but Henry's was smaller, with the kitchen area used for washing-up only, as cooking was done in Frank's cottage; the accommodation was limited but quite enough for Henry. What appeared, viewed from outside, to be a cottage was inside merely a room, with one end partitioned off for sleeping by a large bookcase which, as Henry put it, veiled 'the penetralia of the part sacred to sleep'[8]; it was not tall enough to touch the ceiling and there was space on each side for entering the bedroom. A conservatory which served as a kitchen and scullery was hidden from the main room by a curtain.

Much of Henry's day was spent outside, beginning, as usual, with a run, very different here from his London route through the streets from Chelsea to the Serpentine. Here he ran down steep lanes to his chosen swimming place on Rocquaine Bay at Le Douit du Moulin, where a millstream reached the sea. While the southern coastline of Guernsey is marked by cliffs, coves, and caves, the western coast is flat, with wide, sandy bays and headlands. Of these bays Rocquaine is one of the largest, with rocks and islets out to sea marked by the Hanois lighthouse, built in 1862, as the area was notorious for shipwrecks. Fishing boats used the bay, but there were also two hotels and picnic houses, which provided refreshments for visitors and hot water for their tea. The Imperial Hotel was at one end of the bay and at the other Lihou, a small island, accessible by a causeway for only a few hours at low tide. In the middle was Fort Grey, an old round fortification, known as the 'cup and saucer', also reached by a small causeway. Several small lanes, with steep banks covered with flowers in spring, lead down to the bay, making it difficult to guess which route Henry might have taken when he ran down each morning.

To the local children, watching from the sides of the road as the Englishman pounded past, this daily routine caused great amusement. They had been told by their parents how very clever Henry was, but they thought him quite mad. Running for pleasure seemed very strange to them, as their parents only ran in emergencies. His clothes in particular were a source of delight, for they believed his outfit to be his underwear, not knowing that people had special clothes for running. Henry never looked at them, but ran straight down the middle of the unmade road (with no worries then about cars of course). His old friend Coulton reported that his routine varied with the tide, but local people recall him being so regular that they could tell the time by his approaching footsteps. Frank and James Wilson are not remembered at all, no eccentric behaviour fixing them in local lore. Perhaps it was odd that someone so shy should draw attention to himself in this way.

Despite this exercise Henry walked a great deal too, for there was little alternative to setting out on foot for expeditions to St Peter Port 6 miles away. He was always anxious to get his post and on a Sunday, when letters could be collected only from the main office in St Peter Port, he was happy to walk in to get them. He would set out at 5 for the twelve-mile round trip, in the dark of course in winter. Although he kept no pets at this time, he enjoyed the company of local cats and dogs visiting his house, and described one companion of these walks—

> The collie, who is *grand seigneur* of the settlement, graced with faultless manners, condescends to walk daily with me to the post-office, holding one end of my stick while I hold the other.[9]

Working outside was another benefit of living in the mild Guernsey climate, which Henry always loved, relishing how 'one found oneself quite warm sitting there half-naked in a sea-mist'.[10] His cottage faced south-west and even in winter he could work outside in the porch. He described sitting out on a December day writing an essay, 'with no clothes whatever beyond a cotton shirt & a pair of thin flannels, nor any need of more'.[11]

In domestic matters Henry was very efficient and did all the work of the little house himself, insisting, 'I cook and sweep and scrub for myself, as a hermit should.'[12] Throughout his life he was always prepared to take on these menial tasks, whether washing up in the officers' mess as a soldier or keeping the cottage clean while caring for his dying wife and continuing with his normal dictionary work.

Gordon Coulton, who was a frequent visitor, described the catering arrangements in detail years later in his brief biography of Henry; Frank and Henry cooked alternately with what sounds like considerable skill.

> The ideal was to depend on the butcher only twice a week. On Monday, for instance, he brought a neck of mutton, and two chops were cooked that day. On Tuesday the rest was roasted; on Wednesday (and Thursday?) it was eaten cold. Then beef, on a similar scale and with similar gradations for the next three or four days . . . Sometimes, again, the fare became mainly vegetarian; there was pea-soup put on to cook after breakfast and forming the staple for lunch. Then tea at 4.30; the frugal, plentiful, stimulating tea of the literary man, and work again till supper, a plain cold meal.[13]

In all, this seems a healthy life and an excellent foundation for the hard work which lay ahead for the brothers, both in the market garden for Frank and in the collaboration which they had certainly planned during Henry's visits to Cambridge. But while Frank worked with Wilson, Henry continued with his essay-writing, sitting at the door of the cottage within sight of the sea.

✤ ✤ ✤

Henry's last days in London had been occupied with the considerable excitement of a great competition, announced in *The Times* of 31 March 1903, where it was described quite correctly as 'novel'. This celebrated the publication of the tenth edition of the *Encyclopaedia Britannica*, recently completed with the issue of the thirty-fifth volume, the great index to its contents. The first prizewinner was to be awarded a scholarship of £1,200 to be held for four years at Oxford or Cambridge—or at Girton, should the winner be a woman, a most surprising decision when university education for women was in its infancy; this scholarship could be commuted for a cash prize of £1,000. The prizes continued in decreasing amounts down to the smallest, scholarships for fifty winners of £12 for a year at an 'educational institution' or £10 in cash. The competition was discussed among the Volunteers and of course the £1,000 prize attracted Henry; it was a fortune and he laid plans for it, dreaming that 'it was all to go in good works of a peculiarly noble kind'.[14]

Three question papers were sent out to applicants, each with twenty questions to be answered using only the encyclopaedia, details of page references to be supplied with the answers, and no other source permitted. Sets were lent to entrants without access to one; institutions, and owners who did not wish to take part, sponsored others to use their sets. Henry must have borrowed a set, for years later, when he needed the encyclopaedia for his work, Oxford University Press gave him one, changing it later when a new edition was published. It would certainly have been a rather weighty item for a single gentleman without a settled home to transport from a London lodging to an island cottage.

The question papers were accompanied by a booklet giving rules and specimen questions with answers. Entrants were given one month to complete their efforts and so Henry spent the spring of 1903 working and dreaming. The competition questions were varied:

> A certain boy (A) six years old, offered to marry a certain girl (B) a year his senior. Some twenty years later A was treated with open disrespect by menials, while B was a Queen. After another seven years a certain emperor (C) asked A not to desert him, and at the same time B was perilously unpopular. Two years more and A was buried in a pauper's grave, while B was approaching a terrible calamity. One of A's most brilliant successes was a work of art in which he collaborated with the Abbé da Ponte. Name B and C.

This could be answered with a few words and no dispute; Marie Antoinette was B and C the Emperor Joseph II, while A, of course, was Mozart. Other questions required much longer answers—

> Describe concisely the social progress and increase of comfort due to the
> advance made by science during the last quarter of the 19th century.

Only an essay would do for this, far more difficult to judge than the more
straightforward type of question. There were problems also with others, one
for instance involving a trumpet blown in a balloon in a light breeze! These
difficulties led the *Times* management to decide not to publish the answers
when they revealed the winners, causing great disappointment to many,
including Henry, who had won a fifth prize, £75.

Among the angry entrants was the winner of the first prize, Leslie Ashe
from Acton in West London, who proposed to publish a small book giving
some of the prizewinners' answers, and so wrote to Henry, asking for a copy
of his entry. The *Times* management objected greatly to this and told Henry
so when he wrote to ask for their advice, although eventually, under great
pressure from entrants, they did agree to the publication of their questions,
which Leslie Ashe issued privately with his own answers and one other set.

✾ ✾ ✾

When Henry, by that time in Guernsey, received his cheque from *The Times*,
he had to decide how to spend his prize. As it was only a smaller amount and
'was obviously not enough to be heroic with', he decided to use it to help
with a cherished project; 'it just gave me a lift towards publishing a book that
no-one in the trade would take the risk of.'[15] This book, Henry's first, was a
collection of essays to which he gave the title *More Popular Fallacies*, echoing
Lamb.[16] Some may have been written in London, but references to the *Times*
competition suggest that others were produced later.

In twenty-four short chapters, *More Popular Fallacies* discussed
various proverbs, from 'Children are the best judges of character' to
'Cleanliness is next to Godliness', 'a delicate subject, very delicate',[17] Henry
thought. Some pieces were quite successful, others merely tedious. 'Let them
fight it out; they will be the better friends', as an example, began:

> There is something large-hearted, prize-ringy, and Old-English about this;
> now is there not? It appeals to the man in us; wakes the generous instincts.
> It calls up visions of a blood-stained pair clasping hands, amid the plaudits
> of a crowd which is delighted that the right man has (as usual) won—
> clasping them not indeed without manifest twinges of sprained fingers and

thumbs, but half disguising these by well-meant contortions of feature which would, we guess, but for incapacitating puffiness, be wreathed smiles.[18]

The conclusion reached after much discussion was that 'While men are men, defeat will rankle, and the friendship born of it be precarious.'[19]

The book was published in 1904 by Elliot Stock under the pseudonym 'Quillet' (a verbal nicety—a quibble, or a small quill), and it was not a success. Even Henry must have doubted its merits, not attempting later to get a new edition when a more accomplished collection was reissued. The response from reviewers was unenthusiastic and any praise reluctant, as Henry himself noted; 'a reviewer told me & the world that "the publisher at least has done his part well".'[20] In collaboration with Frank, on the other hand, Henry's work was to be very different. The brothers had decided to cooperate on a translation of a Greek or Latin author and chose Lucian, a second-century writer of Greek prose satires.

✤ ✤ ✤

Lucian was a Syrian, from the town of Samosata on the Euphrates, and travelled extensively as a young man through Ionia, Greece, Italy, and Gaul. Working at first as a 'rhetorician', he earned his living, as the Fowlers described in the Introduction to their translation, by speaking in court for clients, teaching pupils, writing speeches for others, or declaiming his own, perhaps to an audience who proposed subjects on which he would instantly speak. After many years as a wandering orator, Lucian settled in Athens and adopted a different style, composing comic dialogues between characters from history or mythology, which he performed before audiences or occasionally sold as handwritten copies. Dialogues were a form used for philosophical debates but Lucian was the first to develop them as comic discussions, satirical conversations in prose, and they were his masterpieces; although his style was copied, no one surpassed his skill in their execution.

For Henry and Frank there were, of course, sound practical reasons for choosing Lucian, which appealed to Henry's businesslike nature and made easier their approaches to publishers. There had been two earlier major translations, by Thomas Francklin in 1780 and William Tooke in 1820, but these had long been out of print, while smaller selections were considered on the whole inadequate. Lucian had been for many years ignored, but the brothers, explaining their reasons for choosing him, pointed out the many similarities between the Graeco-Roman world of the second century, when he lived, and the early twentieth century. One area of particular interest, for Henry at least, was emphasized by the statement that 'it was questioning the truth of its religion as we are today questioning the truth of ours'.[21] Henry was interested in Lucian's views and in some areas sympathized with them; writing to a friend later about the translation, he explained that he was quite unable 'in spite of seventeen centuries' extra experience, to look down on Lucian's views of life from a superior altitude'.[22]

By early 1904 enough material was prepared for the brothers to feel able to offer their translation to publishers, contacting first the Clarendon Press at Oxford. Henry had last visited his old university city in 1886, when he finally received his degree after his failures with divinity, and he was never persuaded to make the journey again; but some feeling for Oxford may still have lingered and encouraged him to approach the Press. It was of course the obvious choice for this type of book; Oxford was beginning a new series of translations into which Lucian would fit well. Perhaps the decision was discussed with Henry's old teacher Robert Whitelaw, still living at Rugby, although by then retired; his translations of Sophocles' *Antigone* and *Electra* and Aeschylus' *Prometheus Bound* were published by the Clarendon Press in this new series, but not until a year or two after Lucian.

✤ ✤ ✤

The University Press approached by the Fowlers in 1904 was a rapidly expanding institution. At Oxford was the great printing works in Walton Street controlled by the Printer to the University, Horace Hart, and nearby at Wolvercote a paper mill supplying some of the printers' requirements. The Oxford publishing offices produced academic books under the imprint of the Clarendon Press, which was enjoying considerable success. The great *New English Dictionary*, later called the *Oxford English Dictionary*, was its principal glory at this time; publication had begun in 1884 with the first part, A–Ant and had reached the end of L, with parts of O and R and the whole of Q also completed. An article in *The Times* summed up its position and impact:

It is the greatest enterprise which has ever been undertaken by the Clarendon Press, the greatest effort probably which any University, it may be any printing press, has taken in hand since the invention of printing.[23]

In the City of London at Amen Corner in Paternoster Row, almost in the shadow of St Paul's Cathedral, were the offices presided over by the Publisher to the University, Henry Frowde,[24] distributing Oxford books and issuing more general books under the imprint of the Oxford University Press. A bindery nearby in Aldersgate Street produced fine bindings for bibles and prayer books, and there was a warehouse in Old Street. The New York branch of the Press had been opened in 1896, and others were soon to follow in Canada, Australia, and India.

The Press, as a University department, had been since the early seventeenth century under the direction of successive boards of Delegates, chosen from the academic staff and chaired by the Vice-Chancellor. The Secretary to the Delegates, who acted as a chief executive, was at this time Charles Cannan,[25] Dean of Trinity College before his election as a delegate and appointment to the Secretary's position. R. W. Chapman, for many years his assistant and his eventual successor, described him:

> His manner was formidable; his tone was dry, and even cynical; his last weapon, which he used ruthlessly, was silence; his enthusiasms were unspoken; he had a mean opinion of human intelligence in general, and not a very high one of human probity.

Chapman softened this daunting picture by allowing Cannan, among other virtues, 'a singularly tender heart'.[26] His Assistant Secretary at this time was a young graduate, Humphrey Milford,[27] who was soon moved to London as assistant to Frowde, eventually taking over the running of the London Business, as it was called. Milford did occasionally meet Henry, who, despite refusing firmly all invitations to Oxford, would, when in London, sometimes call in to the office at Amen Corner. Chapman also, staying many years later with Somerset relations, managed to persuade Henry to have tea with him once, but no one else at Oxford was ever to meet him.

Henry Fowler's name was, however, not unknown in Walton Street; it had first come up in 1903, quite by coincidence, when James Murray,[28] the distinguished editor of the Dictionary, needed an assistant. Murray had begun his own career as a schoolmaster but had been editor for twenty-five years by this time and lived in north Oxford, working in an outhouse in his garden grandly named the Scriptorium. Charles Cannan, searching for a suitable candidate, consulted an old friend from his time at Corpus Christi College, Charles Lowry, who had become headmaster of Sedbergh after Hart's retirement. Cannan needed 'somebody of fair ability who is weary of private school mastering',[29] but offered a salary of only about £100, noting briskly, 'there are people who do worse'.[30] Lowry suggested Henry, explaining that he had retired and painting a sad picture of him 'doing precarious journalism in London . . . blessed with a very small competency, & lives on porridge or the like'.[31] Cannan had another idea, wondering whether Henry would like to work for Sidney Lee, the Shakespeare scholar and the first editor of the *Dictionary of National Biography*, who wanted 'an amanuensis to keep his affairs in order and do some occasional research for him in the British Museum'.[32] Henry would have known Lee from Balliol days and might well have been tempted to stay in London by this; the work was for mornings only and the salary, much better than what was offered for the dictionary work, would, with his small income, have made him quite comfortable. Presumably he never knew about these prospects.

❧ ❧ ❧

So on 22 April 1904 Henry Fowler wrote to Charles Cannan in Oxford about Lucian: 'Would the Clarendon Press look with any favour upon a proposal to translate Lucian, with the few necessary omissions?' He stated very plainly the aim of their translation, which was not a crib for students and was certainly not intended for scholars but was 'simply an attempt at a version in modern English, natural enough to attract the general reader'.[33] The brothers had clearly been very busy since Henry's arrival, for they had much of the translation ready and some specimens printed to impress publishers. They worked alone and may have been preparing their sections for some time before Henry arrived in Guernsey. Each part of the published work was marked unobtrusively with a single initial, F or H, to indicate the identity of the translator. Very rarely both initials were attached to a particularly difficult passage to show that they had worked on it together. This practice interested friends but proved misleading to others, particularly one reviewer who 'thought the "lady" sometimes more brilliant than her "husband"',[34] causing great amusement to the brothers.

Charles Cannan responded quickly to Henry's approach; he expressed some doubts about finding a market for the book, but after investigation it was decided that it would sell and within a month Cannan wrote to say that the Delegates of the Press had accepted the proposal. Henry plunged immediately into the details of the arrangements with the well-organized enthusiasm which would become very familiar in Oxford, numbering the points in his letters in schoolmasterly fashion. He was soon making suggestions for the contents of the Introduction; the brothers hoped to attract readers who had never read anything like Lucian before and were anxious therefore to include 'popular notions of philosophy & some celebrities-at-home personal details of philosophers'.[35]

The 'necessary omissions' of Henry's first Oxford letter were partly for some passages of doubtful authenticity, but mostly for matters of decency, a problem with Lucian, as Henry delicately pointed out: 'we are occasionally offended by his frankness on subjects to which we are not accustomed to allude . . . the waters of decency have risen since his time and submerged some things which were then visible.'[36] As editor of the plays of Aristophanes for the Clarendon Press, W. W. Merry,[37] the Vice-Chancellor, was considered a suitable arbiter on these matters and was brought in to decide whether there should be further cuts. Henry and Frank, who had left out the most unacceptable passages, were very happy to accept his position as censor with other doubtful sections and were soon satisfied with the results of his efforts; 'as to stopping the mouths of Puritans, there really is nothing, I think, for them to open them over now,'[38] Henry commented. One particularly difficult section was the Dialogues of the Hetaerae (prostitutes), but even this was eventually sorted out, leaving 'little except the title . . . not fit for parlour use'. Henry and Frank believed that the Vice-Chancellor had 'come very near reducing morality to the level of an exact science', allowing 'a singular kiss (& that 'oh, such a kiss', too) . . . whereas six lines lower the plural kisses are condemned'. They promised, however, that they were 'not the naughty non-moralists, devoted to art for art's sake, that translators of Lucian are traditionally taken for; & we accept our chastisement without (almost) a murmur.'[39]

Lucian was published on 2 August 1905 in the Oxford Library of Translations in four small volumes for 14 shillings. Henry sent a copy to the Harts, now enjoying their retirement in Wimbledon, with a letter pointing out the sections which had proved tricky to translate and those which he felt would interest them, although he was sure that Henry Hart would not share his enthusiasm for Lucian.

The reviews were generally most enthusiastic. Humphrey Milford, in the London office of the University Press, while trying to sell the translation to the New York branch, described it as 'remarkably vigorous and lively',[40] and this was echoed elsewhere: 'The editors . . . deserve high praise for the clearness and vigour of their translations',[41] for example. When it was published in the USA the reviewer of the *New York Times*, with the admiring exclamation, 'Who are these Fowlers?', decided that the translators must be women, deducing this from their work, which was described as 'dainty as well as accurate and finished'.[42]

This was the brothers' first experience of the irritating feeling that their aims had been misunderstood, on this occasion by a reviewer in the *Athenaeum* who caused particular annoyance; he was 'rather childishly perverse',[43] they thought, for he had hoped for an edition of Lucian for scholars and when he found a translation for general readers reviewed it as if it were the edition he had expected.

There were many consolations, nevertheless, in the form of excellent reviews. Perhaps the best came years later, when Herbert Read recorded his opinion of the book in a passage of complete admiration which must have delighted Henry, describing it as 'one of the best modern translations ever made' and as a book to which he returned frequently with real pleasure.

> The translation is so perfect that one is never aware that it is a translation: it reads like the work of an original genius—which, assuming a sufficient accuracy, is the sole test of a translation.[44]

5

No Levell'd Malice

⁂

THE potential of 'these Fowlers' was recognized at Oxford as well as
in New York, and when Lucian was ready for the printer, Cannan
was quick to ask whether the brothers had any other author in mind.
Henry replied with evident interest but explained that 'the translator's
hunting-ground' was far more limited than it had been, as most authors
worth translating had been well done; he and Frank had 'regarded Lucian as
a ἕρμαιον [a lucky discovery] not very likely to be matched'.[1] He did suggest
Don Quixote, always a particular favourite; he had written about it with
delight in the article on 'Books We Think We Have Read' published early in
the London years and 'Sancho Panza, that epitome of human wisdom'[2]
managed, with his fellows, to creep into other essays too. Much later, after
Lucian had been published, discussions turned again to translations and the
early Latin comic poets in particular; the plays of Plautus were put forward,
but Frank had already been working on a translation of Terence in 'easy
going blank verse'[3] and Henry offered this to the Press, although it was not
to be a joint venture. Frank had one play ready which was sent in and quickly
accepted, but the translation never appeared, as its completion was
overwhelmed by other work. For the time being the brothers rejected all
these ideas and put forward, tentatively, a suggestion for a quite different
book.

Henry and Frank had begun quite recently to collect materials for this
small book, but accepted that Oxford might not think it suitable. It was to
be, Henry explained to Cannan,

a sort of English composition manual, from the negative point of view, for journalists and amateur writers. There is a vast number of writers nowadays who have something to say & know how to make it lively or picturesque, but being uneducated cannot write a page without a blunder or cacophony or piece of verbiage or false pathos or clumsiness or avoidable dulness [*sic*]. The book we are thinking of would consist chiefly of classified examples displayed in terrorem [as a warning], with a few rules on common solecisms.

These examples were being gathered from well-known authors and from newspapers and journals, *The Times* and the *Spectator* for example, and the brothers hoped that, as well as being useful, the book might also be 'mildly entertaining'.[4]

Charles Cannan was delighted with this proposal and responded at once, expressing his approval and naming the book 'an antibarbarus'. He had long hoped for something like it, and quickly made clear his strong feelings with a collection of examples which he described as 'a heap of filth of various degrees of abomination'.[5] He also set about proposing cases for inclusion—'Pray attack and excise the abominable preposition "in the case of"';[6] Henry never expressed views as heated as these, although he did comment on these compound prepositions, giving a particularly bad example from their collections which was used later in the syntax section of the book—

> 'A resolution was carried <u>in favour of</u> giving facilities to the public vaccination officers to enter the schools <u>for the purpose of</u> examining the arms of the children *with a view to* advising the parents &c' (*Spectator*)[7]

Practical matters had to be cleared away before work could begin. The brothers were asked to produce a specimen of the proposed text and title, which they quickly did, and were offered useful books, including a set of the parts already published of Murray's great Dictionary. They were concerned about acknowledging their authorship of the new book, feeling their lack of authority, and suggested, with typical modesty, that it might be published anonymously. Writing to Cannan Henry referred to himself and his brother as 'two nobodies' when he explained their position:

> we have occasionally to reprove writers of repute, which is more presumptuous in two who are by their names just known to be unknown than in an imaginary one about whom it is unknown whether he is known or not.[8]

At the end of January 1905 the Oxford people expressed themselves 'glad to go on with the enterprise'.[9] They accepted too the suggestion of anonymity, but when the book was eventually published with initials only attached to the Preface, many guessed the identity of the writers.

Of course there were problems for the brothers when the work began. Henry fretted in letters to Oxford about the tone of the book, for he and Frank were beginning to fear that it would be 'more serious reading' than they had intended: 'We try to throw in a little elegant flippancy here & there, but grammar is a very solemn theme, & our hands are subdued to what they work in.'[10] Later, when opinions were expressed about less successful parts of the work, fears about the tone surfaced again, although by then it was not its seriousness which concerned them but anxiety about whether the Press really objected to 'the flippancy, jocosity, or other indiscretions that appear in these parts'. The brothers felt it best to leave it and not try to remove it from some parts of the book only, telling Cannan, ' 'tis in grain; 'twill endure wind & weather. We have in fact tried to be readable rather than blameless, & preferred making readers (even justly) angry to sending them asleep.'[11]

'I dare say we have been playing about too much'[12] was Henry's suggestion when confessing to another problem; the book was becoming far too long and would need cutting down. He felt sure, and assumed quite rightly that Cannan would agree, that to produce two volumes would be 'to make too much fuss over the thing'.[13] The brothers proposed that the work already completed, including syntax and pronunciation, should be treated as a first part. This would be cut down and much of their remaining material included in a much shorter second part with small articles demonstrating particular problems. Here lurked split infinitives, vulgarisms and colloquialisms, and 'wens and hypertrophied members' among many other delights. This was the final shape of the book. During this shortening much material was excised, something about which the brothers had very mixed feelings; 'some rubbish has been cleared out in the process, though we rather regret some of the omissions';[14] presumably Henry saved the best examples for later use. Soon they were receiving printed sample pages from the book and making choices about its appearance, determined that it must not look like a textbook. Meanwhile opinions were needed about the quality of the work, and for these Cannan approached one of the most brilliant scholars associated with Oxford's great Dictionary.

Henry Bradley[15] was a man of immense ability; he had worked for many years as a clerk to a cutlery business in Sheffield while studying in his free time, eventually becoming an expert in many languages both modern and classical. Aged about forty, he had, like Henry, left his job in the north of England and moved to London, where he attempted to live by his literary efforts. A perceptive review of the first part of the *New English Dictionary* brought him to the notice of the Clarendon Press authorities and he was invited to help Murray with the great work. He was quickly made an independent editor and moved later to Oxford, where he lived in a house in the quadrangle of the University Press building in Walton Street. This formidable man was asked to comment on the initial proposal for the book and was later to read the proofs. The Fowlers were told that Bradley would be a most severe critic and were quite rightly very wary of his expertise, although glad of his advice and anxious, with typical modesty, not to claim abilities similar to his:

> we have practically based no arguments on historical grounds, have made no pretensions whatever to technical knowledge, & have occasionally implied that our authority is only that of the half hour's start, or of having made up our minds on some points the readers have probably never troubled their heads with.[16]

Asked to give an opinion on the syntax chapter, Bradley's reply was brief but encouraging: 'I have gone carefully through this admirably acute and solid piece of work, and enclose a few critical remarks.'[17] He felt rather differently when later asked to comment on the index, which he considered, as first proposed, 'needlessly and undesirably elaborate'.[18] Even when it was revised he was still unhappy, but it was to the contents list that he chiefly objected, condemning it roundly when it was shown to him as 'decidedly the most bizarre table of contents'[19] he had ever seen. It did, however, reflect the arrangement of the book with its two very different sections, and the brothers, while declaring themselves ready to make changes, defended and explained their work, declaring the strangeness of the contents list to be quite unimportant. Bradley's disapproval they excused with the assertion that 'much lexicography doth make him—methodic', going on to explain their own system:

> <u>Our</u> method, as we have said in the preface, is to reject method—not to go systematically through the realm of language, as a grammar must in one way,

and a dictionary in another, but, after ascertaining empirically what blunders and minor faults are most frequent, to make opportunities for introducing cautions against these with as little of a desultory effect as is consistent with such a scheme. This being confessedly the character of the book, the Table of Contents must necessarily be guilty of the same shortcoming.[20]

The brothers had been asked to suggest a title for the new book when they sent in their first sample piece of text and had offered a selection—'The New Solecist', 'The Book of Solecisms', or even 'The Clarendon Press Book of Solecisms'. The first of these had been accepted, but without any serious discussion, and eventually Oxford asked for something better, a title to 'compel the public to buy and yet not look too catchpenny'.[21] Henry and Frank had also hoped to insert something on the title page about the book being intended for schoolboys and journalists, explaining to Cannan their reason for including the schoolboys: 'the proud journalist can say "Ah, that is for the boys", as often as he is affronted by such news as that a singular subject takes a singular verb.'[22] They were very concerned about reactions to the book and well aware of the risks they were taking, so this attempt to indicate the broadness of the intended audience might have served as some protection. They felt one problem with the book would be the great variation between the demands different parts of it would make on the abilities of its audience: 'Some readers will say half of it is so simple as to be an insult to their intelligence, & others that the other half is the sort of stuff that no fellow can be expected to understand.'[23]

For months everyone in Oxford was struggling with the title problem and the office was 'divided into several hostile camps on the point'.[24] Henry Bradley was asked for a suggestion, 'something less erudite than "the New Solecist" but not vulgar',[25] but he could only think of 'Bad and Good English: Chapters on Common Faults in Composition'.[26] Henry and Frank made further hopeless efforts—'Solecism & Journalism', 'Solecisms & Minor Literary Faults', 'Solecisms & Literary Blemishes', 'The Unmaking of English', echoing the title of Bradley's recent book *The Making of English*, and even 'The English of the times (with compliments to The Times)'. They suggested that, as they had gleaned many of their examples from *The Times*, the book should be dedicated to it, although permission would be required to make this dedication and they felt they would have to submit all passages which might cause offence for inspection, so that the newspaper authorities could 'decide with their eyes open'. Even when suggesting it Henry described it as 'a mad notion', adding; 'If it would only have the air of a 400-page joke, it had better not be perpetrated.'[27] Finally the brothers decided to return to their first idea, feeling that the original suggestion was the best—'The New Solecist: for sixth-form boys & journalists'.[28]

Eventually someone suggested *The King's English* and the matter was happily solved, with no mention of schoolboys and journalists and no injudicious dedications, only a quotation from *Timon of Athens* on the title page insisting on authorial good intentions:

> No levell'd malice
> Infects one comma in the course I hold[29]

In the event the title proved more popular than expected. After publication a slight flurry was caused by another publisher, who had produced a book three years earlier with the same title. Henry Frowde in the London Office replied pointing out yet another, written by George Washington Moon and issued in 1881, and the matter was dropped with no more fuss.

✤ ✤ ✤

When *The King's English* was published in May 1906, Humphrey Milford in Oxford felt it necessary to sound a warning note: 'I am afraid that journalists will seize upon the K.E. as a chopping block for their . . . wits, and that you must expect cheap nastiness.'[30] This was indeed what happened, for 'the freedom with which the authors had toiled at a few conspicuous shields aroused a certain amount of natural outcry'.[31] Use of newspaper quotations made the brothers very vulnerable to journalistic revenge, and snippets from popular authors incited admirers to anger. Some reviews seemed unfair to Henry and Frank; one critic condemned them for assuming 'an excruciatingly low level of intelligence'[32] in their readers. Again, as with Lucian in the previous year, they were misunderstood and misrepresented, which particularly upset them;

> . . . they <u>will</u> make us out to have said much ruder things than we have, & to have drawn distinctions that we have not drawn between different authors, & generally read themselves into us. This is inevitable, perhaps; I fear we have sailed rather too near scurrility.[33]

In an article particularly noted by Milford as a 'most telling attack',[34] the reviewer of the *Guernsey Evening Press*, not deceived at all by the initials on the Preface, described the authors as 'two clever residents of one of our country parishes'. He went on to recount their grammatical sins, noting how often they made the errors themselves which they warned about in the book. He also attacked their use of examples from the work of Marie Corelli, clearly a favourite of his, declaring them to be 'ungallant' in criticizing the 'little lady'.[35] He suggested that they read her work for pleasure, but Henry certainly did not, for he never looked at a novel, only newspapers; her contributions must have been selected by Frank or gathered from the collections sent from Oxford.

✤ ✤ ✤

Among these reviewers was a voice from Henry's London past; William Archer[36], critic, journalist, and former Volunteer, attacked the anonymous pair, labelling them 'Architects of Babel' in his headline, although commenting in an early paragraph that they were 'acute & competent critics of style, whose views are, in the main, a little too conservative to suit my taste, though here and there they make astounding lapses into radicalism'. He particularly objected to their views on Americanisms, insisting that, if adopted, their ideas would become 'the corner-stone of a new Tower of Babel which would cast its sinister shadow over the future of humanity'.[37] Archer's anger was caused by the assertion in the book that 'Americanisms are foreign words, and should be so treated',[38] which he called 'philologically false and politically foolish'.

As an example Archer chose 'fall', which Henry, who had written the offending chapter, preferred to 'autumn', commending it as 'short, Saxon (like the other three season names), picturesque.' 'Fall' had once been common in English but had dropped out of use, although still appearing occasionally in literary language and used in some dialects, especially in the expressions 'fall of leaf' and 'fall of the year'. Despite preferring 'fall' Henry felt that, following its lapse from English and adoption by Americans, its use in England was 'no better than larceny'.[39] This allowed Archer to point out a problem and suggest that Henry should have made a distinction 'between classical English preserved in America', which of course included 'fall' and new words coming in from America 'pleading for admission into the English language'. He concluded: 'the attempt to set up an artificial barrier, and treat as foreign all words and expressions which originate beyond the Atlantic, is happily foredoomed to failure.'

To Henry this article seemed much less hostile than the reviews they were receiving by every post. Quite sure that Archer would not remember him, he wrote to him at once in London to explain who he was, and to tell him about his present situation and describe his 'foolish hermit existence'. Henry had regarded earlier reviews as 'such rot' and so was glad to see Archer's, which seemed sensible; he could even forgive his attack; '"clotted nonsense" does not strike us as at all overstepping the courtesies of debate, nor as impertinent either in the parliamentary or unparliamentary sense.' There was, however, to be no agreement between the two; Henry went on to speak of the 'degrading effect' of American on English and his feelings about 'cosmopolitan ideals and a universal language', declaring it to be preferable 'to do one's small best for the national language only'. He was particularly anxious to stress that the book was intended to be used by novices, who would learn the skills taught and then do as they wished. He and Frank did not intend to reform the literary figures whose work had supplied them with examples; 'let Kipling himself americanize, in word or in spirit, as much as ever he pleases.'[40]

In reply Archer, beginning an exchange of letters between London and Guernsey, confessed that on the subject of America he was 'a bit of a fanatic'; he outlined the undesirable result of resisting the introduction of Americanisms:

> two nations who start with the same vocabulary, & have in common a rich & splendid classical literature . . . in constant & intimate oral & literary communication . . . deliberately resist the natural transfiltration of words & forms of speech from one to the other, so as to bring about a gradual divergence & final duality of language.[41]

Henry was nonetheless delighted, pleased to find some degree of agreement and clearly enjoying the contact with an old companion: 'How clever of you! I thought we were irreconcilable; & even in the act of emphasizing our irreconcilability [*sic*] you fling me the formula of reconciliation.'[42] In a later letter he explained how he and Frank felt about American English and Archer's attitude to 'the Pan-English' of which he believed they were 'so foully compassing the death': 'We are not world-reformers or millenarians or laudatores temporis prae-Babelii [glorifiers of the time before Babel]; we are only verbal critics of English.'

Henry went on to insist that they lacked the experience to deal with American English, an argument frequently repeated in their later dealings with Oxford; 'it would be the height of impudence for any one to set up as a verbal critic who was not well read in both branches.'[43] Here the correspondence seems to have lapsed, and Henry's last remaining contact with the Volunteers dropped out of his life.

✤ ✤ ✤

The first printing of 3,000 copies of the new book was selling quickly and the decision was taken to produce a second edition, with corrections to protect its copyright in America and make it more useful. Humphrey Milford in Oxford planned a new preface, suggesting that Henry and Frank might attack and thank their critics with their 'wellknown light touch'.[44] The brothers were delighted at a chance to explain themselves and were anxious to add what Henry called a 'controversial appendix', twenty or thirty pages long with about twelve notes, some of several pages, discussing various topics. One was to be what Henry called 'the tendency of books like ours to encourage a dull uniformity of style, or again to make writers self conscious' and another 'the idea that we have impudently undertaken to teach George Meredith his business'.[45] Among them was to be a favourite subject for the Fowlers, the problem of prepositions at the end of sentences.

'The great preposition-at-end question' had been raised by at least ten reviewers and the brothers were particularly irritated by a remark in *The Times*: 'A sentence ending with a preposition is an inelegant sentence.'[46] Henry wrote to Bradley setting out their feelings on the matter in typically self-deprecating manner, seeking advice, while speculating on the origin of what he called this 'superstition'.

> Earlier writers felt themselves (as we ought to) quite free to choose. Some (eighteenth-century?) grammarian made a rule on quite insufficient induction—as with many grammatical rules— . . . Grammatical parrots have repeated it from generation to generation, not making any independent

inquiry . . . This is only conjectural, you will understand, out of our ignorance.[47]

Of course the brothers recognized that there were sentences where a preposition could not be placed at the end, but Henry enjoyed giving examples of the inelegancies resulting from slavish and unthinking adherence to the rule set out in *The Times*:

> It is laid down in a manual known to us, Do not say, Which pond did you fall into? but, Into which pond did you fall? Picture the poor dripping mortal being frozen into solid ice by this barbarous frigidity.[48]

Frank was, Henry told Oxford, working on a concoction intended to persuade readers to accept their argument which would appear in a section in the new 'controversial appendix'.

> my brother is trying to weave a dialogue entirely out of sentences from the best authors (except the immaculate Gibbon) ending that way. His ace of trumps, perhaps, is: 'A fine conformity they will starch us into!' (Milton). But I fear the continuity of it will escape all but rather acute readers.[49]

'. . . don't be too polemical!'[50] Humphrey Milford urged as the brothers began their work, but when the text came in it was certainly controversial. It was read by Charles Cannan who, with a firm dictum, declared himself 'distressed by discovering in it "apologetic remarks" and some polemical argument with specific persons or reviews . . . "The elementary laws do not apologize, neither does the Clarendon Press apologize."'[51] He sent the appendix off to Henry Bradley, holidaying at Lynton, who expressed his disapproval firmly and was sure that the book would be better without the notes. Henry and Frank were forced to submit to this criticism and cut down their work, although they were particularly unhappy to part with the section on the preposition business: 'we think it actually desirable to be controversial on this question, by way of showing that we know the prevailing opinion, & think it wrong on deliberation.'[52]

Eventually the second edition was published without the appendix and with a tiny preface setting out exactly the changes: 'In this edition new examples have been added or substituted here and there.'[53] The original preface was printed again but had been altered by the removal of all references to particular newspapers by name, only the general remarks remaining. Despite all these criticisms *The King's English* sold steadily, nearly

5,000 copies in the first year. Henry was always surprised at its success, but delighted with the yearly cheques from its sales. Twenty years later he had earned about £1,000 from it and felt 'that it has run both stronger & longer than we had any right to expect'.[54]

❧ ❧ ❧

Henry's letters to Oxford were frequent and enthusiastic, so a silence of nearly three months in early 1905 with no communication from the brothers must have been rather surprising. Although perhaps in Oxford they might have been thought to be merely working hard at their new book, in fact they were occupied with the melancholy business of the illness and death of their youngest brother.

Sam Fowler was only fourteen when he left Sedbergh and must have continued his education somewhere, although no hint remains of where this was, except a reference to him on a census return as a student. His early attempts at a career were as fragmented as his school life had been: he tried work on a tea plantation in Ceylon and was in business in London. Eventually, however, he went out to India to work as a journalist, at first for the *Englishman* in Calcutta, an English-language newspaper detailing all the activities of the expatriate community. Sam clearly made a success of this new beginning, being later described in its columns as 'an ideal journalist, bright, ready and well-informed'. He shared the family's love of words and had another skill, shown also by Henry, his 'remarkable talent for versifying, and his parodies, in rhymes and blank heroics'.[55] By 1904 Sam had moved north-east to Lucknow and was editor of the *Indian Daily Telegraph* at its offices in Abbott Road, but this appointment was to be short-lived. Later in the year he became ill and, with a diagnosis of tuberculosis, was ordered to return to England. This was a long slow journey, and by the time the ship reached Marseilles Sam was too ill to travel on to London. He was taken to the Hotel du Louvre et de la Paix, where he died, aged only 31, on 13 February 1905.

Henry was the informant named in the death registers of the vice-consul, so he must have managed to get to Marseilles in time, travelling from Guernsey by boat to St Malo and then across France by train. Frank, who had spent so much of his school life with Sam and was nearest to him in age, would certainly have gone with Henry. He would have needed help on this dreadful rescue mission if they had been hoping to bring Sam home. But they came back without him, and returned to their quiet island life and their work for Oxford.

✤ ✤ ✤

Henry had sent off copies of *The King's English* to Sedbergh, but the response was perhaps not what he expected. Two schoolmaster friends asked him about writing another book based on a system devised while he was working at the school. Henry had drawn up a scheme for helping pupils with sentence analysis, 'the taking of a sentence to pieces and determining the exact relation of each piece to the rest'.[56] This scheme had been set out on cards, printed locally, which the staff had been using for twenty years. Nevertheless his old colleagues were still struggling to impart syntax and explain parts of speech to small boys and they felt in need of help: 'Say something about the difference between a clause and a phrase . . . These dolts often find it hard to tell t'other from which.'[57] They wanted sentences analysed 'in the far-too-little-known (shades of the King's English!) H. W. style'.[58] Henry's cards helped with this and, with the advice and encouragement of his old colleagues, he expanded them into a small book.

With *The King's English* safely launched Henry offered the Press this new project, describing it as 'a tiny book of English sentence-analysis for lower forms—twenty or thirty pages only'.[59] He was of course asked to submit it; on arrival it was promptly sent on to Henry Bradley, who was impressed by Henry's method, feeling it to be 'far more intelligent and profitable than that which is ordinarily taught' and likely to be 'splendidly helpful',[60] although he did suggest that teachers should be asked about its value in the classroom.

Only one small problem stood in the way of the new book. Henry had used at school a text by another author which, although he considered it useful, had been 'unfortunately disagreeable to self-respecting English boys',[61] because of the unappealing small stories used as examples in the exercises. He sought the agreement of this author[62] and was able to acknowledge that he had 'kindly consented to being thus pillaged'.[63]

Sentence Analysis was published anonymously in October 1906, as by 'one of the authors of "The King's English"' but with its preface initialled by Henry. Unfortunately it sold very poorly—'too hard for the ordinary uneducated master,' Humphrey Milford suggested, reporting to Henry that it had rarely left the warehouse shelves 'and even then mostly by desperate attempts to bribe masters into adopting it by the gift of a free copy'.[64]

✿ ✿ ✿

While Frank grew tomatoes, Henry sorted out his essays for publication; these were safely wrapped in the cloaks of anonymity too. The first volume, *Si Mihi!*, was published privately in 1907 under the pseudonym 'Egomet' which can be translated as 'I, myself'. These are autobiographical essays, described as 'lightly touched pieces of self-portraiture',[65] and although sometimes the self-deprecation becomes irritating, they do provide small insights into the man himself. Henry certainly regarded the book as autobiographical and many years later sent a copy to R. W. Chapman, Cannan's successor as Secretary to the Delegates of the University Press, with an explanatory note:

> Under cover of the Xmas-card season I send you a tedious brief document having the Xmas card's authentic notes of costing the sender little or nothing & benefitting the receiver nothing or less. It is my autobiography as I conceived it some dozen years ago, of no interest to you except so far as any good company officer likes to know his men's antecedents . . . Habent sua fata libelli [books have their own destinies]; this one nobody reviewed, nobody bought, & nobody read; so pray waste no more time on it than on other Xmas cards.[66]

The title *Si Mihi!* translates as 'If I had!' and the book is arranged as a series of eleven essays embodying what Henry saw as wishes for himself, with, after a prologue, titles such as 'If I Had Frankness', 'If I Had Ideas', 'If I Had a Sense of Beauty'. Many of these essays were written after the move to Guernsey and there are frequent references to life on the island. 'If I Had a Cat' is the most successful piece, quite different in style from the other essays, with a charming insight into Henry's life in St Pierre du Bois and his little home. After an opening recital of his reasons for not keeping a pet, the essay develops into a description of a visit from a neighbour's kitten for whom he had temporary responsibility during her owner's absence from home. He describes delightfully his struggles to keep out his 'young admirer', ending in typical style: 'If I had a cat, I should recognize the equality of her right-to-exist with my own just so far as to toss up with her—heads, I drown you: tails, I shoot myself.'[67]

Henry's remarks to Chapman were not quite accurate; there were reviews, but these were distinctly mixed: 'a charming little book of confessions . . . Egomet has a cultured mind, a pleasing wit, and a dainty fancy',[68] for instance, but on the other hand 'self-conscious verbose essays'[69] and 'he is merely shallow and—oh! so banal and trite'.[70] There were also readers; Humphrey Milford, by this time in the London office, hinted in a letter to Henry that he had recognized him.

Si Mihi! was reissued in 1929 with a new title, *If Wishes Were Horses*, and the author's name on the title page. Henry had sent his published collections on a tour of publishers hoping for such a reissue, but this was the only one to find a place. The new dust jacket was adorned with a rather surprising statement:

> A commonplace person, painfully (but not too painfully) conscious of deficiencies in his mental, moral, and social equipment, appeals to the sympathy of fellow sufferers from inferiority complex & introversion, those fashionable modern disorders.[71]

In 1908 another pseudonym, 'Quilibet', heralded a very different set of essays under the title *Between Boy and Man*. These were talks which might be delivered by a schoolmaster to senior boys, preparing them for life after school, and were perhaps lectures which Henry might have given had he become a housemaster. He stated his position very clearly in his preface to the book, explaining carefully that these 'sermons', as he called them, had never in fact been delivered;

> To offer such teaching in a public school of the ordinary kind would be a breach of trust on a master's part; and the author ceased to be a public-school master virtually for this reason. This book should not be put into the hands of boys whose parents think it wise to rely on orthodox Christianity as the only sound foundation for moral principles.[72]

The chapter headings show the varied subject matter, 'Money', 'Choice of Profession', 'Openness and Reserve', and 'Bores, Prigs and the Seriousness of Things' among them. Entertainingly but perhaps predictably, reading is the only subject meriting two lectures. Henry's comments seem often sensible and practical, and sometimes surprisingly modern in attitude. On 'Manliness', for instance, he wrote:

> If you can contrive to regard all these characteristics of young-manliness as the symptoms of a sort of disease, making you rather unpleasant to most other people and occasionally much ashamed of yourselves, but about as inevitable and usually as transitory as the measles, you will have the chance of getting over them quickly.[73]

Sex, Henry explained, had never been mentioned to him at school or at home, although he did think that he had perhaps not understood veiled hints in chapel sermons. In his chapter he put the facts far more plainly than perhaps a modern reader expects from a Victorian schoolmaster, although his terminology causes inevitably a little amusement. He began with what he called 'unnatural indulgence', firstly 'the solitary form of unnatural vice'; the resulting ill-effects were graphically described:

> Excessive indulgence takes the vigour out of you, and makes you soft and effeminate, more like girls than men, and unfits you for doing any work, whether mental or bodily, with the keenness and energy that you would otherwise have. In extreme cases it means permanent and incurable feebleness, with perhaps paralysis or madness in the end.

From this he progressed to 'sentimental friendships' between boys, harmless in themselves, he thought, but going on to 'initiating the small boy into vice'.

'Sexual vice that is not unnatural' followed with the problem of a boy who might take advantage of 'some poor girl, one of his father's servants, a shop-girl, the daughter of working people in his village'. Henry pointed out to his young audience that such behaviour, which in Smollett or Fielding might seem acceptable, was unpardonable in the modern world; he urged each listener to make sure that no girl sacrificed 'her whole life to his short pleasure', explaining that 'in such cases nearly all the guilt is the man's and nearly all the suffering falls to the woman'.[74]

Between Boy and Man was not a great success but does usefully reveal Henry's sound practical attitude to the boys he taught, while illustrating the great division which caused his departure from teaching. His old friend Gordon Coulton described it years later as 'a book of great value for any man who dared to use it freely', and believed that it would be increasingly useful to 'students of Victorian thought'.[75]

Many years later Henry sent a copy of this 'threepennyworth of sermons' with *Modern English Usage* to J. S. Phillpotts,[76] who had been a young schoolmaster at Rugby when Henry was a boy. He added a note asking Phillpotts not to bother with writing to him about the books;

> The world has decisively enough accepted one & rejected the other for me to have no hankering after those private opinions which it is such a nuisance to have to write; now as ever, habent sua fata libelli; & now as ever, authors prefer their luckless products.[77]

Life in the Guernsey cottages had been very busy since Henry's arrival, with both brothers working hard together on their joint projects, while Frank pursued his horticultural duties with James Wilson and Henry continued with the essay-writing begun in London. But changes were looming and the lives of the two 'hermits' were to be transformed in both their working and domestic spheres.

6

The Quart and the Pint Pot

'A pleasant occupation for say 3 hours a day' was the prospect put before the brothers in the autumn of 1906 when the ink was barely dry on the pages of *Sentence Analysis.* Humphrey Milford wrote to Guernsey from his new office at Amen Corner in London, where he had moved to assist Henry Frowde and learn the business. His suggestion was that the Fowlers should write two small dictionaries for Oxford, but he would give no details of the work until he received a response, feeling that they might find the idea 'utterly revolting'.[1]

The Clarendon Press had long planned to produce small dictionaries abridged from the published parts of the great dictionary, by this time referred to by Milford as the *OED*, the *Oxford English Dictionary.* Its completion was 'still misty on the horizon',[2] and vast sums were being expended on the project; much-needed income would be produced by two smaller versions, planned to sell at one and two shillings each. The authorities also feared that, if they failed to embark on the abridgement of the *OED*, other publishers would. They had been casting around for suitable editors and Henry Bradley had been evaluating trial pieces; a former Cambridge Fellow had been the most recent to fail this scrutiny.

An editor had already been found for a third, larger abridgement, the '3/6 dictionary', as it was then known, published later as the *Shorter Oxford English Dictionary.* William Little,[3] a Fellow of Corpus Christi College, had undertaken this work and retreated to Cornwall to complete it. He had been a very popular tutor with many distinguished students, including Charles

Cannan, but left Oxford for Lincoln's Inn and a career as a barrister. After a few years he was forced to abandon the Bar when he became completely deaf, and it was then that he was persuaded to take on the largest abridgement. Little was settled in Cornwall and already at work when the Fowlers were approached.

✤ ✤ ✤

No time was wasted; the brothers were interested, tempted to try something new. Frank's work on Terence was put aside and Oxford set out the rules. The *OED* was to be followed as far as it existed and then its collection of material used to finish the job. Obsolete words were to be excised, except those from the Bible, but etymologies were to be kept as full as possible; spellings were to be as in the big dictionary, although, Milford suggested, they might 'always enter into controversy with Bradley and emerge victorious'.[4] Terms were put forward: a lump sum would be paid in instalments as the work progressed rather than the royalties paid for their earlier work; to be sure that the proposed sum would be adequate, the brothers would need to evaluate carefully their speed of compilation before agreeing. Small dictionaries were sent over to Guernsey as a guide to size, with a bundle of trial pieces produced by earlier workers, some still in manuscript but others actually printed; all these arrived with criticisms from Henry Bradley or his colleagues.

The brothers set to with typical enthusiasm, enjoying the wrangling that went with it:

> Lexicography is very contentious business; we fight tooth and nail over a hundred trifles per diem. As long as this lasts we go very slow and get much enjoyment; when we have made all our compromises and settled in drab uniformity, I don't know whether we shall enjoy it, but anticipate moving faster.[5]

Only three weeks after Humphrey Milford's approach Henry sent across their first efforts, page-long pieces of two sections of text, 'M' to 'Macroscopic' and 'Mandragora' to 'Manna-croup'; 'scraps', Henry called them. These sections were intended as exercises which, when printed, would enable the brothers to assess how much space they were using and get a clear idea of the size of the two books. Accompanying these trials were tables of statistics, word counts in other dictionaries, figures about page sizes compared to prices, and similar data, all typical of the brothers' care and enthusiasm when faced with a challenging new project. Milford must have felt pleased with this good start. In fact he was anxious to press on with the business and was annoyed with the Oxford people when the printed pieces were rather late, telling them that he wanted 'to keep the Fowlers up to the scratch' and that they were 'probably panting for specimen pages by this time'.[6]

Just before Christmas 1906 the first small sample finally arrived in print, set up in different forms so that Milford and the brothers might choose which they preferred. It was accompanied by the usual seasonal good wishes and Milford's excuses, using the time of year as a reason for the delay, since 'a tradesman's life during November and December is full to overflowing'.[7] With the scheme set out in their pieces he was happy, finding it 'more exciting than most small dictionaries', but expecting to have some comments on details later. His final remark must have pleased Henry and Frank; their 'native genius', he declared, would carry them 'triumphantly over the OE[D] thorns', presumably in the form of the daunting Henry Bradley.

✣ ✣ ✣

Larger samples of each dictionary had been promised, based on the first 150 pages of the *OED*, and the brothers worked on these, sending in their copy in the early days of January. For the larger, two-shilling book which was eventually to become the *Concise Oxford Dictionary*, they sent text for 'A' to 'Aerolith' and for its smaller sibling, never completed, 'A' to 'Acetabulum'. Henry commented that he and Frank were working very slowly, and this must have caused some amusement to the men who were used to monitoring the creeping progress of the great dictionary in Oxford. Of course Henry and Frank had worries about their work and they asked for advice about particular problems, but they had to wait until it had been read for a response. Milford immediately sent it off to Oxford for examination by Henry Bradley and setting in the style chosen after inspection of the earlier small samples; with it went a copy of Henry's accompanying letter with a wry comment from Milford for Charles Cannan, the Secretary, about the brothers' complete lack of interest in the financial arrangements: 'would that all our authors were like them.'[8]

Henry Bradley believed that only a member of the *OED* staff would be able to tackle the abridgements satisfactorily, and had been very unhappy about the earlier small pieces presented to him. The Fowlers were by then accustomed to his comments, 'Bradleian usages', as Milford described them, and must have been thrilled to be told of his favourable general verdict on these new larger trials and his belief that they would produce very good small dictionaries. His detailed comments on particular points in their material were nonetheless as tough and plain as the brothers would have expected; as an example, he described the entries proposed for the smaller dictionary as being 'rendered repulsive by the excessive use of abbreviations'.[9] It was suggested to Henry and Frank that they correct their samples using the advice in Bradley's comments and that the material would then be printed. Some type would have to be cast specially for the work and so printing was delayed until the style was settled.

The brothers' first response to Henry Bradley's report was fury that he criticized details which they had taken straight from the *OED*; 'H. W. has taken off his coat to the work,'[10] Milford reported to Oxford, suggesting a pugilistic response. The definition of 'aeon', for instance, had been taken by the brothers from the big dictionary, where it was described, in Platonic philosophy, as, 'a power existing from eternity; an emanation, generation, or phase of the supreme deity, taking part in the creation and government of the universe'. Bradley corrected their definition, suggesting that it was a term from Neoplatonic philosophy. Furiously Henry replied that he should discuss the matter with James Murray, who had edited this section of the *OED*; Bradley's disagreement was not with the Fowlers. Similarly, the etymology of 'ab-' was described as 'badly put' and the definition of 'admire' as 'unsatisfactory', but both these were 'almost slavish reproductions'[11] from the parent volume.

Henry Bradley dealt in his report with the concerns raised by the brothers when they sent in their work, and they were able to digest his comments and respond to them. One of the problems presented had been foreign phrases and sentences; Henry and Frank had added Latin and French tags, many not in the *OED*, such as 'bonnes femmes [ladies' favours]' and 'ad verbum [word for word]', and incorporated them into the text of the books, but then wondered whether this bold move was acceptable. To Bradley it was certainly not right in an English dictionary; he stated firmly that these phrases should be put in a separate appendix. This was one area of the report which Henry and Frank could not accept and it was dealt with most efficiently in typical style; Henry typed their arguments for each problem on separate sheets so that these could be sent to Bradley for further discussion if necessary or dealt with simply in the office. Eventually decisions were made; in the matter of foreign material Henry and Frank were successful and the Latin and French tags were incorporated into the text, although in the end the brothers agreed to omit whole sentences and include only words and phrases.

The etymologies Bradley considered too long; most small dictionaries omitted them, but Milford and his colleagues considered that their inclusion might be a useful selling point. The brothers had been unsure about length, but the eventual conclusion was that those in the smaller book should be further abridged, while in the Concise they were judged to be just about right.

The pronunciation scheme was in fact the biggest problem remaining before work could begin properly. Milford had indicated before Henry and Frank started preparing their trial pieces that they should include some indication of pronunciation but must avoid the *OED* phonetic symbols which were not understood, certainly 'by the man who buys cheap dictionaries'.[17] They therefore concocted their own system, which Bradley condemned for errors and inconsistencies. He was also quite certain that the *OED* scheme could not be used in a popular dictionary but declared himself unsure of the best system to follow, before setting out in detail proposals of his own. Milford felt unhappy about these too and told the Fowlers so when he sent out the report. Lengthy discussions followed on the details of indicating pronunciation; marking stress in words, for instance, proved a problem. The brothers had used the turned period, following the *OED*; this was a full stop placed above the line after the stressed vowel as in 'a·ccent'; it was formed quite simply by turning the piece of type which would print a full stop, hence its name. Bradley was unsure about interpreting this in their text as typewriters did not have this symbol among their array. He favoured using accents to mark stress, but Milford disagreed and the turned period was adopted. Henry and Frank, feeling challenged, adapted their typewriters, changing them in some way so that they could type the necessary sign, a feat which they reported to Milford with justifiable pride. Eventually, after much bandying about of obscured vowels, thick and thin accents, turned letters, and other mysteries, a workable system was hammered out.[13]

Other critical eyes had been cast over the specimen in the Oxford and London offices; John Armstrong, the manager of the New York office of the University Press, was in London and was very impressed by the brothers' efforts, giving his approval to the project. This was most important, according to Humphrey Milford; 'the Americans are great Dictionary-buyers,'[14] he wrote to Henry. Clearly Oxford had found the right men for the abridgement, but Milford was becoming nervous and 'afraid of their suddenly diverging to some other work, which would be a great pity'.[15]

✿ ✿ ✿

'A formidable undertaking,'[16] Henry had called this new line of work, when asked to estimate the time required to produce the two dictionaries. He guessed that it would take between two and a quarter and three years, although of course the rate of progress would improve when they had agreed the method and style. Perhaps this long commitment made the brothers nervous, for they asked Milford if the work might be divided into sections and paid for in this way; this would allow them some chance of withdrawing if they had problems. 'An insurance against death, lunacy or boredom,'[17] Milford called it when he agreed to their plan. Although none of these misfortunes interfered with the progress of the Concise, the first two certainly impeded their later work.

Invited to make suggestions about payment, the brothers were as usual silent. Humphrey Milford felt that undertakers of these large projects knew 'best what intellectual and financial damage'[18] they might suffer but was forced to put forward ideas himself. The proposal, agreed without any discussion, was that the work should be divided into three instalments, A–E and F–N, which corresponded each to three volumes of the *OED*, and O–Z, abridged from the last four volumes; in the end the *OED* grew rather large in production and two of the volumes had to be split, making twelve rather than ten. Payment was to be £100 for the first section and £120 and £150 for the next two, with £80 paid when the last page of each book was passed for press. When inviting comments from Henry and Frank on this proposal, which resulted in their inevitable acquiescence, Milford pointed out how 'the pay improves as the shades of the prison-house darken!'[19]

✿ ✿ ✿

The Fowlers completed their revision of the first trial pieces and, while waiting to see the printed versions, settled to work, spending ten hours a day each rather than the six they had planned. Humphrey Milford, describing them as 'indefatigable', suggested to Charles Cannan, the Secretary at Oxford, that they should be held up as examples to the 'feeble Oxford lexicographers'.[20] The brothers were, Henry said, feeling the results of their efforts: 'The perpetual struggle between the quart and the pint pot is having serious effects on our literary style and the color of our hair; but we are maintaining it gallantly'.[21]

They were, of course, having some problems, finding, for instance, the *OED* rather behind the times in some areas as new words or meanings had evolved in the years since the earliest parts were produced. When 'blouse' had been drafted in 1887, it was not commonly used for an item of female clothing but was described as a 'light loose upper garment of linen or cotton, resembling a shirt or smock-frock'[22] and its application to the blue blouse of the French workman noted. During the last years of the century its use for an article of feminine attire had been growing and, when they reached its place in the dictionaries, the brothers felt the need to add another definition; they concocted to fill the gap 'woman's loose light bodice visible only to waist, and there belted'.[23] Similarly the 'blue-water school', a group of strategists who believed that a fleet was the only defence necessary for Britain, had not been heard of when the relevant part of the *OED* was drafted, but by this time Henry and Frank felt that the phrase merited inclusion in both books. It would have been damaging to omit these words, and the example of 'appendicitis' served as a warning to the brothers; its omission from the *OED* seemed ill-judged after the popularizing of the word by the new king's illness before his coronation in 1902, a business in which, of course, Henry had played his own tiny part. Later, when 'appendicitis' was added in the supplement to the *OED*, the earliest quotation proved that criticisms of James Murray were unjust and the word had first appeared in print in 1886, after the publication of the part to which it would have belonged, Ant–Batten. These additions did cause the brothers some anxiety for, although they were familiar, they seemed, according to Henry, 'not so familiar that one can define them in so solemn a context as that of a dictionary without tremors'.[24]

The production of the promised printed samples was being delayed by the need to buy considerable quantities of new type, but this allowed the brothers to continue quietly with their work. They had incorporated all the agreed changes but, on reaching the end of B, had accumulated various points which they could not settle between themselves. Quite naturally they were anxious not to leave things undecided, and feared being forced to go over old ground again to make revisions. They prepared a list of doubtful points, and this was submitted by Humphrey Milford for immediate inspection by Henry Bradley and his colleagues; Milford was anxious that 'the Brothers should not be checked in their career'.[25] Quickly the list was returned with 'Bradleiana and pencilled glosses by inferior philologists'; the feeling amongst the critics seemed to be that the books were becoming 'too clever' for their proposed audience and Milford exhorted Henry and Frank, 'Please be as stupid as you can.'

One matter came up for discussion again on which it seemed that the brothers would never agree with Bradley; this was the problem of the pronunciation system, generally agreed, but still in dispute in the area of foreign words. Different systems were put forward but each appeared satisfactory only to its inventor; finally it seemed best that all attempts to indicate foreign pronunciations be dropped. Milford summed up the situation: 'I can see that you and Dr. Bradley will eventually have a triangular duel (on Sark) over the pronunciation of foreign words'.[26]

The arrival of the eagerly awaited printed sections produced another flurry of opinions from Oxford and London, some from Henry Bradley, of course, and from the Secretary, Charles Cannan, also. Among his comments was one piece of refreshing praise, mixed with inevitable small criticisms:

> I am lost in enthusiasm over the article 'above'—the quotations and instances seem to me most appetizing: I wish there were more of these deft examples and less laborious etymologizing.[27]

Milford also approached one half of a pair destined to become another Oxford institution. Herbert Ely collaborated with his fellow editor Charles L'Estrange to produce children's books under the name 'Herbert Strang', with assistance from ladies in the office to produce books for girls by 'Mrs Herbert Strang'. These gift and prize books, annuals, story-books, and adventures, were to become an important part of the London business for the next thirty years. Milford asked Ely whether he believed that the new dictionaries would be 'intelligible to the plain man likely to use [them]';[28] Ely's most emphatic response was that the smaller book would be 'far above the heads' of its intended audience.

The Fowlers themselves commented at length on their intended changes and the typography. There were many small matters, such as superior numbers; where they had typed, for example, 'AL2,' they had intended the printer to put 'AL²'; more alterations to their typewriters were necessary to ensure that this would not be misunderstood again; some additions by hand would be necessary when preparing copy, although they preferred not to do this. Page size also was a cause for concern; this allowed Henry to indulge in much counting of words and comparing of statistics with other dictionaries. The question was whether to have fewer larger pages or more smaller; 'fatness in books is not to be desired,'[29] Henry remarked. With all these matters before them, the brothers set out to revise the trial sections again and then continue with their work on the first segment of the dictionaries.

More than fifteen months had passed since the first proposal, and the brothers expressed to Milford their concern about the two books. Although they were not dissatisfied with them separately, they felt that there was perhaps not 'enough difference between them to justify the existence of both'.[30] They suggested cutting the etymologies from the small book which would not only reduce its size considerably but would also make a very obvious difference from the Concise. The Oxford people were also concerned, and planned a canvassing of more opinions when the revised sections appeared—on this occasion from schoolmasters who might advise about the suitability of the small book for their pupils. In the meantime they asked the Fowlers to wait for a response.

The first sections of the dictionaries, A–E, were due; they had been promised at first for Christmas 1907 and postponed by the brothers until the middle and then the end of January. By early March Milford was worried: 'I hope its non-arrival does not mean influenza or any other misfortune? We have been so fiercely attacked here that I fear even your balmy isle may not have escaped'.[31] Henry had, however, caught something very different, and it was to this happy occurrence that the delay could be attributed.

✤ ✤ ✤

'I have never fallen in love . . . but I am not tempted to lament over it,' Henry had written in the previous year, making this confession in a chapter in *Si Mihi!* where he described his feelings about his 'sense of ladies' beauty', something for which he cared little; he did show, however, his liking for women, even being happy to talk to them in his 'more sociable moments'. He set out very clearly his feelings about marriage, revealing considerable timidity about approaching suitable candidates—

> But to decide the momentous question which of them, if any, is the one that I should like to contemplate & talk to through life; to plunge into the social vortex by way of qualifying for deciding it rightly; to stay there until the decision could be converted into action; & afterwards to revolutionize my whole life in consequence of it—I stand aghast at the bare thought.[32]

'I am incurably shy';[33] another confession from the pages of *Si Mihi!* explained Henry's failure to develop any relationship with the women he met. It is easy to believe that he had never been involved with a woman when reading his catalogue of fears, revealing his lack of 'social experience'.[34] He had never been to a dance and would not have known how to behave if he had; he wondered, for instance, if it mattered which arm he offered to his partner. He could not talk across a wide table, walk across a room, or express interest or admiration for fear of being noticed, considered presumptuous, or misunderstood. He would not dare to call upon friends uninvited in case they had with them others he did not know. This parade of inadequacies which Henry condemned as a lack of manners, he blamed for his state. Had he possessed the qualities he wished for, he might have been

> a dweller in towered cities instead of in this *angulus terrae* [corner of the world], a diner-out instead of a hermit, a paterfamilias instead of a lone lorn man, a member of Parliament instead of a writer of books.[35]

Henry would of course have met suitable women at Sedbergh, sisters and daughters of his fellow masters for instance. Just before his departure for Guernsey young Arthur had married Ada,[36] the sister of his old colleague, F. P. Lemarchand; she had come north to help her brother when he became a housemaster in 1898. In traditional house photographs Ada's round face smiles besides her younger spouse's gaunt but handsome features as she sits beside him with a small dog on her knees. She was clearly a great help during Arthur's time as a housemaster until cruelly handicapped by ill health in later years. Henry had obviously never met anyone sufficiently captivating or determined to overcome the mental obstacles. But all this was soon to change: the 'lone lorn man' was caught by a plump nurse with a merry laugh and a mass of white curls, and settled happily after a whirlwind romance in a most successful relationship.

✿ ✿ ✿

Jessie Marian Wills was a Wiltshire girl, born on 31 May 1861 on the western edge of Salisbury Plain at Upper Knook in the tiny village of Knook near Warminster in the Wylye valley. She was the seventh child of Mary Ann and Richard Sydenham Wills, who was described on her birth certificate as a yeoman, and was certainly at that time a most prosperous farmer, with 674 acres of land and a large team of men and boys to work it. When Jessie was ten the census, while recording again her father's substantial farming business, revealed that Mary Ann had a cook and housemaid; the children remaining at home, four girls, Florence, Harriet, Jessie, and Alice, and one boy, Turner, were kept in control by a governess. Within a few years all this had gone, swept away by some great misfortune which had clearly overwhelmed the family.

These were dreadful years for farmers; Europe was plunged into a great agricultural depression caused largely by an influx of grain grown on the prairies of North America. Innovations in farm machinery aided production over there and much cheaper and quicker transport by sea and rail made it possible to send the grain across to Europe. A series of bad summers added to the disaster and the British farming industry was in ruins. Labourers left the land for emigration or work in the growing cities, and the farmers themselves lost their businesses and homes. The disappearance of the Wills family from the Wiltshire countryside during these years may well reflect the situation of many farming families reduced to poverty by the agricultural decline.

The family was scattered across the country. Richard, the eldest son, was a bank clerk in Lewisham and Jessie became a governess herself, caring for Robert, Mary, Ruth, and Edwin, the four small children of John Leiven, the rector of Burnham Thorpe in Norfolk. Her parents settled in the seaside town of Seaton in Devon, where her father worked as surveyor for the local council. His changed circumstances were reflected in the will left at his death in 1891; in touching language he expressed his regret at being unable to provide for his eight children, feeling that 'as there is so little' he should leave it all to their mother and ordering, with the lack of punctuation normal in these documents, 'that my funeral may be as plain as possible no unnecessary parade such as hearse hatbands &c but a simple plain coffin carried on some kind poor mens' shoulders'.

For many years after this Jessie is hidden from view, working presumably as a governess and later training as a nurse, but she eventually appears again, living in Guernsey. In 1905 she was running a nursing home in St Peter Port when her mother, Mary Ann, died there of bowel cancer, 'at her daughter's residence, Sunnycroft'. This was a large handsome house with four floors and a pillared porch, still standing as 3 Grange Terrace, Grange Road, high above the steep streets and precipitous flights of steps which tumble down to the harbour of Guernsey's capital. Nothing reveals when Jessie arrived; the house had been the family home of a local doctor, Charles D'Auvergne Collings, and his English wife, Laura. He had consulting rooms nearby with his colleagues, one of whom, Dr Carey, lived in 2 Grange Terrace. Perhaps Jessie came out to help with the Collings' children or to superintend a nursing home begun by the doctor. Certainly it was eventually her own business and, before the war, it prospered.

❧ ❧ ❧

Henry had first met Jessie as a patient when he was nursed by her for what Gordon Coulton, later his biographer, coyly described as 'a small operation',[37] but it was when his old doctor friend from Balliol and Chelsea, Terence Woulfe Flanagan,[38] spent time in her nursing home that the great romance began. Flanagan had given up his medical work and was 'drifting about on a small competence'. Diagnosed with neurasthenia, he was admitted to Jessie's nursing home, and while he was there Henry of course called on him; when Jessie 'kind-heartedly lent her own sitting-room to the patient and his visitor',[39] the elderly pair quickly fell in love. On Christmas Day 1907 Jessie invited Henry to share her meal and years later he recalled

> The bachelor guest, the hostess maid
> Of that first Christmas dinner.[40]

The relationship flourished; on 29 February 1908 Henry, putting aside his natural timidity, proposed and was accepted. Eight years later, as a soldier writing from France, he repeated the proposal, the light-hearted agreement being that 'the engagement was revocable as its anniversaries came round'.[41]

> I should perhaps warn you before we start that I shall have a question of some importance to put to you—no less a one than whether you will consent to change your name for mine, & that at short notice (by the way, I wonder whether the censor deals indulgently with proposals of marriage; or does he think it is wrong to let the Germans know that there is a project afoot for increasing to some slight extent the population of Great Britain).[42]

There was no reason to delay the marriage and it took place ten days later on Henry's 50th birthday, 10 March, at St Stephen's Church in St Peter Port, a brisk walk up Grange Road from Sunnycroft. Of course Frank was present as a witness but presumably the other surviving brothers, being trapped at that time of year by the demands of school life, were informed by letter about the sudden decision, as was Gordon Coulton. It seems perhaps odd that Henry should submit so readily to a church wedding, but Jessie was always regular in her attendance at services and Henry never interfered with this; he was indeed always anxious to ensure that she did attend and years later, when she was sick and frail, waited for her in the church porch to escort her home.

Safely married, the happy couple set off on a seven-mile boat trip eastwards for their honeymoon on the neighbouring island of Sark. In March it would have been at its most beautiful with masses of wild flowers, and the honeymooners, who were great walkers, would have enjoyed exploring. The steep climb up from the harbour would not have worried them, although they might have taken a horse and carriage ride on such a special occasion, but for Jessie their arrival did produce other difficulties; the harbour of Le Creux was approached at that time through a sixteenth-century tunnel, and the climb from boat to quayside would have been understandably tricky for a large lady of advancing years. The Fowlers were to be most diligent in celebrating anniversaries, and Henry marked a second honeymoon in 1912 by verses given to Jessie under the title 'Honeymoon No.2', noting her unease at the difficult landing.

> Again we've crossed the seas, and faced
>   That horrid disembarking,
> A second honeymoon to taste
>   And go once more a-Sarking.
>
> First honeymoons are very well,
>   But too experimental;
> For either's energies to spell
>   The other's moods are bent all.
>
> The four years' flight almost has been
>   Too swift for our remarking;
> Before we know't, nineteen-sixteen
>   Will catch us still a-Sarking.[43]

The intention to repeat the trip to Sark every four years was not to be realized; the war of course prevented the next planned visit.

✤ ✤ ✤

Verses such as these were given by Henry to Jessie, hidden under her pillow for her birthday, the anniversaries of their engagement and marriage, and often for Christmas; he sometimes referred to her by her second name, Marian, or named them both as Darby and Joan. Some verses were printed in the *Westminster Gazette* and many were collected by Henry into a small volume, published as a broken-hearted tribute after Jessie's death. Some years before he had offered a small collection to Oxford University Press for publication. 'The doggerel', Humphrey Milford called it, and felt that, although it was 'really quite jolly and touching of its kind',[44] it would be better not to publish it but to print a few copies for distribution to family and friends. Some verses are certainly more successful than others, as selected passages show, but they all reflect Henry's great love for his wife and their happiness in their marriage from the earliest years—

O Jessie, jes' ye think of what I asked a year ago;
O Jessie, jes' ye give me now the answer, if ye know;
O Jessie, jes' ye tell me if ye'd live with me your life;
O Jessie, jes' ye whisper if ye're fain to be a wife.[45]

This never falters until the last lines written after her death, following a gap of some years when her long last illness made the production of verses seem perhaps rather frivolous.

This was a marriage of complete opposites, in appearance, temperament, attitude, and interests. Jessie, for instance, was rather stout and taller than her husband, whose neat figure was of course fit from his athletic pursuits; 'stumpy and plebeian', he described himself. She had a mass of hair which, according to Henry, had gone white years before when she was ill; he had by contrast very little hair remaining, ascribed by him in jocular fashion 'to the daily orgies of soap and water with which in youth we worshipped at the Shrine of Cleanliness'.[46]

A natural perruque she grows
Of silver curls well ordered;
With narrow fringe that sparsely shows
My naked noddle's bordered.

Gordon Coulton contrasted 'her eternal loquacity with his natural taciturnity' and described staying with the pair:

it was good, at their table, to watch him listening to her irresponsible and entertaining babble, with glistening eyes that wandered from guest to guest, saying most plainly 'Isn't this capital fun?'[47]

Coulton was a frequent visitor to the Fowlers' various homes and was by this time married too; Henry had been across to England to be best man at his marriage to Rose some time before his own wedding.

These various differences were summed up delightfully in verses written in July 1911 and published later in the *Westminster Gazette* under the title 'Harmonious Discord'. A selection illustrates Henry's picture of their marriage.

My wife and I we disagree
On every mortal matter;
The Sprats, 'tis said, were odd; but we
Are infinitely spratter.

Of fifty Aprils she's the sum,
  Sunshine and showers together,
While fifty-three Novembers come
  In me to sober weather.

Her fitting throne an easy chair,
  Her joy a motor-car is;
For me a stool, or Shanks's mare,
  A fitter mount by far is.

Words are my study, life is hers;
  We go to different teachers;
I learn from books, while she prefers
  To learn from living creatures.

Yet (though you'd say words had their use
  In speech, as legs in walking)
A sentence rarely I produce,
  And she does all the talking.

A crowning discord only can
  Solve discords so inhuman:
She says the world to her's one man,
  To me it is one woman.

After the honeymoon on Sark, Henry and Jessie sailed back to lexicography and nursing on Guernsey. They lived at Sunnycroft during the week, Henry cycling out to his small cottage each day to work and returning to the nursing home in the evening; weekends were spent in the cottage, where the pair must have felt rather restricted in the tiny space. In 1912 James Wilson, Frank's business partner, suggested an improvement, offering to exchange homes. Wilson's marriage had failed and his wife, Mabel,[48] had returned to her family home in Kent; as early as 1908 court proceedings in Guernsey had made financial arrangements which amounted to a legal separation between the two. Being single, Wilson was willing to settle in the cottage and Henry and Jessie moved up the lane to his farmhouse, then called simply Lihou, in modern times Lihou Cottage. They must have felt rather sad at parting with Henry's home, although it was not sold to Wilson; Henry owned it until his death. Lihou, on the other hand, had real advantages, as he pointed out in rather complicated and not always successful verses written for Christmas 1912 as a conversation between the tiny cottage and the larger farmhouse under the title 'Sighs and Smiles':

Though I'm not so snug to nest in
(Sighs Lihou)
As your well-beloved Cottage,
I've a range to cook your pottage
And a room to stow a guest in
(Smiles Lihou)[49]

Some work was clearly necessary on the new house, and Henry would never shirk the need to deal with domestic matters. By the anniversary of the proposal in February and the wedding in March he could jocularly suggest that he felt rather overwhelmed by chores, in the first verse of 'Floors and Rhymes';

I fain would rhyme, but I am dumb-
My wits so obfuscated
With laying of linoleum
That rhymes will not be mated.[50]

✤ ✤ ✤

Household duties and versifying aside, Henry needed to earn money. Later he commented to R. W. Chapman, Cannan's successor as Secretary at Oxford, on his attempts at making a career as an essayist:

the apple-cart was upset by my unexpectedly marrying at fifty. I had to make a few pounds yearly out of printers' ink instead of spending them upon it; & so came the C.O.D.[51]

7

A Marvel of Condensation

❦

'H E WRITES most penitently and says it shan't occur again,' Humphrey Milford told Charles Cannan, the Secretary, when communicating the details of the Guernsey marriage, meaning of course not the wedding but the delay. The missing first sections of the dictionaries arrived within weeks, and work was then suspended in view of the unease felt by all parties about the two little books; discussions were to take place and decisions had to be made about the future.

Henry and Frank were not left unoccupied while all this debate went on in London and Oxford. Milford's reaction to the news of Henry's marriage had been perhaps an indication of some guilt; maybe, he suggested, they should send a wedding present, 'having made so much more money than he out of King's English'.[1] It was certainly selling well, and a proposal had been made earlier to the brothers that they might produce a shortened version of the book. Of course with their dictionary work they could fit in nothing else, as Henry explained: 'Our leisure . . . is since we delivered ourselves over to these exigent dictionaries non-existent.'[2] They did nevertheless feel enthusiastic about the project, thinking that much in the book was too difficult for its intended audience and would be appropriate only for those who would never use it. By condensing the material they could make it available at a suitable price, about one shilling, for those who really needed it. While Henry and Frank waited for decisions, there was time to begin the work.

The brothers were becoming familiar during these discussions with the dreadful handwriting of a new figure on the Oxford scene with whom they were to have dealings over many years. This was Robert Chapman,[3] a Scot, who had been appointed assistant to Charles Cannan and was to become Secretary to the Delegates after the war. A notable scholar, he was an expert on the works of Jane Austen, preparing the standard texts of her novels and other papers which were published by the Press and also collecting and editing her letters. Similar work on Dr Johnson established his scholarly reputation during his years as a publisher at Oxford. He was also a considerable eccentric, inexpertly rolling his own cigarettes and riding his bicycle in a daring fashion in central Oxford. Chapman took a great interest in the affairs of the *OED*, contributing collections of slips and endless comments which still linger in the files at Oxford, providing a challenge to all who attempt to read them.

'The educational market is a mysterious thing,' Chapman told the brothers, asking for a chapter of the proposed abridged *King's English* to be examined as usual by the Oxford experts. Henry and Frank were quite clear about the book's place, stating that it would 'not be of much use except to the upper stratum of schoolboys' and feeling that they could not make a textbook from it. They were not prepared to change the book completely, rejecting 'radical changes in tone & arrangement', but were ready to shorten to the extent required by the Press. They proposed to cut out the second part, transferring any suitable sections to the first, and similarly to omit the punctuation chapter or heavily reduce it if Oxford objected. 'Elaborate discussions'[4] were to be excised, and wherever possible shortenings were to be made.

There were the usual exchanges between Oxford and London about the proposed reduction. Humphrey Milford doubted that the brothers 'could successfully execute a more methodical work', and felt sure that they should make no attempts to change the style of the book, thinking them 'wise in sticking more or less to their original lack of method'.[5] Chapman eventually responded to the brothers, agreeing on the whole with their plans although unhappy about the excision of the whole punctuation chapter. The hesitation in Oxford about the book was, he revealed, caused by some doubts about its commercial viability, but this Henry happily shrugged aside: 'the suggestion was yours, not ours, which comforts us.'[6]

A few weeks later the completed work arrived on Chapman's desk, with (as usual) accompanying statistics from Henry giving details of their work. It seemed sensible, as he suggested, that the little book should keep its original title with just the addition of the words 'abridged edition'. He rejected descriptive phrases such as 'for the use of schools' which might have limited its appeal; the unfortunate suggestion 'for persons of mean intelligence' was not considered 'attractive'[7] and would surely have been commercially disastrous. The little book was launched on 20 November 1908 and was to outlive its authors by many years, being finally put out of print in 1969 after fourteen impressions and sales of 40,000 copies. It had effectively occupied the brothers while the fate of their dictionaries was decided by the Press.

✿ ✿ ✿

Elementary schools were judged the key at home to the success of the smaller dictionary, estimated by this time to cost two shillings rather than the intended one, as it had turned out rather larger than originally planned. The main questions to be decided were whether it was worth continuing with it and, if so, whether the etymologies, which could be trimmed no more and were causing the length problem, should be dropped. 'Expert schoolmagisterial opinions'[8] had been sought at the cost of a guinea each from several advisers in different parts of the country. When their reports had been evaluated it was clear that the smaller book was not thought suitable for elementary schools, although there was a need for such a dictionary as none of those available really satisfied requirements. Armstrong, the manager of the New York branch, had been enthusiastic about it on his visit to England, and it seemed sensible to seek his opinion before finally dropping it; there was, however, no support for the book from him, so the decision was finally made and communicated to Henry and Frank. Plans were launched for finding someone to produce a small dictionary suitable for elementary schools, but this came to nothing.

The brothers had been prepared for this outcome and so accepted it without argument:

> We are glad the little dictionary's fate is settled, sorry it is settled as it is; to
> have produced an unmarketable article is disconcerting. I wish we could

offer to begin again on a different plan; but small dictionary making except on some such lines as we were going on seems hardly endurable for a self-respecting person.

They were on the other hand concerned about the Concise, feeling that its differences from other dictionaries might make it also unmarketable. 'We have no fancy for being paid for unsalable stuff, &, if you would like to drop both books now, we should have no objection'[9] was Henry's offer, but the Oxford people were quite happy.

The question of payment for their work on the *Concise* remained to be settled, as the original agreement had been for the two books. Frank was quite unable to calculate how much of his time had been spent on the small book, but Henry, who was far more capable in business matters, quickly settled that the fee originally agreed should be reduced by one fifth. Humphrey Milford felt a little guilt about cutting down the payment: 'They are so tractable about money that one hardly likes to talk about deducting anything.'[10] Nevertheless they accepted Henry's calculations. The brothers also offered to give up one half of their fee, proposing that it should be changed to a royalty; if the book failed they would not feel that they had benefited when the Press had lost money, but if it succeeded they would gain financially. 'We think we ought to take the risk,' Chapman told Henry in reply to the suggestion, 'so please let us pay you like honest traders.'[11]

Henry and Frank estimated that the Concise would be finished by the end of 1909. They did find it hard to gauge how difficult the work would be after they passed the end of the completed *OED*, feeling unsure whether they would be able to work more quickly when not referring to it or more slowly when writing entries rather than abridging them. When they finally reached this point and were faced with the prospect of completing S–Z without the support of the big dictionary, their fears were to some degree realized:

we go rather slower, produce rather shorter articles, & have always the consciousness, with the words that really matter, that a third or so of the senses are likely to be escaping us; but we are getting on.[12]

Later the brothers explained how they had used the modern dictionaries sent out by the Press to make up for the lack of the parent volume, adding to this what they 'could get from other external sources or from' their 'own heads'.[13] Having assembled all this material, they then produced their own entries.

They could appeal to Oxford for help if necessary in this more difficult section. They asked Charles Cannan, for instance, to find information which would help them define the phrase 'Windsor uniform', a special outfit worn, with the permission of the monarch, for some state or ceremonial occasions at Windsor by members of the household or guests; it consists of a blue or white waistcoat topped with a blue coat with red collar and cuffs. Henry tried to find the truth about it, but the nearest he got was 'to discover some one whose cousin wears it in capacity & on occasions & in places unknown'.[14] Cannan believed, quite wrongly, that the Prince Consort had introduced it, but in fact it had been first worn long before during the reign of George III. He approached John Fortescue, the librarian at Windsor Castle, to extract the required definition, which, after use by Henry and Frank for the Concise, was passed on to the *OED* staff to await their work on the letter W.

When the fate of the small book had been settled and the style of the Concise set, Henry and Frank were able to work on quietly, submitting material periodically to the Press. In early 1910 the end was reached and the final batch passed to the printer; the *Concise Oxford Dictionary* was finally published on 16 June 1911.

In their almost universal praise, reviewers emphasized points which the brothers had raised in their preface when explaining the principles adopted for the work, setting out the differences between their book and other small dictionaries. Stressing that the book was 'designed as a dictionary, and not as an encyclopedia',[15] Henry and Frank ascribed to this all its 'peculiarities', as they called them, as compared to the current popular dictionaries, which were, as one reviewer described them, 'a blend of glossary and encyclopedia'.[16] The treatment of common words was the greatest difference: in existing dictionaries these words, being used most and therefore known to all, were quickly covered in a line or two, so that 'go', for instance, would take up less space than its near neighbour 'gnomon'. To the brothers these small words needed space and explanation, for they were 'entangled with other words in so many alliances and antipathies during their perpetual knocking about the world that the idiomatic use of them is far from easy'.[17] So conjunctions, prepositions, and pronouns were treated in detail, as were the simplest nouns and verbs, 'run' and 'set', for instance, and 'go', the latter being allocated two columns in the new book. This 'masterly analysis of common words' was singled out by one reviewer as worthy of 'special attention'.[18]

Illustrative quotations were used freely 'as a necessary supplement to definition'. They pointed the distinction between the senses of a word or demonstrated the meaning if the definition was felt by the brothers to be 'obscure and unconvincing'.[19] They neatly summed up their belief about the use of these examples: 'define, and your reader gets a silhouette; illustrate, and he has it "in the round".'[20] The parent *OED* had used quotations, collected over many years by an army of volunteers, to demonstrate the history and development of words, and in their abridgement the brothers had naturally followed it. They used illustrations taken from standard authors, gathered from the dictionary or their other sources; when these yielded nothing suitable for their purpose, they concocted examples of their own. No author's name is given, as the purpose of these sentences was not, as in the big dictionary, to show the historical period in which the word was used or the style of work in which it was employed, but to illustrate its use and exemplify its meaning.

'A marvel of condensation, accomplished by skilful hands'[21] was one opinion, and of course it had been necessary for the brothers to save space to accommodate all their innovations—the lengthy treatment of common words, the illustrative sentences, and also the etymologies, trimmed from those in the *OED* but still occupying space. 'The curtest possible treatment' of all uncommon words had made this possible with 'the severest economy of expression—amounting to the adoption of telegraphese—that readers can be expected to put up with'.[22] 'A miracle of condensed scholarship,'[23] another admirer declared it.

Of course there were critics; a correspondent, lurking in the columns of the *Spectator* under the nom de plume 'Scot', spotted that 'idea' had a symbol indicating that it had only two syllables and suggested that it could be pronounced with a final 'r' as in, for example, 'I had no idea rof.' This was quickly taken up by others and the Press magazine the *Periodical* reported that it had even 'crossed the Atlantic'.[24] One commentator accused his New York newspaper of misleading him with a favourable review as the Concise was the worst dictionary he had ever used. He seized particularly upon the brothers' insistence that 'idea' had two syllables and pointed out that it was of course a trisyllable in all educated speech; nevertheless by showing a dipthong in the second syllable Henry was indicating a pronunciation given a few years later by Daniel Jones in his *English Pronouncing Dictionary*[25], widely regarded as the standard authority on British southern standard English. Henry sent a lengthy note to the Press explaining that he and Frank disagreed with the *OED* on this matter; in the parent work the word was given with three syllables but the brothers believed that in current usage it had become a disyllable and they would not be persuaded otherwise. They felt also that the *OED* editors, two of whom were Scots, were favouring 'a more Scottish view', while they themselves believed 'that Southern pronunciation is the winning horse' and had put their 'money on it'. They pushed this even further (not of course in print, as it would have caused offence): 'What the Scots really dislike is not the sound we mean idea to have, but our assumption . . . that the Southern pronunciation . . . is the standard pronunciation instead of theirs.'[26] Problems with pronunciations were to be a frequent difficulty in later years, and this particular instance continually returned to vex Henry. He described it as 'hapless', and commented many years later that their 'long-memoried critics' were still using it to prove their 'ignorance or ill-breeding'.[27]

Years later, in the preface to the second edition of the dictionary, Henry, by then without his brother, explained how when they began their work they had been 'plunging into the sea of lexicography without having been first taught to swim'.[28] They had, however, succeeded in their untutored efforts and the reviews were glowing with praise: 'it is the best small English dictionary extant,'[29] said one; 'it is not only without a superior, it is literally without a rival,'[30] said another. 'Entertaining reading,'[31] one reviewer thought it, while another declared that 'all other English Dictionaries are now obsolete'.[32]

✤ ✤ ✤

Publication was followed by many letters from readers with corrections and suggestions for words which should have been included. These were to continue for the rest of Henry's life; indeed, letters for him still occasionally arrive at Oxford. Despite a lengthy explanation in the preface of the principles adopted when deciding which words and phrases to admit, readers still asked for the inclusion of obsolete terms. One correspondent offered 'a list of 80 Shaksperian obsoletes' which should have been given in the dictionary with 'all Baconian obsoletes', for, he believed, Shakespeare was 'widely known' as 'an alias for Bacon'. Lists from more discerning critics were useful to the brothers, and they hoped that this interest in supplementing their work, which they referred to as a 'game', 'might become, among persons of discretion, a fashionable one'.[33]

Omissions were pointed out—'blots that we should be glad to have cleaned up', Henry called them. '<u>Good copy</u> should certainly have been in,' he declared, confessing that they had in the early part of the book 'erred very much in the jejune direction'.[34] 'Gorgonzola, mayonnaise, covert-coat, second, boycott, agent provocateur, creme de menthe, creme de la creme, flapper, burble, & pied a terre',[35] all suggested by one contributor, were to be added or corrected if space could be saved, and were in the dictionary by the time a lengthy list of addenda was added in 1914.

'Kiss', as a billiards term, was one problem word, with some uncertainty about whether it meant a touch between two moving balls or between a stationary ball and one moving past it; the brothers were unable to sort out their revision of the definition without help, although they did point out the inadequacy of the *OED* on this word. They received an explanation of the term from Oxford and after some thought decided that 'lightness or weight of impact, accident or design, & the identity of the balls, are all immaterial, & the essence of a kiss is simply "contact between two balls of which both are in motion"'. This ruled 'out the case in which you try to pocket the red & it is obstructed by the stationary white', and the definition eventually substituted was 'impact between moving balls'. The brothers were confused and felt their terminology in this game to be 'very rusty', so had waited for advice with the thought that 'if it is true it is humiliating; but lexicography is full of humiliations.'

Another correspondent suggested an adaptation of the definition for 'cutlet', perhaps to include the word 'chops', but it was left unchanged as 'small piece of meat (esp. mutton or veal) cut off for broiling &c.'. 'I wish we had recognized the nature of mutton cutlets more fully; it was one of our early stinginesses',[36] Henry lamented.

'An enormous circulation'[37] had been prophesied by one reviewer and the book was soon selling well, at three shillings and six pence, not two shillings as originally intended; nearly 10,000 copies were sold during the first month and more than 40,000 by the end of March 1912. Schools were buying the book—not the elementary schools for which the dropped smaller dictionary had been intended, but secondary schools. William Vaughan, for instance, the headmaster of Wellington College, 'issued instructions to the school bookseller' that the boys should 'be supplied with no other dictionary than the Oxford Concise'.[38] There had been encouragement for the book from the educational press; one reviewer had spoken of its suitability as 'a dictionary for the school-satchel,'[39] and elsewhere it was described as 'the last word in school dictionaries'.[40] Sales settled down after that, fluctuating between 9,000 and 14,000 in the years before 1920; but the Oxford people were not happy with the figures and by 1913 the brothers were aware of their dissatisfaction; 'its crabbed compression will be the ruin of it,'[41] Henry thought.

For their work the brothers had been recompensed by the agreed lump sums, amounting to £380, but on completion the Delegates of the Press agreed to grant them an extra payment of £70 because of the time the work had taken. A further £100 was paid in 1914 and after the war bonuses were more frequent, often paid at Christmas. These windfalls were very welcome to Henry in his married state, and his brother too was in 1910 indicating a pressing need for funds. Of course if they had been paid the royalties suggested by Henry when the financial arrangements were revised, they would have been better recompensed for their work. In future for all their work, even *Modern English Usage,* they were paid lump sums and Henry was always naively grateful for the bonuses, which seem very small when compared to the sales of the books. Nevertheless he was earning what he needed for his modest way of living and was perfectly happy with the arrangements made with the Press.

✤ ✤ ✤

Frank Fowler rarely wrote to Oxford or to Milford in London, since all the business arrangements were dealt with by Henry; he did, however, contact Charles Cannan, the Secretary, soon after the last pages of the Concise had been sent in, apologizing for 'this obtrusion of my private needs'. Frank was expecting shortly to marry and hoped that the contacts made in Oxford might help him to find some literary work. He needed to produce an income of £200 a year to keep his intended bride, and was prepared to desert his brother and leave Guernsey for Oxford or London if a post was offered. Failing this he would be happy with 'more or less continuous employment on school editions, translations, etc.'.[42] Chapman replied with suggestions but could offer nothing permanent at Oxford or in London. Work on a new edition of Liddell and Scott's Greek Lexicon was a possibility and there were ideas among the Oxford staff about employment on classical school books. Frank's name was put forward as someone who might 'cut & carve his way through the wilderness'[43] of a particularly dreadful translation of Ovid's *Metamorphoses* submitted to the Press. He was suggested as a partner for William Lowe,[44] who produced successful Latin and Greek readers for schools which were still in the Press catalogue fifty years later. Titles such as *Scenes from the Life of Hannibal* and *The Fall of Troy* were tucked into many school satchels, but about their author Chapman was scathing. He was unsure about 'a combination of F. G. F. who is brilliant and W. D. L. who is stupid',[45] and was certainly unaware of Frank's family reputation for being difficult. Probably it was fortunate that none of these plans went any further than discussions at Oxford.

In the autumn of 1910 the librarianship of the Priaulx Library in St Peter Port was advertised, and Frank asked for a testimonial explaining his association with the Press, to accompany his application for the post. The Priaulx Library is a collection of rare books and manuscripts with an excellent reference section given to the island by a local benefactor, Osmond Priaulx and kept in a handsome house, which it still occupies, high above the town, only a short walk from Jessie's nursing home at Sunnycroft. This post must have seemed most suitable for Frank and Charles Cannan was happy to recommend him, describing 'his high qualifications' as 'placed beyond doubt by the work he has done and is doing for the Press'. Despite promises of 'first-rate scholarship' and 'most laborious industry',[46] Frank was not appointed, and it was as an unemployed man that he was married on 11 February 1911 to Una Jane Mary Maud Godfrey in a civil ceremony at the Greffe in St Peter Port.

Una Godfrey[47] lived at the time of the marriage with her father, John,[48] and, presumably, her mother, Maud, in the Forest parish at Le Bourg, a hamlet above Petit Bot, a tiny bay on the south coast of the island noted for its exquisite scenery. It has steep cliffs and caves and had then an old wooden water-mill, destroyed many years later during the Second World War by the German occupiers. John Godfrey had been a barrister in London, but he and Una were described on the marriage certificate as artists and, after these Guernsey years, he seems to have led a wandering life. Soon after Una's wedding he made a will in London describing himself as 'having now no permanent address'. He eventually died years later in Spain and his death was reported to the British Vice-Consul at Tarragona under the assumed name of John Stuart.

No clue survives as to how Frank and Una became acquainted. The English population in Guernsey at the time of their marriage was small so that it was not surprising that the two should have met. They may have been introduced by some acquaintance of Jessie in St Peter Port or some friend of Frank's partner, James Wilson. The Forest parish was near to the Fowler homes and Petit Bot Bay within walking distance. In fact the walk between St Peter's and the Forest was a favourite of Jessie and Henry, and they loved exploring the cliffs and bays of the southern coast. However Frank and Una met, it seems certain that once married they lived in Frank's cottage at Les Reveaux. This was larger than Henry's and would have had room for two. A later photograph shows a wooden hut next to it, called 'the studio' by local people. There is no mention of Henry and Frank working anywhere but in their cottages; perhaps this annexe was built for Una and the necessary equipment which would have been needed for her artistic efforts.

Frank's bride was very different from the plump, merry, middle-aged farmer's daughter who had been Henry's choice, and his marriage was to be far less successful. Between Frank and Una there was a great chasm; she was only 21 when they married, while her new husband was 40. He had not been involved in the busy world of school and London life as Henry had, but had left Cambridge for Guernsey, where he had spent twelve years working with James Wilson and collaborating with his eldest brother. Marriage may have seemed attractive to Frank, seeing Henry and Jessie and their happy island home, but this difficult, scholarly man was probably not suited to life with a very young woman, artistically inclined, from a distinctly unstable background. By the time of her errant father's death Una's circumstances had declined, from the happiness which must have surrounded her marriage in St Peter Port, to complete tragedy.

❦ ❦ ❦

No trace remains of a honeymoon for this newly married couple, but in the following year, 1912, Henry and Jessie enjoyed their second honeymoon trip to Sark; the older pair managed to spend time away from home in most pre-war years, despite their demanding workload. In July 1911, for instance, Henry contacted the London office of the Oxford University Press, proposing a visit, as he and Jessie were staying in England; Humphrey Milford responded enthusiastically with an invitation to lunch, looking forward to meeting Henry 'in the flesh after so many letters'.[49] He did call at the office, but a chill had kept Milford at home and they were not to meet until Henry, a newly enlisted soldier, called in on his way to join his regiment.

In 1913 Henry and Jessie went north to Yorkshire, where, on her birthday, Jessie was 'drinking the waters and taking the baths' at Harrogate. Although Henry was with her he appears not to have sampled these delights, and his birthday verses for his 'brightest-hearted creature' record his distaste, illustrated by extracts from 'Sulphur at Harrogate'.[50]

> But though we know the odour's so
>   Supremely nauseating,
> These stinks in drinks are winks, high jinks,
>   Of Nature, laugh-creating.
>
> They say salvation's way, for aye,
>   Is entered by a narrow gate;
> And stout health, out of doubt, will spout
>   From sickly founts at Harrogate.

❦ ❦ ❦

At home Frank seemed to have discovered an answer to his money worries, perhaps benefiting financially from his marriage; in 1912 he was able to invest in James Wilson's business, buying a third of the vinery from him.

Perhaps Frank had less time for active work as his collaboration with his brother progressed; it does certainly seem strange that after his earlier anxiety about money he was in such an improved position after his marriage. Wilson's fortunes, on the other hand, had declined; it was at this time that he handed over his farmhouse to Jessie and Henry and moved to the little cottage down the hill. The rent he received and the capital invested by Frank would have helped him to make the necessary payments to his estranged wife.

The brothers, of course, had wives to support too and needed to earn money, but at times they had rather desperate ideas about how to do it: 'we have thoughts of hawking our services among publishers as grammatical correctors of inexperienced authors' MS. on King's-English lines.' This was not to prove necessary: the Oxford people were determined to employ them, and various ideas were as before put forward by both sides for discussion.

❧ ❧ ❧

'Misolexicography' Henry called the malady from which he was suffering at this time; after the years of work on the Concise the prospect of more dictionary preparation was hateful to him. Frank, on the other hand, was more amenable to the idea; 'his digestion is more youthful & able to deal with the unpalatable than mine,'[51] Henry reported. The proposal was that, having successfully completed the Concise, they should return to work and produce the smaller volume still wanted by the Press. Humphrey Milford was very straightforward about the situation, telling Charles Cannan in Oxford that 'they should be compelled to have one more try at the 1/- book'[52]—plainly impatient with the brothers' ideas for more entertaining work. Henry, however, set out their position very clearly:

> Reflection, & the casting of a business eye over a few pages, does not convince us that the abridging of an abridgment is attractive work, but on the contrary that it would be like nothing so much as pulling out the hairs of one's own head one by one; & yet to make a completely fresh start & write a new dictionary on a smaller scale without reference to the larger one, tho' it would be easy enough for anyone who had not written the larger one, would be out of the question for us. On the other hand it is of course true

that we have acquired a modicum of expertry at the job, & natural that it should be thought foolish to waste this; but expertry is not proof against staleness, & we have a hankering for pastures new (or old, for that matter— any but the at present too familiar).

There was, of course, one small problem arising from this rejection of lexicography: the brothers needed to earn money and their married states made it more difficult to dismiss this source of income: 'we should say goodbye (for a year or so at least) to lexicography straight off, if the wages of it were as indifferent to us as they were when we first took it on.'

Henry's ideas were rather more exciting, to his eyes certainly; he had suggested years before a book of English etymologies, 'no sort of scientific treatise, but designed to rouse interest in the subject merely'. For this the *OED* would supply 'an embarras de richesse in the way of material'.[53] Oxford again showed little interest in this plan, resurrecting instead the idea of an idiom dictionary, which they had rejected roundly in 1909 with the stinging remark, 'A Utopian dictionary would sell very well—in Utopia.'[54] This revived interest Henry fell upon with delighted enthusiasm, writing at length in reply and returning an earlier proposal and reports with hopes high.

Then began another round of discussions; prospectuses and specimens were prepared, negotiations begun about time and payment, while the brothers thrashed out with the Oxford people plans for the work which would occupy one of them for most of the next fifteen years.

8

This Heartrending Time

∞

'**Y**ou must certainly keep them employed,'[1] Humphrey Milford advised, writing to Oxford about the Fowler brothers; unoccupied, of course, they might find other work elsewhere. The challenge was to persuade them to produce the smaller dictionary while sweetening the unpalatable work with other small items to 'vary the monotony';[2] Chapman, for instance, suggested school books, not at all attractive to Henry, although acceptable to Frank. Chapman fell delightedly upon Henry's remark, hardly a suggestion, about his brother's youth and inclinations making dictionary work more attractive to him and offered at once to discuss the small book with him; this was again called confusingly 'the shilling dictionary', but was soon referred to more satisfactorily as the 'Conciser', although it was eventually to become the *Pocket Oxford Dictionary (POD)*. Chapman pointed out plainly the nature of the proposed project, '(highly skilled) hack work'; Frank 'should not allow himself to be too scrupulous or to weigh the balance too nicely'[3] when deciding what to retain or omit.

Frank Fowler was far more irascible than Henry, and the surviving scraps of his correspondence with Oxford suggest always some anxiety on the part of the authorities to placate him. Milford, involved with the first dictionary negotiations years before, had written with suggestions for the new attempt, although most of the discussions were being conducted with the Oxford office. He wondered, for instance, whether it might be possible to incorporate some 'encyclopaedic information' into the text of the book, perhaps even with 'neat little diagrams'.[4] This seemed to provoke Frank to fury, and the London manager was soon retreating apologetically. In the Preface to the finished dictionary the brothers could not resist a comment, pointing out that 'a dictionary is a book of diction' which 'absolves the dictionary-maker from cumbering his pages with cyclopaedic information'. Agreement was eventually reached, and the Press waited for Frank's advice about the time to be taken over the work. The brothers would use the Concise dictionary to make the new book and not their old text, referring to other dictionaries only when faced with special problems. Abridging the Concise was difficult, and the brothers noted in their Preface that it had been 'found not to be easily squeezable'.[5] They were, however, by then experienced in the business of dictionary making and the style of their new book was already agreed, so the work proceeded quietly. There were of course some problems, and a new adviser was brought in to comment on samples of the Pocket as Bradley had for its larger sibling.

✤ ✤ ✤

Charles Talbut Onions[6] was a Birmingham man, born and educated in the city, and had made the short journey to Oxford in 1895 to begin work as an assistant in James Murray's Scriptorium. He moved across after a time to Bradley's team and was finally made an independent editor, preparing eventually the last word in the great Dictionary, 'zyxt'. Onions had edited the *Shakespeare Glossary*, proposed by the Press to the Fowler brothers some time before, and Henry was later to work with him on another project, the completion of the *Shorter Oxford English Dictionary*. Onions' final years were spent in the preparation of the *Oxford Dictionary of English Etymology*, and it was about the etymologies in the Pocket that he was now consulted.

Etymologies had always been a problem with the small dictionaries; they had to be kept as brief as possible and it seemed at times tempting to omit them altogether. Onions examined Frank's first efforts and decided that brevity had led him to make misleading statements: 'why give the illiterate public unsound notions?' The Concise, he argued, in following the *OED*, had given 'the public sound etymology', but the cut-down versions in Frank's sample would not do. Onions chose as an example 'nation', for which Frank had suggested as etymology '[L *nascor* be born]'. Onions declared this to be crude, and put forward an alternative which would indicate that it came to English from the French *nation* while leaving in the reference to its roots in Latin; this was, of course, more accurate but much longer. 'What will be the impression on the minds of illit. pub.?', Onions worried, after outlining other errors; 'brevity goes too far in nanny-goat . . . and namby-pamby.' His final conclusion was that if this 'crude etymological method' were 'adhered to', the *OED* could 'hardly in fairness be asked to stand sponsor'.[7] His suggestions, however, would have taken far too much space and could not be accepted. 'Nation' was eventually to have a cross-reference to 'nascent', where the etymology was given as originally planned by Frank. In their Preface the brothers explained that the etymologies were 'little more than bare statements of ultimate origin', noting also 'the consequent abstention from the titbits of desultory information usual in this sphere'.[8]

Frank worked on, setting the style of the Pocket, his careful planning later praised by the Oxford people; while Frank began this new abridgement, Henry was negotiating with Oxford about a book which the brothers had long hoped to write.

ψ ψ ψ

Years before, when Henry and Frank were beginning their first attempt at lexicography, Henry had asked Humphrey Milford about another book. The exchange, dating from 1907, is obscured in a puzzle of missing letters and difficult handwriting, but it is possible to deduce that Henry had asked whether anyone was using the *OED* to produce a certain unspecified book, Milford replying that he would enquire about it. His response was that no one was doing what Henry proposed and that he should collect materials from the *OED* as he worked. 'It should be an interesting book and repeat the success of the King's English,'[9] Milford added. Perhaps this was the first appearance of the book so brusquely rejected in 1909 by Robert Chapman in Oxford as 'Utopian'.

'In the case of my own heart, the warmer corner has reference to your old proposal of an Idiom Dictionary';[10] with these encouraging words, brushing aside the etymological suggestion, Chapman in Oxford wrote to Guernsey in 1911, receiving of course a prompt response: 'we are delighted to hear of its surviving in your memory.' The proposed dictionary, Henry quickly explained, would omit many classes of words completely, scientific and technical words, for instance, compounds, and derivatives, except when used in unusual circumstances. In this way space would be saved and could be used for the treatment, 'without making an unwieldy volume', of the remaining

> hard-worked words that form the staple of general talk & writing; their varieties of meaning, liabilities to misuse, difference from synonyms, right & wrong constructions, special collocations, & so forth, could be liberally illustrated, & approval & condemnation less stingily dealt out than has been possible in the official atmosphere of a complete dictionary.

Henry described the *OED* as 'very chary of pronouncements on the unidiomatic' and felt that he and his brother, being 'irresponsible nobodies', should be 'more courageous & more directly concerned in the matter'.[11] Chapman received his explanation of their plans with further encouragement, asking for the usual sample pieces and estimates of time and the length of the book, and declaring that he and his colleagues were 'unanimous in preferring Idiom to Etymology'.[12] So were the Fowler brothers, and their etymological hopes were forgotten.

A sample was quickly produced and sent to Oxford, where Henry Bradley was as usual asked to provide comments. He gave to the new book the title of 'Contextual Dictionary' and, while approving of the intention, thought the plan had not been fully worked out and found fault with the method of its execution. He particularly disliked the arrangement of definitions and examples for each word, suggesting that when the brothers reached particularly complicated words there would be 'a repulsive congestion of examples'; he proposed that they should prepare an article for the word 'go' and attempt to reduce it to 'manageable compass and to lucid arrangement'.[13] If the proposed book were produced on the lines set out it would be a very large book indeed.

Henry and Frank had known that there would be 'many bickerings'[14] before the work was finished, but found Bradley 'courteous & candid & critical at once' as usual, although quickly indicating their disagreement with some points when they received his report. They felt that he had misunderstood their aim and the audience at which their work was directed. Bradley referred several times to the appeal of the book to foreign readers but the brothers were very clear about their public: 'the half-educated

Englishman of literary proclivities . . . who has idioms floating in his head in a jumbled state & knows it'.[15] Bradley had attached remarks about particular words based mostly on the assumption that the book was for foreign users, and Henry's comments on these, written on the manuscript in red ink, begin firmly in most cases 'we dissent'.[16]

The brothers had always known and had warned the Oxford people about the size of the book. Their estimate was that it would have about three-quarters of the words treated in the Concise but because of its arrangement would be as long or slightly longer. They could not give a 'trustworthy estimate', thinking it 'a question that solvitur ambulando ['it is solved by walking', i.e. the question could only be settled by making a trial], '& we cannot walk fast'. They were designing 'not a mere phrase-book, but a dictionary'—one that would, Henry told Chapman,

> not perplex the half-educated reader with a brevity attained by giving him only a set of bare definitions that he has not imagination or time enough to translate into the concrete or clothe with flesh & blood; the flesh & blood is to be there ready for him in the shape of examples, & the space is to be got for them by not treating shortly, but absolutely omitting, all the words with which examples of usage would be a mere ornament or luxury.

With these lengthy remarks Henry returned the red-pencilled report and of course the requested treatment of the word 'go' to Oxford. He did mention money, not usually a great matter to the brothers. They hoped for £150 a year between them while they worked at the book and would accept, as Henry put it, 'any stipulations that seemed desirable to prevent our going on at it for many years in a comfortable leisurely manner'. In Oxford the brothers' comments were examined and the sample shown to various people, 'representing the scholar and the plain man', before the decision was made that the proposal should be rejected. Charles Cannan, the Secretary, wrote to Henry explaining the decision, based chiefly on the size of the proposed book; but he was still interested in a smaller book, perhaps 'a companion to the King's English doing for words alphabetically arranged what that does for words and constructions classified'.[17]

Henry and Frank were not perhaps surprised at this rejection, for they described their feelings as 'not worse than mixed'.[18] They had already confessed that, after the publication of the Concise, there would be 'less opening for the Utopian' as they called the idiom dictionary. They themselves had wanted to write it instead of the Concise, but now there was less desire on their part to do it, because they had 'been to some extent approximating to Utopian methods' in the dictionary. In the new book they would be extending the work they had done, using 'exposition by example rather than definition' and omitting 'the useless & the obvious'. 'It is undeniable that the Concise to some extent cuts the ground from under our feet,'[19] Henry had said, and so they quietly accepted the rejection of their plans for the idiom dictionary.

✤ ✤ ✤

The brothers were, however, not so easily put off. While indicating in the letter of rejection his interest in a companion to *The King's English*, Cannan had suggested that they should let him know if they had any ideas for something on 'lesser lines'.[20] Of course they had, and within a fortnight a new sample was on its way to Oxford, promising a book about one seventh of the length of the Concise. Whereas the original proposal had been for a book recording 'all uses that could be described as idiomatic', the new one would only warn 'against the unidiomatic'. The sample showed a section from E–Euphuism and included 'short general articles, placed alphabetically' which would 'save saying the same things many times over'. Discussions would be avoided in these pieces and 'conclusions stated authoritatively as far as possible'.[21] The Oxford people were delighted; they considered this sample of what they called the 'Reduced Idiom Dictionary' to be 'excellent reading', and were unanimous in asking the brothers to go ahead.

In practical matters Henry and Frank proposed two possible arrangements: they might work together on this reduced book, which was later to become *Modern English Usage*, and then, when it was finished, produce the Pocket dictionary or they might each work on his favourite book separately, Frank on the Pocket and Henry on *Modern English Usage*, and then change over when half-way through, if Henry's 'misolexicography' permitted. They would not consider beginning together with the Pocket because of Henry's distaste for the work. The second plan was preferred by the Press, as it would mean that the eagerly awaited Pocket would be ready first. Payments were agreed for each book, to be paid in quarters as the sections were sent in. Henry, writing to accept the terms, hoped that his own new book would not 'turn out either much longer or much shorter than our estimate & hurt you or us in purse or conscience'.[22] Length was not in fact to be a problem, but time; these books, so enthusiastically begun, were to take many years to complete.

⚘ ⚘ ⚘

When Henry began work he was showered with advice from Chapman in Oxford, for his proposal had struck a chord with the scholarly publisher. Chapman sent what he called 'a collection of my favourite vices' with a covering letter mentioning some of his particular hates. He hoped, for example, for 'a general article of an analytical nature'[23] on the 'character' group of words, and Henry did eventually cover this 'valuable and important word' and its degradation by being made to do 'inferior and common work . . . cheapened by familiarity'.[24] He could never become as passionate about these matters as Chapman and, while agreeing that 'character', and its fellow-sufferers, 'case' and 'connexion', were 'very sloppily used', he warned, 'I fear you will denounce us as lukewarm.' On a similar matter Henry described himself and his brother as 'secret heretics, not venturing to acknowledge our heresy', and gently reprimanded his adviser by describing his pet hate as 'a bit of precision for precision's sake'.[25]

Later Chapman urged that spelling and pronunciation should be included in 'the Perfect Englishspeaker's Companion', as he called the new book, although he considered spelling to be 'much less exciting'[26] than pronunciation. Henry did take up many of his suggestions, including notes about the pronunciation of 'apparent', 'gladiolus', 'deficit', and 'idyll' and the spelling of 'judg(e)ment' and its fellows. He regarded the title 'Idiom Dictionary', which was still being used, as merely a leftover from the old scheme, and was sure that spelling and pronunciation should if possible find a place in the new book, although he quickly realized that space might be a problem. He had believed that 'arbitrary rulings . . . were of little value', while 'reasons made good reading', but was being forced at times to 'fall back on mere rulings', while trying to include all he felt necessary.

> Not to tell people that <u>altogether</u> is different from <u>all together</u>, or nail <u>alright</u>
> & <u>all-right</u> to the counter, or distinguish <u>accessary</u> from <u>accessory</u>, or help

chorale to remain disyllabic, or give help on gladiolus & amateur, seems a pity.[27]

Spelling had already been the cause of a small but rather acrimonious dispute with Oxford. The brothers had often disagreed with the *OED*, and Henry felt sure that the Oxford authorities would not expect him 'to avoid dissenting from the great authority' in the new book. He sent in a newly prepared article about 'align' and 'alignment', disagreeing at length with the spellings preferred in the big dictionary, 'aline' and 'alinement'. Etymology was the reason for the *OED*'s preference, 'line' being the English spelling of the French 'ligne' and there being therefore no argument for keeping the 'g' in the derived word; usage, on the other hand, was the reason for Henry's choice, four times as many quotations in the *OED* showing the 'gn' spelling. Cannan himself responded, telling Henry of the alarm taken 'at the scale of your polemic'[28] and employing more bellicose language to express disapproval. Henry did indicate in reply that he might cut the piece, but described himself as 'no philologer' and 'impenitent'. The whole matter seemed to him 'less a question for scientific philology than for common sense',[29] and fifteen years later the article appeared exactly as first written.

The brothers worked on quietly once all was settled and so began the *Pocket Oxford Dictionary* and *A Dictionary of Modern English Usage*; but before they were finished disaster came, not just to the brothers but to the entire Western world.

✤ ✤ ✤

1914 was a dreadful year for the Fowlers; 'Sad tricks our fate has played us,' Henry wrote in Jessie's birthday poem. She had been seriously ill, although there is no hint about the nature of her illness, and may have gone up to London for treatment as she often did later. All this would have been expensive, adding to their grave financial problems; 'united income seriously deficient,' Henry noted. Of course the two new books were paying really very little, £150 for each, which the brothers received in sums of £37. 10s. as each quarter of each book was sent in to Oxford. There may also have been problems already with Jessie's nursing home at Sunnycroft. During the war years there were few patients and constant financial difficulties; English invalids who might once have travelled out to convalesce in St Peter Port would have been deterred by the lengthy journey once the war began, and this decline may have begun earlier with the threat of impending hostilities. The Fowlers were now paying rent for Lihou and supporting the nursing home on a reduced income, but whatever their situation, Henry felt that these 'sad tricks' had only 'momently dismayed'[30] them. Unfortunately this hope was not to be borne out: the outbreak of war was followed by the tragic death in the autumn of his only sister, and at Christmas he described in his usual verses 'this heartrending time'.[31]

✤ ✤ ✤

Edith Caroline Fowler held an unenviable position as the only girl in the middle of a family of seven brothers; she was born fifth, after Edward Seymour but before Arthur, on 27 December 1865. Like the boys she was sent away to school; she went with a young friend, Emily Mary Cripps, the daughter of a Tunbridge Wells solicitor, to a school in St Leonards, about 15 miles along the coast from Eastbourne, and similarly filled with small private schools. When her education was finished she seems to have returned home to her mother, Caroline, by then living in Gratton Road, West Kensington, and to have moved with her eventually to Eastbourne, living in Hartfield Square with her until she died in 1895.

With her mother gone, Edith was quite alone; there is no sign that she ever lived with any of her five remaining brothers, although at that time it would have been quite natural for a single sister to keep house for a bachelor brother. For a time a Miss E. Fowler kept a small school in a house belonging to St Anne's church in Eastbourne, but if this was Edith, it was a very brief experiment, and for some time afterwards her movements cannot be traced. Four years later she was living as a lodger in the house of William Fellows, an electrician, and his wife, Annie, in Clewer, Windsor in Berkshire; here George Jones,[32] a curate briefly at St Anne's in Eastbourne before Edith's mother's death, had moved to a similar appointment at St Agnes, Spital Clewer. In her will made at this time Edith leaves £100 each to Jones and his wife, Ethel, together with all the money in her drawing account at the bank; they were to play a large part in her life.

Edith was without doubt deeply involved in religious matters. During the years when she and her mother lived in West Kensington she had met the curate of the church of St John the Baptist in Holland Road, Sidney Faithorne Green,[33] a celebrated figure from the ritualist movement in the Anglican Church. Green had been prosecuted for the use of vestments and incense during communion services at his church at Miles Platting in Lancashire; ritual practices were at that time forbidden under the Public Worship Regulation Act of 1874 and other clergy were similarly persecuted under its provisions. After a trial he was ordered not to use any ornaments or ritualistic ceremonies; he ignored this ruling and was eventually imprisoned in Lancaster Castle for twenty months. After his release he came to the Kensington church as a curate, and there would have met the young Miss Fowler. Green gave some manuscript sermons to Edith at this time and she left them in her will to her friend Florence Mary Mitchell, who lived nearby in Matheson Road and who with her family must have worshipped at St John's with those Fowlers who indulged in such things. At the end of Green's time in Kensington, George Jones, then a young curate in a nearby parish, St Mary Magdalene, Paddington, was married there to Ethel Leathes Metcalfe, the daughter of a London surgeon. St Mary Magdalene was another parish church where ritual practices had been introduced, and Green and Jones would certainly have met. Edith must have first come across Ethel and George Jones at this time, renewing her friendship with them later at Eastbourne and then following them to Spital Clewer.

The Oxford Movement had begun in about 1835 under the leadership of Keble, Pusey, and Newman, whose intention was to return within the Anglican Church to traditional Catholic teachings; Anglo-Catholicism, it was to be called later. Edith was clearly deeply involved in this High Church world. She left in her will her copies of books by Pusey to one of her Devon cousins, Florence Foss, and asked that the secretaries of two organizations should be informed of her death and a medal returned to one. The Guild of All Souls and the Confraternity of the Blessed Sacrament were both set up for the promotion of ritual practices in the church; the Confraternity, for example, had as its objectives the encouragement of the more frequent celebration of communion and of confession and fasting. As well as this promotion of ceremonial and the use of incense, lighted candles, and vestments, the adherents of the Oxford Movement also founded religious orders, many devoted to the care of the sick and other disadvantaged groups. One of these was the Community of St John the Baptist, first set up at Spital Clewer in 1851. There is certainly no evidence that Edith intended to join the sisterhood when she came to Windsor; she moved to be near George and Ethel Jones and seems to have spent the rest of her life with them.

From Spital Clewer George Jones moved to Sandford St Martin in Oxfordshire, where he spent three years before moving on to a curacy in Croydon for a further three years. There is no evidence that Edith was with the couple during this time but it seems likely. She was certainly in Maidstone where Jones moved in 1906 to become vicar of St John the Evangelist, for one of her cousins gave her address at that time as the vicarage. In 1912 George Jones moved on to Shirley, Croydon, and it was here that the final act of Edith's life took place.

✤ ✤ ✤

On Saturday 24 October 1914, at Hill View, Shirley, Croydon, Edith Fowler died; she had taken her own life by 'drinking Scrubb's ammonia while insane'. No records of the inquest survive, and there are no reports in local or national newspapers to explain this dreadful occurrence. Although events after the outbreak of war had naturally driven many more trivial items from local newspapers, inquests were still being reported. Edith's death was presumably hushed up; no Croydon newspaper was perhaps willing to report the sad story of the suicide of someone closely linked with a local clergyman whose family were wealthy residents in the town.

To piece together the reasons for Edith's suicide is quite impossible after so many years and with so little evidence. Her life at first appears rather bleak: a single woman following a much-admired clergyman from parish to parish and eventually, at the age of 48, taking her own life in lonely despair. But of course this may not have been the true picture. She had certainly known George and Ethel Jones for more than twenty years and perhaps lived with or near them for part or all of her later years, as a valued companion to Ethel, helping with the care of their little girl, Mary[34] who had been born, after thirteen years of childless marriage, when they were living in Oxfordshire. Some interruption to this life might have caused her despair, although there were many other factors which could have contributed to the complex processes of her suffering.

In her will, written long before her death, Edith left books and trinkets, pearl and diamond rings, a gold locket, and other trifles to her girl cousins and friends from her childhood; the months before her suicide had seen deaths among these women which may have affected her badly. The Foss sisters, Annie Maria and Florence, were her cousins, the daughters of her mother's sister Maria, with whom they had remained at home in Devon. Annie and her mother had both died in the same house on the same day in 1913; Annie had suffered from diabetes for some months and lapsed into a coma two days before her death, while her elderly mother had been overcome by pneumonia after a bout of shingles. Another cousin, Agnes Watson, the daughter of Caroline's eldest brother, had died earlier in the year after much suffering from stomach cancer, as Edith's mother had; Agnes and Edith would have met often, certainly during the Fowlers' years in Kensington, for Henry Harris Watson, after leaving Dartington, had moved his family to North London and they had lived in St John's Wood for many years, not far from Gratton Road. Robert Hesketh Jones also, a wealthy man and considerable figure in local life in Croydon and the father of George Jones, had died in the summer. All these deaths, some without doubt more important to Edith than others, may have contributed to her unhappy state.

The outbreak of war had of course caused widespread dismay. Terror at the prospect of the coming conflict and the dreadful news of its first few weeks were given as causes of suicides reported in the newspapers; despair at the horrific events of the late summer and autumn and fear for what might happen may well have proved too much for Edith perhaps already depressed by other events in her life. The newspapers were filled with details of the battle of Mons and the retreat to the Marne in August, the battle of the Aisne in September, and, just before Edith's death, news of the first battle of Ypres. The first weeks of the war had proved disastrous and many must have been terrified by visions of what lay ahead.

Whatever the reasons for Edith's suicide, there is no doubt that this tragic event would have deeply moved her surviving brothers, Henry and Charles in particular, who as executors had to deal with her affairs. Henry, while not sharing her deep religious feelings, would have respected them; he always encouraged Jessie and any visitors to their home to attend church and would never have attempted to dissuade his sister from her beliefs. If terror and despair at the developing conflict were known to have influenced her this may have affected Henry's own attitude to the war. At the end of this dreadful year, 'this heartrending time', as they prepared for a 'melancholy Christmas' the festive verses were certainly not at all cheerful and their opening words showed Henry's despair:

> Birthday of the Prince of Peace,
> Fire and slaughter, loot and ravage,
> Shall not from their havoc savage
>   At thy this year's coming cease.[35]

✤ ✤ ✤

Evidence for Henry's feelings about the war comes only from Gordon Coulton in his brief biography written years later. Coulton seems at times Henry's most unlikely friend, being possibly as different in temperament as he was in appearance. His tall thin figure must have been a striking contrast with Henry's short, stocky frame, and his views on the war, as on other matters, differed greatly from the opinions of his friend. Coulton was a great lover of debate, and one of the topics on which he had long expressed strong views was the case for compulsory national service about which he wrote many books and pamphlets, fiercely opposed to pacifism; to all this he says Henry 'turned a patient but unconvinced ear'. The outbreak of war was to Henry 'as to most Liberals, a very painful surprise', but he was persuaded eventually, shocked by 'the violation of Belgium and the evident peril of this country', to encourage others to enlist. Finally he became convinced that he should not be 'pressing this sacrifice upon others' but should be taking some active part himself.[36]

Determined to act upon this decision, Henry went across to London in early 1915 and on 6 April, at the Hotel Cecil in the Strand, enlisted in the 23rd Battalion Royal Fusiliers, the Sportsman's Battalion. Frank, who had gone with him, was initially rejected but eventually accepted, despite his less robust health. The brothers' ages, 56 and 44, would appear at first sight to have barred them from military service, but they had discovered how to avoid this obstacle by joining a rather special unit. The Sportsman's Battalion had been set up by a Mrs Cunliffe-Owen, who had been given permission by the War Office to recruit men 'over the then enlistment age, who, by reason of their life as sportsmen, were fit and hard'.[37] The battalion boasted well-known footballers among its numbers, and promised that friends who joined at the same time would be able to stay together living in the same hut and 'need not altogether sacrifice their love of sport while training'.[38] Frank was clearly under the age limit of 45, although it seems that his sporting achievements were probably rather doubtful; he had recently suffered from a bout of pleurisy, which must have caused the delay in his recruitment. Henry, on the other hand, was far too old; with the encouragement of the recruiting official, he falsified his age and was accepted. Decked out in khaki he called in at the University Press office at Amen Corner on his way out to camp a week later and met Humphrey Milford for the first time; 'no further progress will be made till after the war,' Milford reported to Oxford.[39]

At first Henry was sent to Hare Hall Camp at Romford in Essex for basic training and Jessie was close behind. She must have been most unhappy at her elderly husband's rash behaviour, but managed to stay near to him during his time in England, lodging at first in Romford near the camp and seeing him as often as she could. They communicated by telegram and postcard, fixing meetings which frequently had to be changed to fit in with Henry's duties; the superior postal service aided their last-minute changes of plan; 'Impossible to get out today; & tomorrow I am orderly, & cannot be home till 5.30 or 6.0.'[40] In the summer Jessie had to go away, spending a few days in London for an operation, travelling up alone but escorted back on the following Sunday by her husband who, after making the arrangement, had had 'the narrowest possible shave of being put on for guard'. She had been missed, of course, during her brief absence: 'It is a thousand years till Sunday,'[41] Henry had written.

Meanwhile he was attempting to convince the authorities of his suitability for service in France despite his advanced age. When trouble loomed the sergeant-major always protected his elderly charge, insisting that Henry was 'the best shot in the battalion' or 'the best marcher'. His experience with the Inns of Court Volunteers and the weekly rifle drill at Harrow must have helped with this. There were some problems at first with shooting but a change of spectacles helped, and he did win some prizes. The daily running and swimming must have helped too; Henry was always very proud of his fitness, feeling that it made him look much younger than his years. He did have some athletic success as well, coming second in the battalion walking race, although the winner had 'in fact broken pace several times without detection'.⁴² All this effort eventually produced the desired results.

The battalion moved in November to a camp at Leamington and Jessie went ahead to find rooms, but the stay there was rather short, for the Sportsmen were soon sent home on leave. Henry and Jessie retreated hastily to Guernsey and the comforts of Lihou. A few days before Christmas the inevitable telegrams arrived ordering Henry and Frank to rejoin their unit at Leamington and this of course they did, accompanied by Jessie and Una. On 22 December 1915 the Fowler brothers set off for the war. Jessie bore it all bravely, Henry telling her in his first letter that a friend had thought her 'a very plucky woman, to be able to say goodbye as you did'. 'Mind you try to sleep well o'nights,' he foolishly advised her as the train took him south to Folkestone, Boulogne, and the war in France.

9

In France with the Sportsmen

❦

Christmas at Étaples, the base in France to which the Sportsmen were sent, was rather bleak, with eight men in a tent and only a 'quarter of a plum-pudding each, & a present of cigarettes & tobacco', although 'three good blankets & a waterproof sheet apiece'[1] must have been comforting. All these details would have pleased Jessie, staying in Weymouth on her way back to Guernsey. Henry wrote to her daily during his time away, missing only occasionally when his days were too full or difficult for writing and sending two letters at times when events demanded it. Writing was 'done under difficulties'; light in the tent was very poor, with only one candle in the middle, and Henry would have to walk some distance to find a suitable hut, often crowded, where he reported 'no tables to write on; one sits astride on a bench & leans forward to use another part of it as a table.'[2] Posting letters too presented problems; sometimes it involved simply finding an office, but often meant having to hunt round for 'a certain corporal' whose duties included collecting letters and who often proved to be 'an elusive animal'.[3] These letters Jessie carefully preserved, a record of her husband's adventures but also a snapshot of their relationship. Each ends as did the first on Christmas Eve 1915 with a variant of the same signature, 'your own Dux',[4] a pretty pun on the Latin 'dux', meaning 'leader', and the affectionate endearment 'ducks'.

Jessie's letters Henry longed for, reporting delays but eventually receiving them all. He could only keep them for a few days, reading them several times before destroying them, a sad necessity when he was always struggling with a weighty pack. Parcels from home were also a great delight, often filled with edible treats, cakes and sweets which could be shared with the other men, and of course more mundane necessities, such as soap and socks. Jessie's first gift was a great success: 'the flannel lining to my tunic is the joy of my life; it keeps me warm by day . . . & makes a fine pillow by night.'[5] There were frequent requests, a torch for instance, 'meloids' for sore throats, and flannel drawers, for Henry could not 'march in any comfort in the tight army ones'.[6] Keeping a supply of tobacco was always a problem, although the men did receive occasional handouts: Jessie was asked to send three ounces of Taddy's Imperial a week. She supplied too cheroots and 'trichies', Indian cigars made at Trichinopoli, while Henry instructed that cigarettes sent should be Wills or Turkish; Woodbines, much loved by the rest of the British army, were not favoured by the Sportsmen.

Newspapers were also essential for Henry, and to save problems the *Westminster Gazette* was ordered from the office to be sent directly to him in France, but there were always difficulties with it, particularly after moves. Jessie was asked for copies of the *Sunday Times* and *Land and Water*, with her own *Daily News* at times when the *WG*, as Henry called it, was not getting through. Books of war cartoons by Louis Raemaekers were also received with great delight. Henry suffered terribly when without reading matter, describing later in hospital the desperate search for a book:

> There is a novel about in the ward, which I pick up now & then & read a few pages of, & then put down again for fear it should be the property of some one who may be watching for a chance of recovering but politely refraining from claiming it.[7]

Gordon Coulton, with his jibes at Henry's 'physical fastidiousness', as he described it in his biography, felt it necessary to excuse references to washing in Henry's letters as due to this quality, 'natural to a Rugby and Balliol man'.[8] To a modern reader it seems quite understandable that a man would tell his wife about the practical problems he was encountering; for instance, Henry could not remove his clothes for weeks, except for boots and tunic, pulling 'them up & down every morning sufficiently to get a sponge all over'[9] and naturally he told Jessie about it:

> I have come down to a shave every other day now, & glad if I can work that in, but I haven't yet missed my sponge over in the morning darkness—no light in the wash-house except when the moon is shining.[10]

Perhaps age and marriage to a sensible woman had moderated the fussiness which Coulton noted during their expeditions as single men. Certainly Henry's letters from France seem to show, with a few rare exceptions, a very level-headed attitude to the situation. 'Mud here is terrible; fortunately cleanness is allowed to go to the wall in France for the most part,'[11] he told Jessie.

☙ ☙ ☙

Life in the base camp was tough and tiring. At first the men drilled and practised bayonet-fighting followed by route marches 'done faster & with a heavier pack than in England'. Henry and Frank, in the same tent as promised when they joined up, stood up well to the hard work, but were already irritated by 'the apparently universal army mixture of violent hurry & shocking waste of time'.[12] They were all quickly passed as fit for active service and put on to fatigues, shifting timber and putting up tents as well as the endless drilling and one night 'wandering about in deep trenches in the dark, with rockets going up & blank cartridges being fired'.[13] There were lectures too on caring for the feet and skin, bombs, barbed wire, and gas and liquid fire.

Tent life was uncomfortable: no mattresses and a wooden floor meant sore hips for all, and stormy weather brought the possibility of collapses during the night. Meals were, Henry reported,

> conducted on very savage principles; woe betide the unwary private who does not jump up with his mess-tin & rush out for his tea or stew at the first moment of its appearance.[14]

Washing clothes was a ridiculous business. Henry had hoped to be able to send the occasional parcel home, but this was not allowed; chaos would have followed if every soldier had sent his washing back to mother. Jessie must have been appalled at his description of the laundry arrangements on New Year's Eve:

> they marched us out with our dirty linen to a stream three miles off, provided tin basins, & let us do the rest; but as we were expecting to move on that night, & had no means of drying anything, most of us only pretended to wash; I did a towel & a pair of socks, for instance, & kept my shirt & drawers dry.[15]

On 29 December the men were warned of a possible move forward and were issued with their kit, weighed down with service caps, gas helmets, and other necessaries, until they felt it difficult to move with the load. In fact they remained at the base for a few more days and were then sent up to join the battalion resting behind the lines at Busnettes.[16] The journey was hard, for they travelled by train in cattle trucks 'followed by several hours of standing & several miles of marching with very heavy packs over very bad roads at rather a severe pace'. Living conditions on arrival were improved: they slept in a barn with 'a blanket each, & plenty of straw' but a single lantern meant difficulties with letter-writing.

Here for the first time problems arose concerning the ages of many of the newly arrived draft:

> The authorities here are not at all pleased with so many old men's being sent out to them; there was an inquisition into our ages this morning, & I begin to doubt again whether I shall ever be allowed to go into the firing trenches.[17]

There were rumours that no man over 40 would be allowed to proceed, and that a group of the oldest were to be sent back. These thirteen were marched off one morning on an eight-mile trip to see the divisional medical officer, who asked each his age and how he felt. Henry reported his response with some delight: 'he did indeed say Good Heaven! when I told him 57, but remarked that I was a wonderfully young-looking man for my age'.[18] He was greatly offended, on the other hand, by the regimental sergeant major, who indicated that he need not do the physical drill, feeling that he was regarded 'as a poor old gentleman who must be let off easily';[19] he went on with the drill to prove his fitness. A good performance in a brigade route march of 11 miles probably helped his case, for he completed it in good order while others fell out.

The men were soon moved to another barn at Busnettes, where the farmer's wife took a great interest in the elderly soldier, calling him 'Papa' and allowing him to use a room in her house for writing home to 'Madame'. These letters were, however, not very revealing, filled with interesting details but giving little hint of the dangers ahead. There was no mention, for instance, of the endless practising with gas helmets at this time and Henry always reported tales intended to make Jessie see life in the trenches as quite safe, rarely telling her of deaths or injuries. A boy returning to the company after a spell in hospital with trench fever was said to have described his time at the front as 'very little dangerous, except on rare occasions, but highly disagreeable'.[20] Once the company had moved up, Henry managed to add details without making them sound threatening: 'We are now, however, within range, tho' long range, of the Germans, & have this afternoon been watching three of our guns firing away within fifty yards of us'.[21]

Jessie must have guessed something of what her husband was experiencing. She was also extremely nervous, and in his letters Henry was always attempting to reassure her. On the last day at the front he felt able to be a little more frank, even mentioning casualties, but adding a little note to emphasis the quietness of their sector:

> We had a certain amount of excitement when the Germans suddenly hit upon almost our exact range, and landed three fair-sized shells only twenty yards or so beyond where a party of us were working, sprinkling us plentifully with mud; that was yesterday; and we have got quite accustomed to the sound of snipers' bullets whistling past pretty close to our heads; there have been no casualties in our trenches (reserve ones), but a few in the front line; this, however, is on the whole a quiet part of the British line . . . This morning we are in our dug-outs, because we are bombarding the enemy & he is expected to reply; before this began we have seen German aeroplanes right over us being shot at by our shrapnel, & also a certain amount of fighting between their aeroplanes & ours; but none have been brought down. When a hostile aeroplane comes in sight, three whistles sound, & we have to stop still, so that no movements shall be visible.[22]

On 19 January the battalion moved up, marching through Bethune to trench billets at Le Touret. Here they slept in a new hut for a night with just room for twenty men to lie down, clean but unfortunately not for long; 'we are having good practice in mudlarking,' Henry told Jessie, 'seas of mud along the roads & especially all round our billet.'[23] Again they were moved to a barn, with some company this time; 'I had some quadruped wandering over me in the night; other people called it a rat, but I prefer to suppose it a harmless, necessary cat.'[24]

Three days later the battalion went up to relieve the 1st Royal Berks in the front line at Festubert; Frank and Henry in B Company were in reserve in the old British line. The men in the front line had to take up their positions over the top and could not be visited in daylight, so the Fowler brothers were involved in night marches to take up food and supplies;

after dusk we had a most weary walk over very slippery narrow wooden gratings for some miles to carry up the water supply, each having two heavy stone jars slung over one shoulder, & a rifle in the other hand. It was a job I expect long to remember, not so much because we then first had occasional bullets singing by or over us, as on account of its discomfort. The jars were anyhow very ill adapted for carrying, & having no corks they sprinkled us liberally at every stumble, & the expedition lasted four or five hours.[25]

Henry was removed from these duties when made orderly to the platoon captain, not a job he enjoyed; 'orderlying is not in my line at all, & I expect to be kicked out of the job as incompetent,' he told Jessie. He was sent out as a guide with Frank, bringing in parties to repair trenches at night, and there was hard work during the day too, digging and carrying sandbags. Accommodation for thirty was in a large dugout with not enough room to lie down so that the men had to sleep sitting; here they were delayed on their final day at the front by a lengthy bombardment and an attack expected because of the Kaiser's birthday.

Eventually the battalion was relieved and marched back to the tobacco factory in Bethune for much-needed rest; they had spent four days in the front line and were to have eight days' rest before returning to the trenches. For B Company this break was short-lived; after one day they were marched away for repair work to defences, and on their return in the evening were told to pack everything and sleep in their boots and coats as they might be needed as reinforcements during an attack. This was in fact the last evening at the front for Henry, Frank, and the eleven other old men, who were the next morning sent back to Étaples for return to England; 'a disappointing end to our real soldiering,'[26] Henry called it. 'It is something to have had even the little bit of the real thing that we did get.'[27] Jessie must have been delighted to know that he was back at Étaples, thinking that he was safe and would soon be in England. Henry naturally realized this: 'it is a real joy to me to think that in one way you will be glad that we are (militarily) on the shelf.'[28]

☙ ☙ ☙

Henry at first seemed happy to be back in the base camp, 'a good dry healthy place, with tents pitched on sandhills'.[29] There had been some improvements since they were there in December, a hut for laundry supplied with hot water and wash houses for the men. The thirteen were taken before the CO, 'a nice old boy',[30] but he could do nothing and they had to go before a board to decide their fate.

While the men waited they were kept busy with fatigues, coal-heaving, for instance; 'carrying coal-sacks too heavy for one to get on to one's back without help; so you may bestow as much pity on me as you think called for on that score,' Henry told Jessie, all this 'to the accompaniment of cold driving rain'.[31] Washing-up as officers' mess orderlies was another occupation, described as 'the way a grateful country rewards respectable old gentlemen of 57 who are fools enough to think they can fight for it'.[32] The orderly duties he condemned as

> disgusting work; the boy who runs it is a stupid oaf, & the appliances for washing up are miserable—no proper cloths, nor anything like enough of the old towels & things used as substitutes, so that nothing can be really dried; no one who likes to feed off clean plates himself can help feeling sick at the beastly state we have to leave things in, & no self-respecting person can go through the farce we perform for the whole day & several times a week without feeling degraded.[33]

When they were later offered the chance to choose more suitable work ('toy jobs'[34] Henry called them), some men accepted police work or clerical posts but Henry, followed inevitably by Frank, refused to volunteer, preferring 'to protest against being kept on as a non-combatant at all'.[35]

The atmosphere in their tent was also rather difficult; two men from the original thirteen caused annoyance as they were 'bad at putting up with adversity, & the air was full of their lamentations & quarrels from morning till night'.[36] Their departure improved matters, and it became 'a nice quiet pleasant elderly tent',[37] although a robbery while they were on a night-time fatigue did unsettle them all, Henry losing most of his possessions.

After inspection by the board the men expected to hear their fate, but nothing was said and they continued in the same state with only rumours to enlighten them—usually that they were to be designated as 'permanent base' men and kept at Étaples for the rest of the war. To Henry this would have been, as he told Jessie,

> obviously a scurvy trick to play upon people whose only offence is to have been more patriotic than many of their neighbours & enlisted early when

the need of men was greatest, to convert them against their wills into labourers doing work that they are neither fitted for nor accustomed to.[38]

After days of waiting the brothers managed to get an appointment with their divisional CO and were able to state their case, but were disappointed to be told that nothing could be done. It was suggested that they prepare a written statement which could be forwarded to the proper department, and they set about this with renewed hope. Beginning with their military details, they set out their belief that they should either be discharged or returned to active service, and this they followed by a clear statement of their position.

> Pte H. W. Fowler (M.A. Oxon., late scholar of Balliol: age 58) & Pte F. G. Fowler (M.A. Cantab., late scholar of Peterhouse; age 46) have been engaged for some years in Guernsey on literary work of definite public utility for the Oxford University Press (Secretary, C. Cannan Esq., Clarendon Press, Oxford). They enlisted in April 1915 at great inconvenience & with pecuniary loss in the belief that soldiers were needed for active service, being officially encouraged to mis-state their ages as a patriotic act. After nine months training they were sent to the front, but almost immediately sent back to the base not as having proved unfit for the work, but merely as being over age— & this though their real ages had long been known to the authorities of their battalion. They are now held at the base at Étaples, performing only such menial or unmilitary duties as dish-washing, coal-heaving, & porterage, for which they are unfitted by habits & age.
>
> They suggest that such conversion of persons who undertook purely from patriotic motives the duties of soldiers on active service into unwilling menials or servants is an incredibly ungenerous policy on the part of the military authorities, especially when the victims are advanced in years & of a class unused to the kind of work imposed on them, & that such ungenerous treatment must, when it becomes generally known at the end of the war, bring grave discredit on those responsible for it.[39]

To this was added a list of their joint published work, and they handed the statement in with high hopes. The following day Henry was summoned by the CO who had rewritten their piece as a letter and rephrased it more tactfully, 'the more lively expressions—dish-washing, discredit, &c.— eliminated for fear of offending the big-wigs'. He hinted that return to England was more likely than discharge; to Henry's preferred option, to return to the front, replied firmly that 'nothing was so utterly out of the question as that'.[40] Jessie must have been delighted to read this news.

Yearnings for a return to the front were all very well for Henry who was fit, tough, and resilient; 'a comic experience tother day', recounted to Jessie, illustrated his strength and athleticism.

> we were loading the ration waggon, & I was standing in it arranging the things when it started forward, & I pitched out at the tail in a graceful header, landing on my hands in the road. They all said it was a marvel I had not broken my neck, but I had neither bruise nor scratch nor sprain.[41]

For Frank, despite his youth, things were rather different.

From the earliest days in France life had been a struggle for Frank; Henry remarked at Busnettes on his permanent tiredness 'as shown by some snappiness of temper'.[42] In one part of the barn which served as their billet the farm people beat flax all day and, while this caused sore eyes for some, including Henry, Frank coughed a great deal at night. On their return to base he became seriously ill with the same cough, falling asleep when he sat down even if only for a minute; he was unable also to put in his false teeth and as a result could not eat. Henry reported all this to Jessie but was unable to persuade his younger brother to go sick, and believed that he would not stop until he had pneumonia. After a week Frank submitted to brotherly pressure and reported to the doctor, who gave him no medicine for his cough and only two days off fatigues, which left him 'to shiver all day in a cold tent'. Henry's thoughts about doctors were very plainly expressed; 'These idiots are possessed with the notion that every soldier must be a malingerer.'[43] The authorities were in fact attempting to empty the hospital for large numbers of wounded expected shortly.

Confinement to the tent did help Frank a little and he was able to eat but, as Henry told Jessie, 'a tent in cold weather . . . is no place for a sick man'.[44] After two days there was a fall of snow and Frank's condition deteriorated. The doctor this time realized the serious nature of his illness and he was taken into the hospital with a fever; 'seems much debilitated' Henry managed to read on his notes.[45] On his visits to the doctor Frank did report his earlier attack of pleurisy but writing home on each occasion Henry spelt it as 'plurisy', a mistake he was particularly to condemn in *Modern English Usage*;[46] Gordon Coulton felt this error should 'be noted among the effects of the Great War'.[47]

Henry had written to Una as soon as Frank was taken ill, and he was able to write himself as he improved. Una had left Guernsey and volunteered for munitions work, although she did return for visits to Jessie, going across while Frank was in the hospital. At that time she was moving into lodgings in Chiswick where she was continuing in munitions, working ten- or even thirteen-hour shifts in the factory. Henry hoped that Frank's illness would bring about his return to England, but he quickly improved and the opportunity passed. After three weeks in hospital he was sent on to a convalescent camp to recover before being returned to the tent and regular fatigues.

✧ ✧ ✧

Henry was very anxious to reassure Jessie about his own health when Frank became ill. He revealed that he had lost weight while at the front, but since his return was eating very well and had put it on again. His confidence about his health was unfortunately not shared by 'two bullying cads' who examined him as part of a medical board and entered in his pay-book 'P.U.', standing for 'permanently unfit' and also 'senility'; 'look that out if necessary in the Concise Oxford Dictionary,' he told Jessie. It was in fact, he added,

> on other people that they chiefly exercised their brutality, scolding men with bad sight, deformed feet, & bent spines, for having ever enlisted, & calling them frauds & bad bargains & such choice names, whereas of course it was the men of their own confounded service, the doctors, whose business it was to prevent unfit men from enlisting.[48]

Henry's anger had seeped into many letters to Jessie from the earliest days, mostly 'the result of incompetence rather than intentional tyranny'.[49] Occasionally this anger produced longer passages which caught the censor's eye, some words still visible despite his blue pencil;

> Life is a fearful rush, not because it need be in the least, but owing to the [silly] [incompetence] of the [authorities], who insist on treating us like mischievous children whose time must be filled up & who must not be allowed to know beforehand what is going to happen.[50]

Henry was intrigued by this censorship, and asked Jessie to tell him in her replies what had been struck out and whether in fact some letters had been stopped altogether. The description of the medical board which he felt was 'all true & justified, but a little indiscreet'[51] did in fact pass through without a mark.

'The rottenest job imaginable'[52] fell to Henry at this time; he was posted as orderly for two days to a group of doctors while their permanent man was away. This was 'a soft job'[53] and consequently hated, but led in the end to more congenial employment. On the eighth anniversary of his proposal to Jessie he described in jovial fashion his new prospects; he had already explained 'Blighty' to her as 'armyese for England'.[54]

> It is true that Pte H. Fowler is accused in his pay-book of senility (poor old thing) & marked P.U. to show him that he is a worthless rag of humanity,— so that he might fairly expect to be shot with other rubbish into the dustbin called Blighty; but for all that he has been summoned this morning to the orderly room & told that he can do most valuable service by putting his trained intelligence at the disposal of a branch of the R.A.M.C. that concerns itself with tracing the facts about dead & wounded & missing men for the benefit of their relations & the War Office.[55]

The work was to be with the Red Cross, interviewing all men immediately on their return from the front to discover what they knew about the fate of their comrades. Clearly this was just the thing for Henry, and he regarded it as useful work which he would happily do even if it delayed his return home. He was soon issuing detailed instructions to Jessie about preparing his typewriter to be sent out if necessary but still thought of getting home, for he asked her also to send out two old kitbags to hold their possessions should he and Frank be discharged. A rumour that stretcher-bearers were to be recruited from among those not fit to fight gave him some hope of getting back to the front and must have filled Jessie with horror.

Living was at this time more uncomfortable, for a group of eighty more older men had arrived and they were squeezed in, 'packed like herrings, ten to a tent'.[56] There were luckily some other pleasures; Henry could escape when he had a little time for a walk or to lie and write his letters in some secluded spot away from the camp, 'sitting on the sand under the pines'.[57] Safe in some solitary place he could read and write happily feeling not 'in the least like a participator in the greatest war that has ever been fought'.[58] In romantic mood he described to Jessie an evening walk in the early spring;

> Have a look now & then at the stars between six & seven in the evening; they & the sun & moon are the only things we have a chance of looking at at the same time. My present job gives me very little exercise, so I have to provide myself with it, which I do after my fashion in exactly the same way every

day—namely a four-mile walk at full pelt along a certain road & back usually starting at six o'clock. Tonight there was a tiny boat of a moon floating in a clear sky, with the evening star close by as the buoy to which it might be moored; there was a little frost in the air, but not a breath of wind, & everything was so tranquil that I could not help wondering whether you were looking at it too.[59]

All this romance was occasioned by a rush of spring anniversaries, the engagement on 29 February and on 10 March the wedding day and Henry's own birthday. These led to a flood of poetic and flirtatious letters, although there was not enough time for verse; writing a letter for the engagement anniversary was in fact a very difficult operation.

> . . . you are to picture me tired with one of the hardest fatigue days we have had, & writing this on my legs in Tipperary hut, which is so full that there is not a seat to be had, & so ill lighted tonight that I can hardly see what I am putting down.[60]

There were as usual repeated proposals, although this time with a warning addition; 'I can see no sure prospect of our being able to live together for some time.' There was even a jocular threat; 'If I hear of your carrying on with your curate between now & the tenth of March, I shall withdraw my offer.'[61] Countering this came a small tale about Frank's nurse, who, commenting to Henry on her patient's state, remarked, 'he has not got cheeks like yours.' 'I will try to abide in the paths of virtue,'[62] Henry promised.

For his birthday there were two large parcels from Jessie, which arrived early and had to be hidden in the tent until the day itself; although Henry resisted opening them, he did read the customs declarations as soon as they came, a lesser sin. Butterscotch, tobacco, chocolate, cheroots, cake, a cigar-holder, and other treats were unpacked after breakfast on the great day and he wrote a cheerful letter home to Jessie. She was soon to need comfort, for events were moving swiftly at Étaples.

✤ ✤ ✤

'Ah! there are the Sportsmen; & which are the famous Fowler brothers?' had been the greeting when Henry and his colleagues, after a visit to the doctor, were brought before another board. The appeals to the War Office had resulted in an immense correspondence; as a result Henry was marked

'Active' again, and the slurs on his fitness which caused such offence were cancelled in his pay-book. Groups of older men were still being sent back, so he did feel that he was unlikely to go up to the front again. Breaking the news to Jessie was difficult; he tried to express some regret, but his pleasure did break through; 'I am so sorry, dear, to be sending you this news just when you were hoping for some of a very different sort; but a soldier is a soldier, after all.'[63] Jessie's response had not arrived when Henry heard that he was in fact to go up with the next draft. When he sent on this further piece of bad news he was able to reassure her that the battalion was just coming out of the trenches for rest so that he would not for a time be 'actually at grips with the Germans'. He did feel that his time at the front would again be brief; 'the absurdity of sending back hundreds as too old & letting me go up is too glaring',[64] he told Jessie.

While Henry was waiting he continued working with the Red Cross people, but introduced Frank to them when he returned to the tent from his convalescence, managing to arrange that he should take over the work. The brothers were to be separated for the first time, but Henry did know that Frank had work which he could easily manage and would not be returned to coal-heaving or other unsuitable fatigues.

On 24 March the draft set out in heavy snow with 'hunches of bread & cheese as provisions';[65] they travelled by train in a draughty horse truck, with afterwards a march of 8 miles to their billets in the village of Sains-en-Goelle. Here life was difficult, with a water shortage, poor weather, and eleven men sleeping on the floor in a small room. The place itself, a mining village, Henry thought, was not at all attractive, 'consisting entirely of cottages almost of one pattern & arranged in twenty-six small roads all crossing one long one with mathematical symmetry—extremely uninteresting'.[66] Work would have helped, but there was nothing, and Henry always found inactivity very hard to bear.

> I have spent three days here without being put on to any work except quarter of an hour's fatigue, & there is nothing to do but sit on one's valise with one's back against the wall & look at other people doing much the same thing round the room & wish it was dinner or tea time.[67]

Fortunately they were as usual quickly moved on; marching to Hersin, they travelled by train to Houdain, reaching their new billets in a large barn at La Comté after another short march. Although the other men preferred a place where there was fun to be had, Henry regarded this as paradise, 'a nice clean country village with blessed dry roads & hedges just sprouting, & cowslips behind them, & pretty views all round'.[68] His letters became for a time full of 'botanical & ornithological remarks',[69] describing the birds and flowers in the fields as he walked or swam. He could sit in the sun in the farmyard to write to Jessie or lie in the meadow behind the farm outlining the pleasures of this rural interlude; one morning, for instance, he had swum in the millstream, 'a real bathe this time, all clothes off at once & myself right into the water'. Eating out was also possible; Henry and a friend spent a pleasant evening in an estaminet dining on 'an omelette & bread & butter, beer & coffee'.

There were of course drills and some fatigues, although orderly duties were light here when they came and meant a pleasant day free of work. Henry described practising with gas-helmets, 'gasping for breath & trying to see & aim through misty eye-pieces',[70] and 'throwing some live bombs at some toy trenches'.[71] Fatigues were of course at night; Henry told Jessie about one dreadful journey which involved travelling 'standing up in a jolting lorry in the dark with no strap-hanging provision' for two hours, then spending four digging in the trenches, followed by the same unpleasant journey back to their billets. Marches provided the opportunity to add to the lists of local flowers and birds, 'blackthorn & pear blossom, elm & chestnut leaves'.[72] After one march they were taken 'to hear promulgated the sentence of a court martial on two men who had been caught asleep when on guard in the trenches—two years imprisonment with hard labour.' Henry described it cheerfully to Jessie: 'Well, we must do our best to keep awake when our turn comes.'[73]

There had been a small delay to Henry's letters because of a case of measles which put the men in quarantine for a few days. They were not allowed into the village and letters were not collected, a great annoyance to Henry, who felt sure the silence from France would cause alarm and that it would have been a simple matter to disinfect their letters. The business was settled when a 'great disinfecting motor' was brought up to steam all their clothing and bedding; '"Les Anglais font beaucoup de précautions" (the English are a careful folk), said the farmer's wife.'[74]

The usual trips to the doctor to discuss Henry's age were quickly arranged. The first, who had sent Henry back in January, said still 'that in his opinion 58 was too old for trench-work', while conceding that he 'was fitter than some who were younger'.[75] After this Henry felt sure he would soon be back at the base, but another inspection was arranged, this time with the doctor and the colonel. Henry described to Jessie the following exchange with the CO:

> . . . he chaffed me a little & said I looked so disgustingly well that he hadn't the heart to send me back, but . . . he would not have me in the trenches because old men like me needed dry beds (I said I didn't, without mentioning your passion for airing sheets), & he was not going to have my grand-children told that I had died of unnecessary trench foot (I said I was not going to have any grand-children), so he should find me some outside job; what was I at home?

Henry would have preferred 'actual soldiering' but he went home 'with modified joy',[76] glad that he was not to be sent back to the base again. This happiness was, however, to be very short-lived.

The next morning the men were assembled to march away for four days of brigade manoeuvres and, while Henry waited with the others, he fainted. His time at the front was over; he was whisked away to the field ambulance, where he spent one night, and was moved after that to a rest camp at Bruay for three miserable days. Having been so elated at his success in getting what he wanted, he was very depressed, finding himself 'the sport of the medical organization, which is amusing itself by kicking me this way & that like a football'.[77] He was then sent straight back to the base, assured that he would be in England very shortly, but himself convinced that he would stay in France.

✧ ✧ ✧

Life at the base quickly returned to the old routine. Henry was back in the tent with Frank, who was a little better but still had a dreadful cough—'a very distressing one to hear,' Henry told Jessie, 'so suggestive of extreme feebleness'.[78] Frank did begin to improve as the weather grew a little warmer. He was working as before with the Red Cross, but there was not enough to occupy Henry too, so he was left to the normal fatigues, quickly finding a permanent place in the dining hall performing with others 'the combined duties of scullery maids & waiters for some four hundred men'. This work he liked for the company was pleasant and there was 'none of the dawdling about' which he found his 'great bugbear in the military life, but on the contrary very brisk work indeed for rather too many hours a day'.[79]

Henry began again his evening walks and was able to find his usual spot for letter writing, 'just out of earshot of camp . . . pines & sandhills & solitude, that is all, with a hot sun & a cool breeze'.[80] As the weather was improving he decided to sleep outside, telling Jessie that it was more comfortable than in the tent: 'you scoop a hollow for your hip in the sand, & then lie on your side.' On the first night a Zeppelin raid disturbed his slumbers when a bomb, which failed to explode, fell just 100 yards away from the tent. After hearing very firmly from the doctors that he would never go up to the front again, nor would he go home unless really sick, Henry had accepted his fate. He seemed to be adjusting to life in the camp, but as usual this was not to last.

Henry was moved on with fifty other older men to a section of the camp called the Base Details, 'a disagreeable place, where people scramble & fight for their food, & the main occupation . . . is navvy work such as road-making'.[81] The men surrendered all their equipment and Henry felt it to be 'an inglorious end to our soldiering'.[82] There was talk of a future as stretcher-bearers, not at the front but in various hospitals in France, and Henry was clearly relieved at the prospect. He was summoned by the CO, who spoke to him kindly and then revealed that he understood him to be an Oxford professor; 'I disabused him of that notion,'[83] Henry told Jessie.

The fatigues were now much harder, shifting sand, chalk, stone, or iron pipes, mostly for roadmaking in the area. Fortunately Frank had remained with his Red Cross work, for this would have been too much for him. His brother seemed quite happy with the life in the beautiful spring weather, but found the incompetent young officers very irritating; 'silly boys,'[84] he called them, but the censor took no notice. Henry reported to Jessie a delay in the change to stretcher-bearing, but in fact he was not to begin the new work at all. On 3 May, after a few days of discomfort in his left foot, he found himself unable to pull on his boot and was speedily taken to hospital with gout.

'They may consider this a good opportunity of getting rid of me,'[85] Henry wrote to Jessie, and they did, telling him the next morning that he was for England. On the following day he arrived in Folkestone on his way to the Queen's Canadian Military Hospital, housed in Beachborough Park near Shorncliffe Camp in Kent. 'You may rely on me to represent that wives & homes are the best nurses & hospitals,'[86] he had already assured his wife, but pressure to send him home to Guernsey did not succeed. He was soon sleeping between sheets for the first time for months 'in the lap of luxury, in a big country house used as a hospital, with pretty nurses, plenty of hot & cold water, good food, & less red tape than in the army type of hospital'.[87] Jessie must have been very relieved to receive his telegram sent from Folkestone on arrival: 'England with gout not serious letter follows Henry.'[88]

10

Partings Full of Pain

❦

At home in Guernsey Jessie must have been thrilled to hear of her husband's return to England, but a shortage of boats to the mainland meant a lack of information, and she bombarded Beachborough Park with telegrams until Henry explained gently that all was well and she could rely on letters for her news.

When Henry left for France in 1915 Jessie retreated to Weymouth to stay with her sister Florence, a single woman who had looked after their mother until her final illness; Florence was living at that time with another sister, Norah, a widow with one young son, Rodier, known usually as Rod. After Christmas and New Year with these three, Jessie went home to Guernsey and back to work, although the Weymouth family did come across to visit while Henry was away. She divided her time as usual between nursing at Sunnycroft and the cottage, Lihou. She needed an able assistant to care for the nursing home while she was away with Henry or her family, and she was fortunate to have found a woman who was to be a loyal friend throughout her life. Florence Shayer[1] was a Guernsey girl who, although not trained, was able to deal with the business even when left unsupervised for some time; she was often the supplier of the socks in Henry's parcels, and his thanks to Nurse were recorded at the end of many letters.

There were frequently questions about Jessie's health when Henry wrote home and requests for information about her ailments. 'Please let me know in every letter how it is going on,'[2] he instructed, asking about trouble with an eye which often caused problems. He also asked about her hands, eventually commenting when struck down himself with gout that it seemed odd 'that the same enemy should have gone for us both, you in the hands & me in the foot'.[3] There were other periods of ill health not clearly identifiable from Henry's replies, but Jessie may have suffered some major episode during the winter which had left her weak and finding it difficult to walk far. Henry was clearly delighted when she could return to gardening and walking. His responses to her worries were usually bracing; when Jessie referred to herself as his 'old wife', he reprimanded her firmly: 'I am quite a brisk soldier lad, & expect to find my gal corresponding to me in youthful vigour when I get home.'[4]

Jessie also had considerable money troubles, continuing from the dreadful year before Henry left home. Sunnycroft was still not attracting enough patients and there were discussions about giving it up, although Henry insisted that this must be Jessie's decision and hoped that she could continue at least until he came home. By the end of his time in France these financial problems were clearly becoming even more serious and he devoted paragraphs to money matters. He urged Jessie to use his bank account and to make sure all bills were paid. On one occasion asking her to check his bank book, he added a warning; 'don't be frightened when you find there is a large deficit; you knew that before, I think.'[5] So life in Guernsey was not at all easy, but must have been considerably improved by the news that Henry had escaped from France and would soon be home.

✤ ✤ ✤

Meanwhile at Beachborough Park Henry made rapid progress and was full of praise for the hospital and the staff; the nurses in particular earned an accolade, for they were, he told Jessie, 'all ladies I think, though the pronounced Canadian dialect makes that rather difficult to judge of'.[6] He blamed his misfortune on the poor army diet, sugar in tea and jam, and green vegetables only appearing once in his diet in more than four months in France. He was soon allowed out of bed, however, and was put to floor-sweeping and potato-peeling. Eventually he was sufficiently recovered to be allowed into the delightful gardens and could describe them to Jessie, thinking no doubt of the delights of home; 'double white arabis, fine long & deep lines of forget-me-nots, lots of periwinkle, some crimson wall-flowers,

espalier apple-trees now in blossom, montanas on the walls, & so on . . .'[7]
Jessie sent across a box of Guernsey sweet peas which delighted the whole
ward, as there were enough to share with several of the wounded too.
Henry's letters were filled with descriptions of flowers they might grow if he
could only identify them; he pursued the gardener enthusiastically to
discover details of their names.

Entertainments were laid on regularly for the sick and wounded,
concerts, for instance, and hymn-singing sessions which Henry joined with
an enthusiasm which would have amazed Jessie. He particularly enjoyed
drives into the countryside, although 'not ordinarily an enthusiast for being
drawn about, in motors or otherwise', and described his first trip into the
Kentish spring as 'a most exhilarating business altogether'.[8] A visit to
Canterbury, which of course he knew well, was particularly enjoyable;

> it is the moment of the whole year to be motoring—all the trees in leaf, but
> many of them only in tiny leaf (so that you look up through lace-work at the
> sky), & none of them having lost the first freshness of their colour.

The pleasure of the other men seemed also to delight him; 'how those
boys enjoyed it, after their fashion!—singing choruses nearly all the way.'[9]
One unofficial entertainment was at night, when after going to bed they
were 'deliciously lullaby'd' by

> a Scotch boy in the ward, Bobby Reid by name, with an exquisite alto voice,
> with which he sings very softly . . . one Scotch song after another for three
> quarters of an hour, perhaps; Annie Laurie & Mary of Argyll were the only
> two I know, but there were several others; the contrast between this & the
> roughish jokes & talk that ordinarily prevail at bed-time was something to
> remember for a long time.[10]

Although Henry noted in a letter home that there were no patients 'of the
educated sort', he did greatly enjoy the company of the men; 'one can't help
being rather proud of the material of the British Army if this can be taken
as a fair average example,'[11] he told Jessie. Life at Beachborough Park was
certainly very pleasant, but Henry only wanted to be at home in Guernsey.

Communications with the island were difficult because of the
shipping situation; there were no longer daily boats, which caused delays in
letters and the sad demise of one box of sweet peas. At the beginning of the
war all the Weymouth boats were taken by the authorities for minesweepers
except one, the *Ibex*, who provided a service alone, with occasional

assistance when she needed inspections or boiler cleaning, the cause of the extra delays experienced while Henry was in hospital. After an attack on a cargo boat she was fitted with a gun and later just escaped a torpedo attack, but finally triumphed by sinking a submarine before the end of the war.

Delays in letters meant for Henry difficulties in keeping Jessie informed about his movements. He would be sent to headquarters at Leith in Scotland before being discharged or reassigned for duties elsewhere, but was unsure about the leave he would get before travelling north. He might be sent home straight from hospital or could be transferred for convalescence first and, if this happened, was uncertain whether it would last for a day or two or for some weeks. There were as usual endless rumours, but as his health improved Henry's letters became more optimistic. He hoped to be home for Jessie's birthday and, as his letters stop abruptly on 24 May, he clearly achieved this dream, spending ten days with his wife.

The military adventure was in its final stages when the correspondence was resumed with a note from the *Ibex* as Henry returned to England after his leave. He went up by train to London, after tea with Florence in Weymouth, and travelled overnight from King's Cross to Edinburgh, picking up news on the way of a great sea fight later known as the battle of Jutland. After a day at Leith he was moved to an old rink, Olympia, in the city itself while he waited for a medical board, constantly postponed in usual military fashion. After his final examination he was still unsure of the result, although hoping that the doctor's verdict, 'Well, I think you have done your bit',[12] meant that he would be discharged; plain words would have suited Henry far better. Delays continued and, while others departed, Henry, assured of his discharge, waited about for his papers.

Work during this spell was rather mixed, an expedition to the Zoo, for instance, and an afternoon spent in a picture gallery, as well as a trip to a swimming bath; 'they make things easy for us returned heroes,' Henry told Jessie; 'the nuisance is that it is all such miserable waste of time.'[13] He did, however, learn how to use a scythe, reporting that, although it was 'not an easy business for a beginner',[14] he was glad to get the chance.

Free time was spent exploring, although the hard granite paving did not always suit the gouty toe. Jessie had never visited Edinburgh and so Henry could describe the sights; 'what makes the place so grand is the combination of hills with streets,' he wrote at the beginning of a description of Prince's Street. 'I shall not find a few days here as dull as I should elsewhere,' he thought, but by the end of his time felt that he would be happy never to see Scotland again. The newly returned battle fleet in the Firth of Forth was of course the great thing to visit at that time, and Henry had been told that it was possible to see the *Warspite*, which the Germans said they had sunk, 'all over hits like the top of a pepperpot'.[15] With a friend he spent a good afternoon enjoying the walk and the view of the Forth Bridge. Although they saw the assembled ships they 'could not get near enough to tell which were whole & which damaged, nor guess their names & kinds',[16] a great disappointment. They had chosen for their visit by chance the day when the King travelled up to meet the fleet commander, Admiral Beatty, and their return journey was delayed at the station as he was expected; once again Henry failed to see the King, as he had missed his father at the Review at Aldershot years before.

'These delays are very maddening,'[17] Henry told Jessie, but matters deteriorated further when measles was suspected among the men; 'from worse to worser' was his message when the quarantine period was announced as twenty-one days. The crisis quickly passed and loitering about continued; his last day of military action he described for Jessie:

> the essential thing, you see, is to get us out of the way; so this morning we marched a mile & a half to the foot of Arthur's Seat, sat on the grass for two hours, reading the paper or writing letters or doing nothing according to taste, & then marched back to dinner; & immediately after dinner we marched a mile to a public garden, stayed there similarly for two hours, & marched back to tea.[18]

The next morning Henry was summoned to fill in his discharge papers, after at first being accidentally omitted from the party, and on the following afternoon, before yet another medical board, received his discharge. In his last card to Jessie the final words sum up the situation; the doctor had said to him that men of his 'age & class were ill-advised to enlist'.[19] Henry had really come to no harm from his adventure, but in France his younger brother still endured the military life and was quite unable to escape.

❧ ❧ ❧

Reunited, Henry and Jessie must have spent the summer in their Guernsey garden as planned in their letters. In the autumn Henry went up to Sedbergh to teach, encouraged by the Clarendon Press people, who had put forward the plan when he had asked them whether he and Frank should continue with the dictionaries if discharged. At Oxford they still wanted the two books, of course, but accepted Henry's move to Sedbergh, since schoolmasters were so badly needed. Henry had written from France to Arthur, still teaching at Sedbergh, to ask about the possibility, and his letter had crossed with one from Arthur along the same lines, but Henry's hope, that he might be discharged to take the place of a young schoolmaster who had joined the army, came to nothing.

Jessie travelled north with Henry; he had asked her to think about this when the teaching plan was first discussed, suggesting that she either give up Sunnycroft or put Nurse Shayer in charge. By the time they came to leave she had let the home go, for a maternity case, hoped for while Henry was in Edinburgh, had gone elsewhere and this disappointment meant the end of her career as matron. After the home was closed Florence Shayer parted from the Fowlers and left Guernsey to begin formal nursing training at Salisbury Infirmary. Her records[20] survive, showing her to have been, although a little slow at times, kind, attentive, and completely dependable, qualities which the Fowlers were later to appreciate greatly. Her qualification allowed her to become one of the first registered nurses and to continue with her career until after ten years she returned to the Fowlers.

At Sedbergh life must have seemed quite grim; the *Sedberghian* records the dreadful story of the continuing loss of old boys, including many who had just finished their school careers. During the term Arthur's wife, Ada, became seriously ill, possibly after a stroke, and was from that time paralysed; he was able to continue as housemaster for a time, but in 1920 retired early to move south and care for his sick wife. Henry remained at the school for only a term and then moved on to munitions work, although no hint remains of where he did this or whether Jessie was able to work too. Certainly the Fowlers spent Christmas away from home in 1916, but they were back in the spring of 1917, by which time Frank's problems were becoming more severe; Henry's efforts were quickly directed to trying to rescue his brother.

✤ ✤ ✤

After Henry's discharge Frank remained at Étaples engaged on Red Cross work as before, but spent several spells in hospital. Eventually, after enduring another winter, he was sent back to England in May 1917 to a convalescent camp at Shoreham. From here he would have been given leave and must have gone back to Guernsey, for he and Henry wrote together the Preface to the Pocket dictionary; probably they hoped soon to be back at work, for Frank's discharge must have seemed a possibility. Unfortunately, when sufficiently recovered, he was returned to his battalion and sent to Dover as a telephonist; by then he was so weak that he could only work for 'a few hours on alternate afternoons' and had great difficulty with the hills in getting about the town. Here he was again in hospital several times, and Henry described later Frank's dreadful 'coughing and blood-spitting.' He applied for discharge but was rejected.

Henry meanwhile wrote to the medical officers in charge of his brother both at Shoreham and at Dover, 'representing that he was worn out, likely to be killed by continuance of Army conditions, useless to the Army, and far from useless in civil life'. He was 'sent reassuring answers and promises of special care' and was told in January 1918 that nothing serious could be found wrong with Frank's lungs; this opinion was not shared by the doctor who examined him four months later, and Frank recounted his words to Henry when he 'ultimately discovered his real state':

> Yes, there is a considerable cavity on the right and one less developed on the left . . . The first thing is to get you out of the Army . . . And *if* you were really fit on enlistment, you are entitled to claim that the Army has got you into this state; but *a cavity like this is a good deal to have developed in three years.*

Frank was not discharged; he died on 27 May 1918 in Castlemount Military Hospital, Dover, with Henry by his side, and was buried in St James's Cemetery. His death certificate stated that he died from tuberculosis, from which he had probably been suffering since 1912.

Henry was immensely angry at his brother's treatment by the Army, and after some thought felt that the best way to help other victims was 'to make public protest in flagrant cases'. His decision was probably prompted by an exchange of letters in the *Westminster Gazette* about the grading of older soldiers, but was finally stirred by the story of a young boy with tuberculosis whom the authorities were pursuing and grading fit for service, relentlessly determined to take him as a conscript despite his precarious health; his case was going to appeal as he was clearly unfit to serve. After the publication of this sad tale Henry wrote to the *Westminster Gazette* and his letter retelling the events of Frank's military career was published under the title 'A Soldier's Story'.

> The relentless persistency of the Army in clinging to its used-up human material, which it will not even be at the pains of sorting out and flinging on the scrap-heap when the expense of its upkeep is greater than its military worth, has doubtless cost the country many lives that deserved keeping in existence for their peace-time value.[21]

This was how he began the tale, and his bitter unhappiness ran through the whole recounting of the tragic events. But there was far more to Frank's disastrous story than his military sufferings, and Henry had more difficulties to face as the war drew to a close.

✢ ✢ ✢

Una Fowler had been working in munitions while her husband was in the Army, but at some time after his return to England she became ill and was admitted in September 1917 to Camberwell House, a large private asylum in south London. Here she remained until two weeks before Frank's death, when she was discharged marked 'recovered'. Whether she was then able to be with him before he died is not clear, but she and Henry seem to have been on friendly terms immediately afterwards; Henry acted for her, with power of attorney, when the vinery was sold in August 1918. There was a change, however, when Una remarried in October less than five months after her husband's death. Henry wrote hastily to Oxford for an estimate of the value of the rights in all the books he and Frank had written together. 'It would be a great convenience both to myself & to my brother's widow (now married again) if we could be relieved of future communications by my buying her share,'[22] he explained. With advice he was able to make an offer to Una and the payment was made; he informed the Oxford people and was asked to obtain her signature on a statement of purchase to make all clear. This he sent to her, but it was returned with the signature of her new husband and a note telling Henry that she had been readmitted to Camberwell House. It must have been a bitter blow for Henry, so soon after Frank's death, to have to buy from this man the rights to books written with his much-loved younger brother.

Una had married a man known to the Fowlers for many years, George Dent,[23] a pupil at Sedbergh while Henry was teaching there, although in a different house. At school Dent had been a great success, an excellent sportsman and talented musician, and had left for university at Cambridge, arriving at Peterhouse, where Frank had been a student, in 1897. Frank was still in Cambridge at that time, earning his living by taking private pupils, and the two young men may have met, perhaps for coaching and maybe becoming friends. After completing his degree Dent went out to South Africa for some years and later worked as a musician, but with the outbreak of war he enlisted, like the Fowler brothers, in the ranks. He was wounded in 1916 but not discharged and at the time of the marriage was a private in the 5th London Regiment stationed at Shoreham.

This was the second time that Una had married a 40-year-old bachelor, although the age gap of eleven years was smaller than the nineteen years which had separated her from Frank. It is impossible to gauge the state of the Fowler marriage before her breakdown, only to deduce, from a slight hint of surprise in the older couple when noting that Frank and Una were in regular correspondence, that all was perhaps not well between them. There was just one reference to George Dent in Henry's letters to Jessie, obviously in reply to a question from her; he had heard nothing of him, he wrote, adding, 'I think I wrote to him at Oxted months ago, but I never got an answer.'[24] Clearly there was some relationship with the Fowlers, but there is no suggestion of any involvement with Una before Frank's death.

Una returned to Camberwell House in late January 1919 and there she remained for the next seventeen years.[25] She would surely have been well treated, although remedies at that time would probably seem appalling to modern observers. The asylum stood in twenty acres and accommodation was in separate houses in the grounds; the illustrated brochures promised sports, entertainments, outings, and even a house in Brighton for holidays for suitable patients; the fees were of course considerable. Una lived at Camberwell House for the rest of her life, dying there aged only 46.

George Dent lived on until 1959, and the final twist in the tale comes with the arrangements made by him for the distribution of his assets in his will. He left a sizeable sum from his estate, and the whole if the main beneficiary had predeceased him, to Violet Cripps, who, as a niece of Arthur Fowler's late wife, had been the only heir when Arthur died as the last of the Fowlers. Dent may have met Violet as a young girl at Sedbergh when she visited her family, but it could have been a way of paying back the sum taken in such dreadful circumstances from Henry Fowler forty years before.

✿ ✿ ✿

After the term at Sedbergh and their munitions work the Fowlers were back together at Lihou for Jessie's birthday in May 1917. The celebratory verses had begun again when Henry came back from France and on this occasion showed their relief at the safe return to home life:

> Love's bond to test and harden,
>   Two years behind us lie
> Of war's alarms, and wanderings, and partings
>   full of pain;
> But here we are, and here we are, and here we are
>   again—
>   The cottage and the garden,
>   The dog and you and I.[26]

This happiness at Lihou was short-lived; in spring 1918 James Wilson sold the cottage to another Englishman, George Francis, who was later, after Frank's death, to buy the vinery too. The agreement allowed the Fowlers to remain as tenants, but when their lease expired the new landlord doubled the rent and they could not afford to stay. So in early 1919 they were homeless; the nursing home had long ago been given up and the original cottage was much too small for their needs.

The anniversary verses, celebrating the engagement eleven years before, reflected their predicament with the title 'Evicted Birds'.[27] It began as always with a proposal:

> 'Tis spring, my Chuck; your ear, dear duck, unto
>   my song incline
> The time is due to tell me true if you'll once more
>   be mine.

Then it turned quickly to the business filling their minds at the time, finding a home:

> With me you'll live? And you'll forgive, sweet Bird,
>   if I allude
> To where 'twere best to fix the nest, nor think me
>   bold and rude?

After much searching the Fowlers found at last the ideal spot, Le Moulin de Haut, a large but neglected mill house in the neighbouring parish of Castel which they were able to rent from a local farmer, Pierre Daniel Ozanne. They may have been helped in their search by Henry Rule Wetherall, the Peterhouse student who had come out to grow tomatoes at the same time as Frank; his group of growers was based was only a few minutes walk away from the new house.

Le Moulin de Haut had been empty for many years and had an overgrown garden of about three-quarters of an acre and an old orchard, 'plenty of apples and a splendid pergola of figs'. The millstream ran through the garden and supplied water for the mill house, which was beyond the public supply. In appearance it was a typical Guernsey granite farmhouse, probably built in the late sixteenth century but with later additions. It was set across a small lane from the mill itself, notable because it had two mill wheels; it is now disused, but was then still worked by the Lainé family, millers there for many years. Le Moulin de Haut stands in an area once noted for its mills and known then as Les Grands Moulins; the mill house of Le Moulin de Milieu still remains, although Le Moulin de Bas has not survived.

The situation of the house is charming, set in the beautiful Fauxquets valley where a footpath follows the mill stream among woods thick with bluebells and wild garlic in spring. The wooded hillside forms an amphitheatre behind the house and garden, with a large rookery still remaining on the rising ground; Gordon Coulton, a frequent visitor there as at Lihou, described an autumnal exhibition by the rooks and a family of kestrels, 'a wonderful drama' which could always attract Henry from his desk to watch.

> ... the rival forces would skirmish in labyrinthine evolutions; now intermingling and again dispersing; never actually coming to grips as it seemed, but always threatening and manoeuvring for position.[28]

Inevitably with such a rundown property there was plenty to do to sort it out but, by the time Henry's *Nursery Rhymes of the Furnishing, Garden,*

Stream, Livestock, and Landlord of Moulin de Haut recorded the work at Christmas 1919, Henry and Jessie were settled and making progress.

> There was an old couple that lived at High Mill;
> They had a many chambers that they didn't
>   know how to fill;
> Their floors had no carpets, but lino instead,
> And, to save sheets and blankets, they slept in one
>   bed.
>
> There is a little man, and he does the best he can,
>   (Though he makes his fingers sore, and his
>   thumb, thumb, thumb)
> To please his darling wife by slicing with his knife
>   At bits of dirty old linoleum-um-um.

The Fowlers had always loved gardening and references to it filled the war letters, particularly as hopes of discharge grew. Jessie had felt sad at leaving her roses at Lihou but found a suitable challenge in her new home.

> Marian, Marian, tell me, contrary one,
>   How does your garden grow?
> I've bindweed galore, and of nettles good store
>   And tall docks row upon row.[29]

Jessie set out to rescue the overgrown garden and orchard with Henry, 'clearing the brambles and digging up the whole neglected plot',[30] and they were soon able to transform their surroundings. To an enquiring friend Henry later described their rural life: 'my wife & I live out in the country, an elderly Adam & Eve labouring with pickaxe & spade & hoe to restore a ruined paradise.'[31]

At Moulin de Haut the Fowlers settled back into their old life, gardening, walking, entertaining visitors, and of course working. Here, as before, Henry ran down to the sea each morning to swim at Vazon Bay on the west coast, a run of about a mile down from the house. Although 60 in 1918 he was still fit and strong, and was to continue with this routine for many more years.

Perhaps the enforced move from Lihou and St Pierre du Bois was in fact fortunate. Here the Fowlers could begin again and start a new life after all the horrors of the past years, beginning with Edith's tragic death in 1914 and ending with the loss of Frank in 1918. With Jessie's support giving him quiet security, Henry could continue with the work begun with his brother and return to his quiet country life.

✤ ✤ ✤

Perhaps Henry was never aware of one final bitter blow attempted to Frank's memory. The parishioners of St Pierre du Bois, when planning their war memorial by the village church, argued against the inclusion of Frank's name, feeling that, as he had died rather than being killed, it should be omitted; the rector, however, insisted and Frank's name is on the front of the memorial.[32] Henry would have been appalled if his brother's great sacrifice had been rejected in that way when he could have stayed quietly at home and perhaps lived for much longer enjoying his work and a comfortable island life. As it was Henry may well have known nothing of all this, for the loss of Lihou had taken him away from the village by the time these discussions took place. His completion of the work they had begun so optimistically together was the greatest memorial to his brother.

1. Henry watching the Ten Mile race at Sedbergh in 1899.
2. Henry relaxing on the deck of an unidentified ship. Photograph taken
from a lantern slide.

3. Studio portrait of Henry probably taken in St Peter Port at about
the time of his marriage.

4. Jessie Fowler. A studio portrait probably taken before her marriage
to Henry in St Peter Port.

5. Henry's Cottage at Les Reveaux.
6. Moulin de Haut in the early twentieth century.

7. Henry and Raven.
8. Henry and Jessie, taken in the garden of Le Moulin de Haut in 1924.

9. Henry in sporting attire.

10. Florence Shayler,
devoted nurse to the elderly Fowlers.

22 Ap. 1928

Dear Mr Onions

I feel I should
be a churl if I did not
make one in the multi-
tude of your felicitators
on the great event of
last week — though doubt-
less the sight of 'April
1928' at the top of the
cover was not an un-
mixed joy; endings sel-
dom are.

I hasten to add what
my business postcards
end with — No answer needed.

Yours very truly

H. W. Fowler

11. Henry's letter of congratulation sent to C. T. Onions when the *OED*
was published in 1928.

12. Henry in old age.

11

A Dumpy Little Book

*Well, if one undertakes to get a book done in a year, & it is not out
by the end of eight, there is plenty of time to box the compass, loop the loop,
& circumnavigate the globe.*[1]

T he Fowler brothers had agreed before the war to produce the Pocket
dictionary quickly for the Press, and Frank, not suffering from
Henry's 'misolexicography', had begun work on it, while his brother
planned *Modern English Usage*, his own pet project. All this they had left for
army life, intending to return when the conflict ended. While they were in
France there had been an attempt to poach them from the Clarendon Press,
when a Bombay publisher offered them £50 for an edition of *Robinson
Crusoe*. When forwarding the letter to Henry the Oxford people added a
note advising the brothers 'to stick to them rather than go elsewhere',[2] but
Henry and Frank had no intention of straying, regarding their work as set
aside, not permanently abandoned. At last Henry was able to take up the
threads again, returning first to the book his brother had left on enlisting
and seeming unruffled by the long delay and the hard work before him.

At Oxford there had inevitably been changes; Robert Chapman had
spent the war with a commission in the army serving in Salonica, while
Charles Cannan continued as Secretary with the help of his three daughters,
pressed into service as volunteers when most of the staff enlisted. There were
later two new figures in the office, both unfit for military service, John
Johnson appointed as Assistant Secretary in 1915 and Kenneth Sisam, but
these two Henry was not to encounter until later. When Cannan died in
December 1919 Chapman, back from the war, was appointed as Secretary,
and it was with him that Henry had to discuss the progress of the Pocket
dictionary.

After initial satisfaction with the Concise, there seemed to be disappointment by that time with attitudes to the book and consequently its sales. Although Chapman assured Henry of his admiration for its 'deft economy', the general impression seemed to be that the book was 'difficult' and 'over-academic', and that this had caused its disappointing results. The aim with the new book was to apply the lessons learnt from the Concise, and this led to changes particularly in the treatment of pronunciation and sensitivity too towards the American market, which had not been greatly considered when the bigger book was being prepared.

In the Pocket every word was to be given its pronunciation, unlike the Concise, where only those considered most important had been included, and stress was to be marked with accents, not the turned periods of the earlier book. The difficulty was the positioning of these accents, and this led to a disagreement with Oxford. The placing of accents could be syllabic, that is at the end of the stressed syllable, or vocalic, 'after the letter or letters that give the syllable's vowel sound',[3] as Henry explained it. The Press had decided that the accents in the new book would be syllabic but Henry was most unhappy about this system, feeling 'no inclination . . . to attack . . . the hopeless & useless task of saying where syllables end'.[4] He gave long lists of words which produced problems, such as 'bonnet', 'commission', 'chargeable', 'horrid', 'hostess', 'Homeric', and 'strengthen', for instance; bonnet, as an example, might be divided as bon'net, suggesting, Henry thought, that the second 'n' had a separate sound, while the division, bonn'et, might imply that the right place to divide the word at a line-end was after the second 'n'. Travellers operating from the London office were asked to canvass the opinions of booksellers and schoolteachers about the preferences of the general public, referred to as 'the G.P.'. Robert Chapman from the Oxford office explained to Humphrey Milford, still in the London office, that Henry, who regarded 'professional lexicographers with suspicion might be converted by a cloud of witness from schools and office-stools'.[5] Henry, on the other hand, was not at all happy and felt bullied; 'my own belief is that not one in a thousand of the G.P. cares twopence where his dictionary puts its accents',[6] he declared. The results of the survey were as expected and syllabic accents were accepted; Henry had to adjust to a system he hated.

The pronunciation of foreign words was also a problem, but had been discussed and settled with Frank before the war. He had reluctantly agreed to a suggestion from Oxford that he should present a list of foreign words to be pronounced and a phonetician would do the work to be published in an appendix. Thinking about it again Henry had doubts, and by January 1919 he had prepared and presented to Chapman an 'Appendix of unEnglish pronunciation'[7] intended for the Pocket. Henry feared that the Oxford expert would 'with curly mysterious symbols & too many distinctions of sound, repel the man in the street'.[8] Prompted by these fears Henry had prepared his own system, but the response from Chapman was not encouraging: 'any attempt to present French in an intelligible shape will lead pedants to blaspheme, & will leave the ignorant very much where they were.'[9] To Charles Onions of the *OED*, who was advising on the Pocket, it seemed best to return to the old Concise method of marking words with an (F) and doing no more; if an appendix were to be used, he found Henry's scheme too difficult. In London the position seemed quite clear; 'as a tradesman who has his finger on the public pulse',[10] Humphrey Milford hoped for a key to French words. These pronunciations were eventually given in an appendix, but Henry's scheme was not adopted; the International Phonetic alphabet was used, with extra symbols added for unEnglish sounds.

The arrangement of compound words and phrases in long entries in the new book was to be alphabetical, to help the reader quickly discover required items. In the Concise it had been necessary to read a whole entry to find one word or phrase. Accessibility of the most important items was to be aided further by printing them, like all the main words, in clarendon, defined by Henry as 'thick-faced type (**thus**)'. Decisions had to be made about which words needed clarendon and which could remain in italics, quietly overlooked. Henry was rather disconcerted by 'the unanimous cry that exciting words should be prominent',[11] wanting to 'know what makes a word exciting'.[12] Onions, in reading these comments, felt Henry to be 'not quite in touch with the Ordinary Man',[13] having spent so long using the *OED* to make his abridgements. Henry attempted to persuade Chapman to leave the matter alone, but he could not be moved, although eventually he seemed quite happy to accept some inconsistency in the allocation of clarendon. Henry finally settled to make his choices, inclining 'not to be niggardly, but rather to be over lavish with it',[14] which seemed to settle his concerns.

Onions had seemed a little critical on the use of clarendon, but he could be generous in praising Henry's work when it deserved praise. The introduction of 'literary', to be inserted in brackets after certain words, was one such occasion; Henry had introduced it rather late in the work but felt it to be important. He defined a literary word as 'one that cannot be called archaic, inasmuch as it is perfectly comprehensible . . . but that has dropped out of use . . . except in writing of a poetical or a definitely literary cast'; as examples he gave '<u>chill</u> for <u>chilly</u>, <u>eve</u> for <u>evening</u>'. Adding this 'literary' label to words was intended by Henry to 'warn writers with a tendency to verbiage that they would do well . . . to consider whether something more familiar would not serve their purpose as well or better'.[15] All this Onions admired, regarding Henry's distinction as 'entirely to be commended'.[16]

'Yankeefication', as Henry called it, was another matter which caused him problems. Resistance in America to the Concise because of its British English spelling had persuaded the authorities to bring out an American Pocket with corrected spellings. 'America makes me feel very old; it will bring down my grey hairs with sorrow to the grave' was Henry's opinion on the matter. He felt quite unable to do the work, and was grateful for the suggestion that an expert should be employed to deal with the spellings. An appendix of American words was also suggested and this too he approved, feeling that to put American words into the English text 'would be not less than a crime—an offering to English readers of the sight of means to do ill deeds'. He felt 'no dislike or contempt for the American language' but was aware that he did not know it well enough to do the work, suggesting to Oxford that if they wanted him to do it they should first shut him 'up for six months with a hundred selected Yankee books & a supply of food'.[17]

Complaints from America about the omission of common words from the Concise had prompted the decision about an appendix. 'Crotch for the fork of a tree, of the human body, bifurcation of a road, etc.' had been suggested for inclusion and Henry knew that there were many others to be added by the expert, words current in America but obsolete at home. There were also endless other proposed additions; the war in particular had introduced many new words, 'ack emma' and 'pip emma', for instance, for 'a.m.' and 'p.m.'. Advice was sought as usual from Oxford and London; Milford, numbering 'literary cricketers among his friends', was able to help with defining 'cow-shot' as 'an exaggerated pull or hook, generally made in a crouching position',[18] while from Oxford came encouragement, readily supplied, for the omission of all the trigonometry terms, 'a bold bad deed'[19] according to Henry.

There were still complaints about words already in the Concise which, although they could not be changed there immediately, could be adjusted if necessary in the new book. The Boy Scouts Association, for instance, objected strongly to the use of the word 'military' in the definition of 'boy scout' and Henry made the change, although pointing out that they seemed to him 'to ensue the thing & eschew the word'.[20] The Concise had of course been published in 1911, and Henry was surprised that objections in some most serious matters had been delayed for so long. There are racial and religious words which cause trouble constantly for lexicographers, trying to reflect honestly the way in which words have been used without appearing to promote uses which will inevitably cause offence to some. This perennial problem Henry encountered while working on the Pocket.

The definition of 'Antichrist' in the Concise, for instance, included as one of its meanings 'the Pope', unobserved for many years but eventually noticed and objected to by the Westminster Catholic Federation. Henry's response to Chapman on the matter was robust; 'You make me feel very old. Why, I was brought up to half believe that the Pope, & no other, <u>was</u> Antichrist.' He had 'imbibed' this from his father but they had both given up the belief, for the older man had 'relaxed in the severity of his protestantism before he died'. Henry did feel it to have been common in his youth, and thought that it should be retained but marked so that readers recognized it as a historical usage, or with 'in ultra-Prot. use'[21] perhaps, adding evidence of its history to convince Oxford. While admitting the use to be defensible historically Chapman told Henry firmly that it was not 'a familiar sobriquet for his Holiness',[22] and it was removed from the Pocket before publication and from the Concise by the second edition in 1929. Chapman reported his decision to the objectors, pointing out that lexicographers should not be concerned 'with the propriety of usage' and omit items because they contravened 'truth or morality'. The Federation had by then discovered also the definition of 'Jesuit' as 'dissembling person, prevaricator' and were preparing a libel case against the Press, but Chapman's advice that their action should be 'against the English people and not against any lexicographer'[23] settled the affair.

Similar problems were raised by the definitions of 'Jew' after the publication of the Pocket. The business began with an anonymous letter to the *Jewish Chronicle* objecting to the definition 'unscrupulous usurer or bargainer'; this was accompanied by an article discussing the matter, including a quotation from a private letter written by Henry to the Chief Rabbi, Dr J. H. Hertz, whose advice he had sought before publication on several words and whose help was acknowledged in the book. Henry had explained to him the position of the lexicographer when dealing with words of this type; he had to put on record what people actually said, not what he believed they should say, and decisions about definitions were made by considering not whether a word or phrase was offensive but whether it was current. When trimming the *OED* entries to produce the shorter definitions for the new dictionaries, Henry, forced to cut harshly to save space, had omitted the lengthy explanation that the word in this sense was used as 'a name of opprobrium and reprobation'. As a consequence the definition was regarded by the writer of the article as unnecessarily insulting and he felt that dictionaries should not be maintaining the currency of a meaning which was both untrue and vicious and had first been introduced at a time and in circumstances which had long since changed. An acknowledgement that the word was used offensively with this meaning was suggested as being the least that should be done.

Henry replied with the same explanation previously offered to the Chief Rabbi, but he was vigorously attacked; at the Stoke Newington synagogue, for instance, the Rabbi declared that a cleverer or more determined attempt to promote racial or religious hatred could not be imagined.[24] One of Henry's advisers, Leslie J. Berlin, wrote supporting him, which reassured Henry, who was certain that, as a Jew and a most careful observer of misprints, Berlin would not have missed 'any animus against the Jews'.[25] After consultation with the Delegates of the Press, Chapman agreed to add the word 'figurative' to the definition to avoid misunderstanding; this was quickly done, '(fig.)' appearing in the third impression in January 1926 and satisfying the critics. Henry, however, was unhappy at the injustice of the attacks on him, regarding his arguments given to the *Jewish Chronicle* as correct and stating his feelings very plainly to Oxford: 'I have neither religious, political, nor social antipathy to Jews; the J.C.'s notion that I have is the merest moonshine.'[26]

Untroubled by promises about time after so long Henry was able to continue quietly with his editing, but other distractions disturbed his main work, even occasionally compelling him to set it aside for a time. *Modern English Usage* had long since been abandoned, to be picked up again when the dictionary was finished.

⚘ ⚘ ⚘

Copying of dictionary material by rival lexicographers was difficult to establish, but very annoying at Oxford, where so much had been invested in dictionaries. The Oxford people were convinced that a new book, Cassell's *New English Dictionary*, edited by Ernest Baker and published in 1919, had made extensive use of the Concise without any acknowledgement. In this way a much cheaper book could be produced and it was, according to Henry Bradley, 'deliberately intended to "cut out" the Concise Oxford Dictionary'. In producing their own books the brothers had of course used others for comparison, but they had been quite open about this, noting it in their preface to the Concise. The notion of piracy was quite new to Henry and he was himself rather puzzled by the whole business, feeling the absurdity of having to avoid the best way of putting a definition because it had been used before. His initial response when he was asked for help with the collection of evidence was, after comparing the two volumes, to decide that the case was proved as far as he was concerned. More careful examination, 'Baker-hunting' he called it, and the comparison of a group of dictionaries persuaded him that proof was very difficult and he decided that it was in fact hard to see who had borrowed from whom; 'most men are thieves,' he concluded, setting aside the work until the lawyers had pronounced on it; 'God forbid that time should be spent on so desolating a pursuit.'

Piracy was in fact established by checking all misprints and mistakes recorded by the brothers after the publication of the dictionary and comparing these with the entries in the new book. This did produce positive results, but the quality of Henry's examples was often criticized and he was urged to find more, a very time-consuming business. The real grievance was not the taking of small items of this sort, but the use of whole articles or rather their underlying structure with the illustrative phrases omitted, 'unreasonably free reproduction of the framework of COD articles'.[27]

Chapman eventually felt that, although the case was doubtful, it would be sensible to get the best legal advice, and the whole complicated business was handed over to the lawyers, who in the end advised that the matter be dropped as too difficult to prove.

✤ ✤ ✤

The decision to produce an American Concise was another distraction for Henry. As this would obviously involve resetting the book to include the American material, it seemed sensible to Chapman to bring it up to date by making corrections and in particular setting straight the etymologies in the last part prepared without the help of the *OED*. A young American, George van Santvoord,[28] a lecturer at Yale, had been engaged to produce the American Pocket and seemed suitable to work on both dictionaries. Chapman's initial proposal was that this young man should do the revision too, but Henry's hostility quickly put a stop to that. He felt the idea of revising to be foolish, and thought that the work should wait until the whole book could be recast; but if it had to be done, he would do it himself. In fact he really believed the Concise to be so inferior that it would be squeezed out between the Pocket on which he was working and the much larger Shorter being prepared by William Little in Cornwall. Nevertheless Chapman required the revision of the material, and Henry set to work on this further task while continuing with the preparation of the Pocket.

The business was a lengthy one, 'interminable' according to Henry, because of the etymological tinkering, very small changes mostly but essential. When the work was finally completed he declared himself 'not ashamed to face the American philological music'.[29] There was also the comforting thought that the prepared corrections were ready for any new English edition, but until then America would have, it seemed, a better Concise than England. Unfortunately this was not to be; the American Pocket was published after many delays in 1927, admired by Henry as 'a nice little book in its American dress',[30] but it was not a success, as many customers preferred the English version. This failure, and the excellent American sales of the Concise, 'despite its very British flavour'[31] about which some had complained earlier, persuaded the Oxford people in New York to abandon the American version.

By the end of April 1922 Henry had sent in the last batch of work on the revision of the Concise and the final instalment of the manuscript of the Pocket. For some months he was involved in proof-checking, occasionally even squeezing in new words, but finally on 3 July 1924 the book was published at 3s. 6d., a considerably higher price than the 1s. originally suggested. The little volume seemed genuinely pocket-sized, measuring only 4 inches by 7—'a dumpy little book' one critic called it.

Reviewers were very kind, the inclusion of new words being particularly admired; 'the compilers have taken pains to keep up with the times.' The passing years have cast a rather grim sadness over one commentator's assertion that war slang should not have been included as it would have 'only a temporary place in the language'.[32] 'A book that has all the qualities, every virtue, every grace,' another reviewer declared; 'one of the most delightful as well as one of the most useful books.'[33] While another, in slightly more florid style, felt: 'As the smallest possible compendium of a great language for the use of the hurried but intelligent we cannot imagine how this book can be surpassed.'[34] The successful completion of Frank's work, acknowledged of course in the book, must have given Henry great pleasure; with this safely done after so long, he was able to leave lexicography with relief and turn again to *Modern English Usage*.

✤ ✤ ✤

Over the years spent working on these projects Henry's friendship with Chapman had developed and they had begun to address each other by name rather than with the usual formal 'Sir' of earlier correspondence. Chapman confided to Henry his ideas about the development of dictionaries at Oxford, musing about supplementing the *OED* on completion, the impossibility of keeping the great work up to date, and the sad prospect of a series of supplements which could never be incorporated into the work itself. Chapman was concerned particularly about the collection of new words and the monitoring of the developing language; the *OED* lexicographers were, he declared, 'still too deep in the fifteenth century to have much time for modern collections'. As a result he was thinking of assembling a group of amateur observers to 'keep tap of the language'[35] as it grew, and was anxious to learn from Henry's experience with his own collections, knowing that he was the only person systematically gathering new words. Henry was constantly sending in material for the *OED*, noticed as he worked through it for his own books, but Chapman urged him to do it more formally by copying or pinning interesting items to slips and sending them to Oxford, even offering a little payment. 'Would it add <u>very</u> much to your toil?' he asked rather foolishly, excusing his request with the explanation that 'you have taught us to expect a great deal'.[36] Henry did agree to try the work although warning Chapman, 'I shall not be much good, because I never read anything but the newspapers.'[37] Sending on his first bundles to Onions the Secretary felt rather differently, telling his colleague, 'H.W.F. has such an eye and nose that he is likely to spot just the things that subsequent and duller readers would miss.'[38] Henry was able also to put him in touch with other suitable word collectors among his correspondents; one retired army surgeon gave him valuable help and another military correspondent living in Jamaica, a great enthusiast, sent lengthy letters with sometimes sixty foolscap pages of suggestions. Perhaps with his own work done, Henry was relieved to divert their attention to the *OED*.

❀ ❀ ❀

Henry must have enjoyed friendships such as these, even if only made on paper, since the death of Frank had deprived him of his collaborator. He seemed anxious always to find a replacement, and in these years at Moulin de Haut he began to exert pressure on his brothers to join him, not living in Guernsey but taking their share of the work in their own mainland homes.

Charles had always found it possible to resist his brother's firm hand, and continued to do so. After his temporary teaching post at Sedbergh he had moved south to Wimborne in Dorset and was still at the grammar school there after nearly forty years; he had obviously no time for more work and firmly refused advances from his brother. The two seem to have had a rather difficult relationship; Henry, for instance, commented to Jessie after hearing from him during the war; 'Charles's letter is so unusually human that, if I remember, I will enclose it for you to see.'[39] Perhaps a little sympathy should be felt for this second brother, whose great size was noted at every appearance of his name from schooldays at Marlborough and college at

Christ's until his death, when he is reported to have weighed twenty-seven stone. Gordon Coulton delightedly repeated tales of the stout student, recalling how he tipped up boats and was impossible to tackle on the rugby field, 'a phenomenon of undergraduate obesity'.[40] He was without doubt a man of considerable courage, indulging in so much sporting activity and fearlessly withstanding his eldest brother.

Arthur was not so tough and gave the matter more thought; perhaps the younger brothers found Henry harder to resist. Arthur had retired early from Sedbergh aged only 52 to care for Ada, paralysed since her illness while Henry was teaching at the school during the war. The couple had settled in Parkstone in Dorset, a small town on the coast between Poole and Bournemouth, since then absorbed as a suburb of Poole; perhaps they were tempted by advertisements describing the town as a suitable home for invalids, 'the Mentone of England',[41] with 'a climate so equable that it forms part of every good doctor's prescription to convalescents'.[42] For whatever reason, they were extremely happy in their new home, and Arthur only left eventually with great reluctance. At first he was interested in the proposal, and Henry asked Oxford to send some materials for him to use in a trial of the work, but after three months Arthur decided that dictionary-making was not possible while caring for Ada. He did, however, join in Chapman's scheme for the collection of new words, sending frequent packets to Oxford; Henry no doubt noted that this younger brother was well suited to the work and would make a useful recruit when he had time.

✤ ✤ ✤

Jessie was no help in this area, insisting that she had no knowledge of grammar at all, remembering only one snatch from her childhood:

> A *Pronoun* is used instead of a *Noun*
> As: 'James was tired, and *He* sat down.'

Her contribution was the maintenance of their happy home life, enabling Henry, despite the pain of past years, to settle back into a comfortable working routine. There were still some holidays, but after settling at Moulin de Haut Henry rarely left home. Jessie went off to shop in St Peter Port and visit elsewhere, bringing 'back all the news of the capital and, more especially, the gossip of the market-place'. Gordon Coulton, speaking of her 'dramatic sense', described her as Henry's 'local newspaper and his picture-palace'.[43]

Henry's appreciation of her good qualities still showed in endless praise in his anniversary verses; he risked her wrath at one postwar Christmas celebration, but no doubt only raised her merry laugh, when he called her an 'old woman' comparing her to modern 'new women' in naughty verses; he did promise in a note that the temptation was fictitious:

> New Women are not to my taste,
> And I'm tempted to say in my haste
>   'Oh, Astor be durned!
>   Bonham Carter be burned!
>   And for Christabel Pank
>   To be drowned in a tank
> Were a much better fate than she's earned'.[44]

Although both the Fowlers were reported by observers to have liked children, they had of course none of their own. One set of verses for Jessie's 48th birthday was a succession of wishes, all perfectly sensible until the last:

> May soon a boy, her crowning joy,
>   Be heard to call her mother!
> And after that, I know not what
>   To wish, except—another.[45]

This may well have been a joke between the pair or a foolish hope on the part of the elderly husband, but it might just represent the only record of a short-lived pregnancy which briefly delighted the Fowlers.

One small story remains of Jessie's kindness to children and impetuous good nature, preserved in the memory of the family of a small boy from the mill, D'Arcy Lainé, well known to Jessie, often running errands for her, fetching milk and post. Sent into St Peter Port one Christmas to shop for his mother, D'Arcy was tempted to stop on his way back and spend his own small fortune at a penny arcade in the Victoria Road. On turning round to resume his journey he discovered that the bags he had put down on arrival had been stolen. He ran all the way home to report the misdeed and was rewarded with a good hiding from his father; the loss was obviously a disaster for a large family at any time of year, but particularly at Christmas. Jessie, hearing the boy's sobs, arrived at the mill insisting that the child's father stop immediately and asking what was wrong with her young protégé.

She settled the matter by providing enough money for the shopping to be replaced. Young D'Arcy adored his stout defender, recounting throughout his long life the story of her kindness to his family.[46]

❧ ❧ ❧

The walks around Moulin de Haut were a great delight to the Fowlers and their visitors, and there were always dogs to accompany them; Jessie's pets, Scamp and Joyce, had been followed by the handsome retriever-collie cross, Raven, seen in a photograph with Henry. His fondness for animals had been shown much earlier when he wrote about the dogs and cats living around his small cottage at St Pierre du Bois. He described for instance the 'black dog', an outcast in the local community who, besides his 'unprepossessing looks', was 'both a coward and a bully'. Encountering his hostile behaviour, Henry realized that the dog was acting only 'on the strategical maxim that the best defence is offence'. For some time he rejected advances in the form of 'mutton-chop bones & other dainties' but finally, according to Henry, came to regard him 'as the only human being whom he may jump upon or come within reach of with impunity'.[47] For some years then Henry had his own dog for company on walks in the woods around Moulin de Haut and Raven was even on occasion a promising poet, especially when thanking holiday hostesses for care while Henry and Jessie were away in England.

Jessie's walking and gardening had been severely curtailed in the spring of 1923, when she fell breaking her ankle and was laid up for some months, making her husband 'idle with the pen and busy with all sorts of other things'. Henry too had been 'convicted of glaucoma' some time before and was beginning to feel apprehensive, telling Chapman that 'cautious estimates of the remaining eyesight are indicated'.[48] Gout too afflicted them still and the Fowler diet was strictly limited by the doctor; the atmosphere of their home was 'murky' with 'meat-hungry moans, fish-sated groans':

> Bacon's tabooed, and meat eschewed;
>   We can't buy, steal, or borrow
> Eggs to abate or mitigate
>   Our fishy mealtimes' sorrow;
> It's fish today, fish yesterday,
>   And fish again tomorrow.[49]

Shadows were gathering as the couple aged, but Henry was doing his best work at Moulin de Haut and, with the text of the Pocket safely delivered, he was able to turn back to his favourite project, *Modern English Usage*.

12

A Heterodox Expert

ome from the war, Henry had set out at first to work on both the Pocket dictionary and *Modern English Usage*, his own book, of which only a quarter had been prepared before the brothers enlisted. He was soon approaching Robert Chapman at Oxford for 'a little paternal advice' about new ideas for the book which, if incorporated, would increase both its size and the time needed to complete it; Henry realized that this would cause him financial problems and would probably not please the Oxford people. 'Is your possible approval of the increased bulk & longer time expressible in money?' he asked, explaining that, with his working pace slowed by the additions, he would be earning only ten shillings a week until it was finished. Chapman was sympathetic, increasing the total for the book from £150 to £200 and ordering that the difference for the first quarter, which had been paid long before, should be sent at once to Guernsey.

Henry made two suggestions for additions to *Modern English Usage*, suitable he felt for 'a general vade-mecum of English writing', as he described it. The first of these was for 'a list of mythological, biblical, & fictional names to which reference is common in books & newspapers' to be arranged as one alphabetical entry under the title 'Generic Names'; Henry had collected about 1,000 and hoped to increase that by three or four times. His second plan was to provide 'a running apparatus of synonyms', more generous than the provision in most dictionaries, which he felt to be 'on a very niggardly scale';[1] readers looking up an important word would find either a set of synonyms or a reference to one elsewhere. He did admit that this addition might overwhelm the other contents of the book but offered for inspection the letter H, which he had just completed. As he had only compiled these lists for F, G, and H this plan would clearly involve considerable extra work.

At Oxford the idea was greeted with enthusiasm, but the general feeling was that the additions would perhaps be better as a separate book or booklets; *Modern English Usage*, Chapman told Henry, 'is so dear to our hearts . . . that we are reluctant to delay it or risk overloading'.[2] The specimen of H was 'read with avidity',[3] and Charles Onions was sure that it would make a remarkable book. He welcomed the 'racy style' but doubted the propriety of some of Henry's comments: 'the freedom of the smoking-room is best avoided in a book that should find its way into all sorts of schools, even convents.'[4] The final decision was that synonyms should be 'abandoned to lighten the ship'[5] while Henry continued with the Generic Names.

His workload was clearly very heavy at that time and, with the intrusion of the other distractions which disturbed his work on the Pocket dictionary, he was forced to set aside *Modern English Usage* until he had finished with lexicography. When at the end of April 1922 he sent off the final parts of the dictionary and the corrections for the proposed American Concise he was able to turn back to his favourite project; 'I will busy myself with brushing off the fifteenth-months dust from the . . . papers,'[6] he told Chapman.

✿ ✿ ✿

This spell of enforced delay in work on *Modern English Usage* did see the first airing of some entries already prepared for it as articles published in various journals. 'Only' appeared in the *Westminster Gazette* and 'morale' as part of a letter to the *Times Literary Supplement* in which Henry objected to the attempts to substitute the French 'moral' for English 'morale' during the war, causing confusion with the English 'moral'; he noted with relief that 'morale' was still used in newspapers 'that had to use a tongue understood of the people' and that it was gradually returning 'timidly and occasionally, even in select quarters'.[7]

These articles appeared mostly, however, in the Tracts of the Society for Pure English, of which Henry was a member. The Society had been founded in 1913, but on the outbreak of war the committee, which included Henry Bradley, decided to suspend publishing plans 'until the national distraction should have abated', and it was not until 1919 that the first tract appeared. In a Preliminary Announcement the principles of the Society were set out; it would aim at 'preserving all the richness of differentiation' in vocabulary,

> its nice grammatical usages, its traditional idioms, and the music of its inherited pronunciation: it would oppose whatever is slipshod and careless, and all blurring of hard-won distinctions, but it would no less oppose the tyranny of schoolmasters and grammarians, both in their pedantic conservatism, and in their ignorant enforcing of new-fangled 'rules', based not on principle, but merely on what has come to be considered 'correct' usage.[8]

This was clearly the best place for a trial of Henry's work. His first tract was published in 1921, 'On Hyphens, Shall & Will, Should & Would in the Newspapers of Today', followed the next year by a note on 'as to' and a tract on 'Grammatical Inversions', well received by reviewers. 'Metaphor' was the subject of a later issue, with essays on the subject by three authors, Henry's contribution a piece on metaphor in journalism; in a leading article in *The Times* a critic commented that 'journalists would not sin more than other writers if they had as much leisure'.[9] 'Preposition at End', already discussed in *The King's English*, was another topic submitted by Henry, although escaping the notice of the critics because it shared a tract with an article discussing the merits of the terms 'Briton', 'British', and 'Britisher' and other names for inhabitants of the British Isles, always an interesting topic.

Henry discussed all this work with the principal figure in the Society, the elderly poet Robert Bridges,[10] since 1913 the Poet Laureate. In presenting his first articles to this formidable Oxford figure Henry described his own forthcoming book as 'comparatively elementary, & addressed to less instructed people than read the Tracts', adding that he would not be offended if the papers were returned unused. As to a fee for his work his response was as usual modest: 'I had no thought of asking payment for the privilege of airing my views on the points of grammar & idiom & typography that excite my small mind.' He eventually agreed that he would accept something if the Tracts proved to be self-supporting, seeming to be not in the least offended by Robert Bridges' suggestion of poverty: 'when you accuse me of being a poor man I cannot honestly repel the horrid imputation, & am not unwilling to do for pay what I was (& still am) willing to do without it.'[11]

✤ ✤ ✤

'If I can aspire to expertise in anything I suppose it is in split infinitives' was Henry's response to Robert Bridges, when he sought advice about a troublesome sentence, but there was a warning: 'it must be borne in mind that I am a heterodox expert, something like a nonconformist Doctor of Divinity.' Henry went on to explain his own position and the current general attitude to this controversial subject, ending in true schoolmasterly fashion with the possibilities arranged in a class-list.

> My notion is that, in your sentence, 'to fully apprehend' ought in 1923 to be the normal thing to say; it isn't yet the normal thing, of course, & centuries ago it neither was nor ought to have been. Secondly, that nothing should induce me to write 'fully to apprehend' instead, that having nothing to recommend it except that it saves the pusillanimous from infinitive-splitting. Thirdly, that 'to apprehend beauty fully' is, on the other hand, different in effect from 'to fully' &c., laying a much heavier stress on <u>fully</u>, whether it is better or worse than the 'to fully' form depends on whether apprehension & feeling are an antithesis sufficient in itself, so that <u>fully</u> is of no great importance & can be allowed to hide under the wing of <u>apprehend</u>, or whether full apprehension & not partial is the point, in which case all the emphasis that can be got by putting fully late & apart is desirable. Class-list accordingly: <u>α.</u> to apprehend beauty fully; <u>β.</u> to fully apprehend beauty; <u>γ.</u> fully to apprehend beauty.[12]

Henry's entry on this subject prepared for *Modern English Usage* was presented at that time as a Tract on 'The Split Infinitive'. In it he divided the English-speaking world into five groups, reflecting their attitude to his difficult topic. The first was made up of the majority who neither knew nor cared what a split infinitive was; they were, Henry felt, 'a happy folk to be envied by most of the minority classes'. The next group consisted of those who did not know, but did care very much; 'bogy-haunted creatures' Henry called them. They 'would as soon be caught putting their knives in their mouths as splitting an infinitive but have hazy notions of what constitutes that deplorable breach of etiquette'. This group would avoid placing an adverb between the word 'be' and a passive participle, believing 'to be really understood' to be a split infinitive. 'Those who know & condemn' made the third group, mostly undetected because they avoided the sin, combining 'with acceptance of conventional rules a reasonable dexterity'. Only those unable to manipulate their work with this ease were discovered; 'it does not add to a writer's readableness', Henry declared, 'if readers are pulled up now & again to wonder—Why this distortion? Ah, to be sure a non-split die-hard!' He had many examples of cumbersome sentences which should have been completely remodelled by writers determined to resist the temptation of using a split infinitive; 'Both Germany and England have done ill in not combining to forbid flatly hostilities', for instance. The fourth group, who knew what a split infinitive was and approved, were also difficult to recognize; a splitter might be a member of the first group happily splitting infinitives without a thought or from this group 'deliberately rejecting the trammels of convention & announcing that he means to do as he will with his own infinitives'. In the final group were 'those who know & distinguish'; they felt that although a split infinitive was not desirable in itself it was 'preferable to either of two things, to real ambiguity, & to patent artificiality.'

After all this Henry wondered whether he had revealed his own opinion with 'indecent plainness'. He finished his article with a split infinitive, described by an anonymous reviewer as 'deafening', but Henry nevertheless italicized it in case his readers should have difficulty spotting it; 'Its main idea is *to* historically, even while events are maturing, & divinely— from the Divine point of view—*impeach* the European system . . .'[13] To this he added his piece on the position of adverbs, feeling the absurdity of concentrating only on the split infinitive and ignoring similar problems. The article drew differing opinions; one critic wrote, 'on the whole, "Don't split your infinitives" is so sound a maxim that it would be regrettable if this witty pamphlet had the effect of discrediting it.'[14] Others were more approving: 'all the super-Dreadnoughts of prose do it sooner or later.'[15]

⚘ ⚘ ⚘

An article on 'Subjunctives' followed this and notes on various words, 'fasci', 'fascisti', 'broadcast', among them, but it was a selection of prepared entries, published just before the completion of *Modern English Usage* was announced, which caused trouble for Henry. Among these was a piece which brought protests from several readers including Otto Jespersen,[16] a distinguished Danish professor of English, who indicated his intention of replying in an article which the Society agreed to publish in another Tract.

The cause of this furore was Henry's condemnation of the fused participle, demonstrated by him in the sentence, 'Women having the vote reduces men's political power.' In other words this participle was joined to a noun or pronoun but there was no clear indication as to whether it was used as a participle or a verbal noun.[17] Henry called the fused participle 'grammatically indefensible',[18] and upon this remark Jespersen fell, scornfully condemning his opponent as an 'instinctive grammatical moralizer'[19] and going on to discuss the historical development of '-ing' over many pages.

Henry was upset by this attack but felt bound to reply. 'He greatly disliked controversy, and was disturbed by it,'[20] a friend recorded, but the assault could not be allowed to pass unchallenged and Henry's paper replying to Jespersen was also published in the Tracts. In it Henry pointed out that much of Jespersen's argument was based on a misquotation of a passage from the original piece, 'an oversight of his in abridging', as Henry generously put it. He accepted the title 'instinctive grammatical moralizer', examining it word by word and turning what had been intended as an insult into a compliment, going on to demonstrate the differences between his own work and that of Jespersen as a historical grammarian; 'the ability to distinguish between the right and wrong in speech does seem to me much more a matter of instinct than of history.'[21] The two men clearly approached the business from completely different standpoints and would never agree.

Before the publication of the new book Henry had decided to stop producing articles for the Tracts, writing to Robert Bridges with, as he put it, 'the to me painful announcement that I shall have now to retire from contributorship'. He had been asked to write a piece on 'Words People Are Afraid to Use', but although he regarded this as a very tempting subject, he could not find time to do it. 'I have confessed or professed to you before that the complications of the simple life, together with the compilation of dictionaries, leave me no time for originalities,'[22] he told Robert Bridges. He did, however, submit much later one final small item, an entry for the word 'comprise', accidentally omitted from *Modern English Usage*.

Henry's surviving letters to Bridges are lively and interesting, suggesting a developing friendship with the elderly poet. He had mentioned a possible visit to Guernsey when they were first acquainted, but Henry had replied to his request for advice about lodgings, not with an invitation to Moulin de Haut, as Bridges may have hoped, but with a list of names and addresses and an offer to investigate, when lodgings were found, whether the proprietors were 'decent people'. Henry explained that he and his wife lived quietly, rarely seeing anyone else, while restoring their garden, 'a ruined paradise', but offered, if Bridges and his wife should be in the area, to show them 'the remnants and the capabilities'.[23]

Years later Robert Bridges, by then 85, published his long poem *The Testament of Beauty*, his greatest success. Henry dashed off impetuously a long letter to the poet admiring the work;

> I am entranced by (not to say your purple) your iridescent patches, your vigilant robin, your Brasidas, your Ur of the (pre)chaldees, your visible perfumes, your chorister, & the rest.

Despite this Henry was puzzled and told the poet, 'I am nursing a grudge against you',[24] for he could not fit Bridges' statements about the metre to the lines. Henry had been reading the *Testament* aloud, a favourite occupation, and sent a long discussion of the metre, eventually deciding that it was based on *Piers Plowman* and transcribing many pairs of lines to illustrate his point. Bridges must have been offended by this long letter for he replied quickly, indicating that the matter had already been discussed at length in *The Times* and suggesting that it was perhaps better not to wrestle with understanding the metre but just to read the verse. Henry was then forced to apologize: 'I am sorry I inflicted my bright idea upon you—& at such length. I did not know that it was a stale one . . .'[25] He was often impetuous in this way, writing quickly when he might have waited a little and after thought responded differently.

❧ ❧ ❧

Returning to *Modern English Usage* after finishing the Pocket dictionary Henry found a great deal to do and, although intending to finish in August 1923, was unable to send in the text until the end of the year, delayed by Jessie's accident and the need to take over some of her duties. He felt sure that he would be required to cut down the size of the book and was quickly challenged by Oxford about the content of the Generic Names article, which they had not seen. Henry felt that it 'had better be sacked'; he regarded it as 'too miscellaneous & too incomplete to be satisfactory' and had not spent enough time or effort on it to make him 'repine at its loss'. 'I shall probably not be refractory', he told the Oxford people, 'if it occurs to you that any other articles & the references to them could be equally well done without.'[26] The loss of this lengthy piece and cross-references to it would make a considerable difference to the size of the book, but despite Henry's assurances, there was at Oxford no 'desperate desire to reduce the bulk'[27] and it was believed that it would be a very successful book even if it proved rather expensive.

Henry was by then dealing with a new figure in the Press office, Kenneth Sisam,[28] a New Zealander who had come to the university as a Rhodes Scholar and remained for almost his entire working life in Oxford. Henry first came across Sisam when he was moved to the position of Assistant Secretary from Junior Assistant on the appointment as Printer of John Johnson, who had previously held the post. On Chapman's retirement Sisam became Secretary, finally retiring to enjoy island life like the Fowlers but on the Scillies. He was a notable scholar of Early and Middle English, lecturing while still an undergraduate, and his *Fourteenth Century Verse and Prose*, published by the University Press, remains in print after nearly eighty years.

'Terrible!'[29] was Sisam's reaction, written on the bottom of the letter in which Henry suggested *Oxford Pedantics* as a possible title for his work, still known to all as 'the Idiom Book'; a decision on the title was clearly rather urgent as work continued on preparations for printing. Henry knew how Sisam and Chapman would react, but the title and an accompanying hastily written preface for the book were responses to an insult, as Henry saw it, published in the *Glasgow Herald*.[30] Dr Bulloch, the editor of the *Graphic*, had mentioned Henry and Frank in passing in an article on the Scots; he referred to the brothers as pedantic, and this 'bit of insolence' had infuriated Henry, who described it as 'naughtily casual'.[31] Appealing to Dr Bulloch to explain his definition of pedantry, Henry had written an angry letter to the newspaper; in it he wittily described the vice as the opposite of an elephant, an animal difficult to define but easily recognized if seen; pedantry, on the other hand, might be quite easily defined, but was more difficult to recognize, especially in oneself. The newspaper printed the letter, but there was no response from Bulloch. Henry had not expected that his quarry would retaliate, but had foolishly hoped for some small expression of regret from the two editors. The proposed preface quoted the entire letter with further discontented remarks and a challenge from Henry to his readers that they should decide whether his work was 'sound advice or foolish pedantics'.[32] Kenneth Sisam responded sensibly to all this, assuming that Henry had sent the material to amuse the Oxford office and urging him to 'let the little dogs bark unnoticed'.[33] The title was rejected, but it was suggested that he might make use of some of the material in his final preface.

Charles Onions of the *OED* had pointed out, when commenting on a sample years before, that it would be very hard to find a 'suggestive and comprehensive title'[34] for the new book, but eventually an acceptable idea was put forward, *A Dictionary of English Usage*. After much thought Henry suggested the addition of 'Modern', feeling that without it readers might expect something more than he was offering. *Modern English Usage* might, he thought, be the best title, with an explanatory subtitle, perhaps '*A dictionary of idiomatic grammar* (or *of grammar & idiom*)'.[35] The final decision was for *A Dictionary of Modern English Usage* without a subtitle, but the first part is normally omitted and the title given as Henry would have liked.

There were other hurdles before the book came to publication. Henry's view of pronunciation, for instance, again caused problems, as it had long before with 'idea' in the Concise, and on this occasion too he proved unwilling to be persuaded. The combined force of Robert Chapman and Kenneth Sisam descended on 'for' chōōn', Henry's recommended pronunciation of 'fortune' in *Modern English Usage* but he would not be swayed. He brushed the business aside, commenting that he had nothing to say about it and adding that with this book he was 'less in leading strings'[36] and might give his own opinion on these matters. In a note to Sisam, Charles Onions objected to the suggestion that the use of 'illustrable' was preferable to 'illustratable'; this protest was also passed on to Henry, but he would not be moved and no changes were made in the text. Onions added also to his note a few general words about the book with which, he said, 'I have so many quarrels, and which will sell so well'.[37]

With work on the text finished Henry had no difficulty about finding another task, for his next project had already been planned. He had been approached some time before by Robert Chapman asking for help with the biggest dictionary being prepared from the *OED*, at first called the '3/6 dictionary' but by that time known as the Abridged and soon to become the *Shorter Oxford English Dictionary*; at Oxford it was referred to jocularly as 'Billy Little' because of its editor's name.

William Little of Corpus Christi College, Oxford, had been engaged to produce this dictionary and had retreated to Cornwall to do the work, but on his death in 1922 the book was not finished, with U, W, X, Y, and Z still to be prepared; there were also some problems with the existing text, which had been in preparation for many years and needed to be brought up to date. This revision of the text was being done by the *OED* staff at Oxford, but they were experiencing problems with their own work, as the death of Henry Bradley in 1923 had been a great blow to the project. No one from the Oxford team could be released to finish the Shorter without interfering far too much with work on the *OED*, and so Chapman approached Henry, promising a good price if he would set aside his dislike of lexicography and take on the work. Time would not be a problem, for progress on the *OED* was rather slow, with the loss of Bradley adding to the problems. Although parts of U and W and all of X, Y, and Z were ready for abridgement, the appearance of the remaining parts was likely to be delayed.

Receiving this invitation from Chapman Henry declared himself 'neither strongly attracted nor violently repelled', with the reminder that the only dictionary work which still appealed to him was the revision of the Concise, which he had always hoped to transform by adding modern material and making it easier to use. Believing that it might be destroyed by the success of the Pocket and the Shorter, he recognized the wisdom of waiting to see the effect of the Pocket at least on the Concise. He felt also that the pleasure of writing a dictionary lay for him in setting out the plans for the work and carrying it out himself; the prospect of having to stick to a model determined by an earlier editor was not at all attractive to him. Nevertheless he was prepared to consider the proposal, but only after *Modern English Usage* was finished; he would not put it aside again or work on two projects at the same time. It was at this stage in fact that he approached his brothers for help, hoping to give them some of the work but guaranteeing to revise all their input himself. Working on the Shorter would clearly be a sacrifice for Henry; as he pointed out, 'the thing will not be a labour of love by any means.'[38]

Chapman was of course happy to wait for the work, and also to accept Henry's choice of assistants if he needed help. The financial offer from Oxford was very generous; unusually, Henry accepted it without argument and agreed to prepare a section of the abridgement for the usual inspection when he had finished his own book. There was, however, one considerable handicap in setting out on this project; William Little had left nothing in writing to help with the work; 'he merely performed,' Chapman told Henry. There had been discussions about method in the early years of the project but no trace remained of these; Henry would have to examine the prepared work and draw up his own set of principles for proceeding.

Henry's trial of the work was examined at Oxford by Charles Onions, whose report to Kenneth Sisam, by then in charge of the project, was very critical. Onions described the piece as 'disappointing and unpromising',[39] and predicted a poor outcome for the dictionary if Henry were involved, suggesting that he would never manage to pick up the principles of the work. Fortunately Sisam understood Onions, who had just given a similarly harsh report on a trial by another possible editor for a French dictionary. He objected 'to all upstarts in lexicography', Sisam wrote, reporting on the business to Robert Chapman. Onions' comments were mostly on small details of style which could be quickly picked up, and Sisam was convinced that Henry would soon understand the methods of his predecessor. On the first page of the trial Onions had unfortunately written 'unscholarly'[40] among his comments; returning it to Sisam, Chapman pointed out that this must be erased in some way before the text was sent back to Guernsey. In a letter to Onions he commented on the matter too, suggesting that Henry would be lost to them if he saw the unfortunate word and pointing out that the *OED* staff were already very busy and could not undertake all the work on the Shorter; he rejected Onions' criticisms as not surprising in a first attempt: 'you can hardly expect an abridgement to spring in panoply from the brain even of a Fowler.'[41]

Sisam was left to explain to Henry the faults in his trial piece, and all the small corrections caused some alarm: 'I feel like a boy, told that his new school is the devil of a place for things that new boys must & mustn't do, but

that he can't be told a priori [from what is before] what they are,' he replied;
he would eventually find out 'by kicks on the behind for not knowing'. Sisam
had suggested also that the *OED* staff who had just finished W for the big
dictionary should take over this letter for the Shorter, leaving U, X, Y, and Z
for Henry. He was most annoyed at this, feeling that the effort expended in
sorting out and learning the style of the book would be wasted if he had so
little to do, and so he offered to stand aside, leaving the whole task for
Oxford; he was, he declared, no more the new schoolboy, but rather like one
of the 'newspaper bridegrooms who fail to turn up for the wedding', and
attached a cutting from a newspaper with the story of a shy Yorkshireman
who left his bride waiting in the church. Sisam quickly recognized this anger,
cloaked in jest, marking the letter, 'Keep him sweet!'[42]; he wrote back to
Henry suggesting that he should begin with U, X, Y, Z and then follow with
W, unless the *OED* people had finished their work before he reached it, in
which case they would do it; in other words Sisam proposed a race, but
insisted that there was very little chance of the *OED* staff managing to finish
their work so quickly that Henry would miss out on W, the most interesting
part. This he accepted, and set to work sending questionnaires to Oxford in
an attempt to discover any clues that might be gleaned about the style. The
work was, however, to take far longer than at first planned, for the Fowlers
were again to lose their home.

✢ ✢ ✢

By the autumn of 1924 Henry and Jessie knew that Ozanne, the landlord,
had decided that their lease on the Moulin de Haut, which was to run out in
the following year, would not be renewed; Henry marked the event by
Christmas verses with the title 'The Song of the Evicted'. Ozanne's son was
to marry and would live in the house, so long neglected and at last restored
by the Fowlers. They would have remained there happily if allowed, enjoying
the garden which had cost them so much work, but, although they both
loved Guernsey with its splendid climate, faced with the prospect of finding
another home, they decided to move back to the mainland. This decision,
never contemplated when they moved five years before, was made at that
time mainly because of Jessie's deteriorating health, which made it desirable
to be nearer to the advice of her London doctors.

Jessie had throughout the marriage suffered bouts of illness, staying sometimes at home but on other occasions in hospital in London. At the time of her birthday, for instance, in 1914, a dreadful year for the Fowlers, she had been seriously ill but at home, and ten years later Valentine's Day saw her in hospital in London while Henry remained at Moulin de Haut. Gordon Coulton, who by that time as a frequent visitor knew her well, felt that she had never been as fit as her robust appearance and cheerful demeanour suggested. He believed that the first symptoms of the breast cancer from which she was suffering had appeared soon after the Fowlers' marriage, but it seems difficult to imagine that she would have survived for more than twenty years with the treatment then available.

Henry, on the other hand, was certain that the trouble had begun when Jessie fell and injured her ankle in the spring of 1923, missing all the new season's gardening. After her death he assembled a collection of his anniversary verses and added a final few lines describing her illness; here he blamed this accident which he believed

> Left in Joan's breast a bruise that lurked
> Unseen, and creeping havoc worked.

Treatment at that time was harsh but not very effective; Henry wrote of the surgeons 'plying their ineffectual art'.[43] Jessie would have endured a radical mastectomy, or perhaps mastectomies, going far beyond the scope of modern operations and removing much more tissue than now considered necessary during such procedures; after this she would also have been treated with radium, probably in platinum rods inserted into the site. All this she endured with her usual brightness and courage; but it seemed sensible to the couple nevertheless to move back to England and make contact with her doctors easier.

Choosing a place to live was rather difficult, but the decision to move to the west country seemed to have been made almost immediately; Henry's Christmas verses, after discussing the possibility of other areas, finished with the words—

> If west, there best
> May pass life's evening time.[44]

Perhaps the memories of travelling westwards for childhood holidays influenced the Fowler brothers, for Arthur on retirement had moved south to Dorset, where Charles had lived for many years; Henry and Jessie settled in Somerset, at Sunnyside in Hinton St George, a village just outside Crewkerne which Jessie may in fact have known from early visits to her family, for her mother, Mary Ann, had been born in the town.

By November 1925 Henry and Jessie had moved into their new home after shipping their household goods across the Channel from St Peter Port to Weymouth and then travelling the short distance of 30 miles inland to Hinton St George. This was to be their last home; as before, they had managed to find a charming house in a most beautiful situation.

13

A Fascinating, Formidable Book . . .
and a Peach

'This very exquisite village of old stone & thatch' was the description Henry gave to a friend enquiring about Hinton St George. From his study he could see the ancient parish church just across the road, and from his dressing room a 'vista of thatched gable windows'. Gordon Coulton still visited his old friends and described later in his biography of Henry the charming village street with the George Inn, a medieval cross in front of it where children played on the steps after school, and a group of fine chestnut trees. About three miles away was the ancient town of Crewkerne, once known for producing cloth, particularly for sail-making. In more modern times it had gained a railway station and Jessie was able to travel up to London frequently for treatment, taking a taxi from the village to catch the train. It was also near enough for shopping trips, and while she was fit enough Jessie would walk in rather than take a bus, sometimes with her husband but more usually alone, calling frequently on a friend for coffee on the way. She could do some shopping in Hinton St George, which then supported a butcher as well as the traditional village store, but other purchases needed a visit to the town.

The house itself, although much smaller than Moulin de Haut, was just right for the elderly couple and the garden also was more manageable, a small piece in front with a larger walled plot behind the house where they could sit out and eat in summer. Here there were neighbours in thatched cottages on each side and the Fowlers seem to have made friends very quickly. For his morning swim Henry was allowed to use two pools set deep among trees in the garden of a handsome house just along the lane. For running he could at first use the park attached to the great house in the village, but after access to this was closed he ran on the roads, as he had since his Sedbergh days.

✤ ✤ ✤

The move to England inevitably caused great delays in Henry's work; searching for a home, packing, travelling, and then unpacking took about a year out of his schedule. 'We have been digging ourselves in for the remainder of our days in a new country—a long process,'[1] Henry told the Oxford authorities when explaining the delay. The poet Robert Bridges wrote to enquire about progress, asking whether Henry had finished 'nailing linoleum', words which delighted the expert; 'you have surely hit upon the best tongue-tripper of the truly-rural kind that ever was,' Henry responded, adding, 'Try it half a dozen times in quick succession; it ought to be patented & offered to Scotland Yard for use in police-stations.'[2]

While work on the Shorter was delayed, there was progress in Oxford with the production of *Modern English Usage*, and soon after the Fowlers' arrival in Somerset proof correcting was finished. Henry sent an appreciative letter expressing his admiration for the skill of the printing house staff and their careful work, while praising the appearance of the title page, which he declared brought a blush to his cheek. There were to be further blushes when the book was finally published on 22 April 1926 to reviews which Humphrey Milford from the London office described as 'numerous and splendid, like wedding presents'.[3] Henry, on the other hand, confessed to a friend that he would 'have liked to see the words "terrifying" and "sarcastic" and "sardonic" rather less often'.[4] When *The King's English* came out critics had picked out sentences to which they objected and suggested that the brothers should look to their own faults before commenting on others. With the new book the response was very different, culminating in a leading article in *The Times* under the title 'The Fowler's Net', where *Modern English Usage* was described as a 'fascinating, formidable book'.[5] Sales were impressive: more than 10,000 copies were sold in the first three months and 60,000 in the first year, after which the figures dropped back to a more modest level. The Clarendon Press journal, the *Periodical,* reported the rapid rise of *Modern English Usage* to the 'dignity of competition with the novels of the moment as a "best-seller"'.[6]

In the *Times Literary Supplement* the reviewer, while describing the book as 'delightful', noted that Henry at times attempted 'to reinstate the irretrievable' or pursued a fad; the writer added in an aside that he had almost used 'idiosyncrasy', condemned by Henry as 'pretentious and absurd'. Nevertheless the review praised the book's 'sterling soundness and essentially English common sense' and ended with the assertion that in its presence 'every journalist must tremble'.[7] Others felt this too; it was described as inhibiting 'the confidence that has hitherto greased the wheels of the reviewer's pen', while Henry's attitude was seen as 'that of the keen observer of tangles and obscurities, of the deliberate resolver of involutions, of the advocate of clarity by way of simplicity'.[8]

There were harsher critics; one American, for instance, condemned Henry's poor knowledge of phonetics and historical grammar, stigmatizing him as 'unscientific' and 'a learned and charming dilettante' and his work as 'a collection of linguistic prejudices persuasively presented'. This critic, however, did believe that the book should be on every shelf and that readers would find it, despite its faults, 'highly enjoyable and highly stimulating', praising the author's mastery of the material and in particular the general articles with their 'seductive titles';[9] he singled out 'Malaprops', 'Cannibalism', and 'Unequal Yokefellows'. Elsewhere a commentator described some entries as 'stiff reading . . . not for the railway train or the pillow'.[10]

A stream of appreciative adjectives marked other reviews, 'admirably conceived', 'astonishingly cheap', 'brilliant', 'comprehensive, thoughtful, thorough', 'extremely valuable and extremely amusing', 'fresh and pungent', 'lively, challenging, inspiriting', 'most entrancing', 'wise, witty, vigorous, absorbing', 'simply enchanting',[11] and so on. Kenneth Sisam sent from Oxford extracts from the review in the *Methodist Recorder* which described the book as 'a volume on table-manners, good breeding, purity of mind, cleanness of habit, self-respect and public decency', going on to praise its humour as 'broad, sly, dry, and quaint.'[12]

There were in addition more personal testimonies to the book by those who bought it; a distinguished judge reported that he had been kept from his bed by it 'to a very unusual hour', adding that it brought 'a terror to living and writing'.[13] There were endless letters too and all tempted Henry into replies; he told a friend that he was 'too much flattered by questions from strangers to treat them summarily',[14] always giving full answers when he might have acknowledged suggestions in a brief reply.

One notable correspondent was Lytton Strachey,[15] who wrote (in a letter now lost) to discuss Henry's comments on the correct use of 'that' and 'which'. Henry responded by explaining that *Modern English Usage* was not intended for well-known writers but for 'budding journalists', and suggested that Strachey should not waste his time on it: 'I forgot to put up a board warning off trespassers',[16] Henry wrote. He accepted that Strachey considered him to be extreme in some of his opinions but was glad that they were in agreement on other matters.

Many of course disagreed with him completely, and raised questions which needed discussion and often advice from others before they could be resolved. A representative of the Institute of Secretaries, for instance, wrote very soon after publication to ask about the correct meaning of the abbreviation 'per proc.' or 'per pro.', perhaps more commonly seen as 'p.p.', used at the end of letters when an agent signs for an absent principal. The question to be settled was the meaning of the complete phrase, 'per procurationem'; this might mean 'by the agency of' or 'by the authorization of'; the names of the agent and principal would be differently arranged according to the meaning assigned to it. Henry believed and had put forward in *Modern English Usage* that it meant 'by the agency of' which would indicate that the name of the agent should immediately follow 'p.p.' If it meant 'by the authorization of', the principal's name would be in that position and this was the arrangement normally used at that time and accepted by the Institute. It was this difference of opinion which had prompted the approach to Henry and he asked Kenneth Sisam to find a reliable expert to decide on it. Henry hoped to be proved right, but would 'be willing to eat humble pie' if wrong, feeling it to be 'a real crime to mislead about a formula used thousands of times a day.'[17] 'What a troublesome trade yours is!'[18] was Sisam's comment on enquiries such as this.

The pronunciations in the new book had already caused Henry problems with his Oxford critics and after publication made more difficulties in a wider arena. Henry's heavy workload was perhaps eased a little by Kenneth Sisam, who dealt with some letters; he responded, for instance, to a comment about Henry's pronunciation of 'postscript' which differed from that given in the *OED*. Sisam pointed out that Henry was giving what he considered to be the most usual pronunciation in ordinary speech and could not fit in all possible correct alternatives. There was an attack also in *The Times* on the pronunciation of 'clothes' in *Modern English Usage* which Henry had given as 'klōz', pointing out that it should not be pronounced as written, while accepting that the *OED* condemned his version as vulgar. The assailant was actually attacking the BBC and stressing its responsibility for the encouragement of good pronunciation and, in attempting to suggest a possible source of advice for announcers, condemned *Modern English Usage* as very weak in this area, using 'clothes' as an example. Henry feared quite rightly, when hearing this, that his book was being used 'as an awful warning of the possibilities of degradation', and when asked to write an article or be interviewed about it 'preferred to lie low & say nuffin';[19] by the suggestion of an interview he put an exclamation mark, knowing that Kenneth Sisam in Oxford would understand his feelings. Robert Bridges, asked to reply as Chairman of the BBC Advisory Committee on Spoken English, made matters worse by attacking the Concise dictionary for not following the *OED* in pronunciation and accusing Henry of encouraging the very pronunciations which were being attacked. 'The siege of Kloz' Henry called this business, and he was pleased that the critic had picked in 'clothes' a subject so easily defended; there were many possible items he might have attacked with 'less of the boomerang about them'.[20] Henry was thrilled with Sisam's response, published in *The Times*, which demonstrated the antiquity of the pronunciation of 'clothes' without 'th'; he was delighted too with 'the impudence & cocksureness' of his own entry in *Modern English Usage*; in a most uncharacteristic moment of self-congratulation he declared himself 'lost in admiration'[21] at it.

There were more newspaper letters which Henry dealt with himself— a scrap, for instance, with A. A. Milne[22] in the *Times Literary Supplement* about 'no mean', as in 'no mean writer', which he would have liked to see condemned by Henry in the new book. Milne was by then a considerable figure, enjoying the great success of *Winnie-the-Pooh*, published also in 1926. He addressed Henry by name in this newspaper letter, and so he was forced to reply and defend the usage which he felt Milne had misunderstood. Milne, in response, could not accept Henry's argument that the adjective 'mean' might have the meaning 'poor' or 'inferior' in addition to 'low, base, sordid', or 'middle, average, moderate', and after an exchange of letters the two agreed to differ.

Modern English Usage was to continue its successful career in America, a publisher arranging to buy large quantities for sale by mail order. He did, however, insist at the very last moment, as printing was about to begin, on a small list to explain Henry's abbreviations and also the use of the ampersand. Sisam, believing it wrong that any other hand should touch Henry's book, wrote to ask if he could get something together very quickly, which of course he did. A small squabble then began about money when Sisam announced his intention of sending a cheque for five pounds which Henry rejected, condemning it as ridiculous and asking for two pounds instead. Sisam had been grateful for the work and insisted upon proper payment for it, which Henry had to accept.

All this business had suggested to the American branch of the University Press that they might, after selling all they could of the English edition of the book, produce an American edition. Kenneth Sisam asked Henry's opinion about this proposal and he was quite happy to accept it, although not willing to have any part in the work. He did feel that it would be very difficult to Americanize the book, as many matters discussed would be of no interest to American readers, while others omitted from the English edition would be of great importance to them. Henry believed that *Modern English Usage* was effective because most of the examples used in the text were genuine and recognized as such by English readers. This would not be so for its American public, and to replace the English examples with American substitutes would be an enormous task. Examples made up particularly for the case would, he believed, be a disaster, and were a reason for grammar's reputation as dull. It was not until 1935 that a *Dictionary of Modern American Usage* appeared; this was not in fact an adaptation of Henry's book but an original version by H. W. Horwill, inspired by the English book but otherwise quite independent of it.

✤ ✤ ✤

While all the excitement of the successful launch continued, Henry, settled in his new home, had taken up again his work on the Shorter. Among the miseries of moving house he had mentioned to Kenneth Sisam at Oxford the possibility that he might relinquish the work on W which he had earlier fought so hard to retain, but he was persuaded to wait and see how things were when he had settled in Somerset. Before leaving Guernsey he had completed the whole of X, Y, and Z and about a fifth of U, which left, he believed, a year's work to finish it; this would mean that W would have to be abandoned, as the *OED* people would reach it first.

On resuming work Henry's first task was to prepare a section of Un-words for inspection at Oxford, offering it to Charles Onions of the *OED* not as 'lively reading' but for approval of the treatment which Henry called 'more or less revolutionary',[23] a description unlikely to appeal to the Oxford lexicographer. Henry was clearly well aware of Onions' probable reaction, mentioning his possible outrage and dissatisfaction in the accompanying letter, but indicating that he was unwilling to change his plan for these words, as it would be heart-breaking to have to begin the section again. After nearly three months Onions appealed to Sisam for help in explaining to Henry that it was not possible to change technique for one section of the Shorter alone, reminding Sisam of his fears when Henry's inclusion in the project had first been proposed. When the manuscript was eventually returned Henry sent a chastened reply, insisting, with a jocular use of the abbreviations for the Concise and Pocket dictionaries, that he had 'tried not to CODize or PODize the austere but comely decencies' of the Shorter. He was left to continue, but was asked to use the accepted style not his own and in reply gave a promise to Onions: 'I undertake that, as a sheep before her shearers is dumb, so shall I open not my mouth when in revising you snip & trim me into congruity.'[24]

After this Henry set aside for a time the work on the Shorter, which he had always regarded as a dreary task, to spend some months on a project which appealed far more.

✤ ✤ ✤

Long before the move from Guernsey, when the Oxford people had first sighted the end of work on *Modern English Usage*, they had made moves to ensnare their elderly author into another scheme. Robert Chapman had written first proposing various possibilities, dictionaries of phrase and fable, quotations, or synonyms. Henry's response to this was quite firm; he had only ever been interested in lexicography from one angle and he had said in *Modern English Usage* all that he wanted to say on that matter. When he had finished with the Shorter he might feel interested in something new, but until that time he would not discuss it, declaring, 'I am hopelessly incapable of training my thoughts upon the future before it is at point-blank range.' Henry finished his letter by returning to a long-cherished plan, the revision of the Concise, which he believed to have many faults and longed to recast completely; this was the only lexicographical project likely to arouse his interest. He told Chapman that when he had finished with the Shorter he would put together a sketch of his ideas for a revised Concise, and ended his letter with a prospect which must have chilled Oxford hearts; 'I will . . . if you don't like it or don't want it, take my leave of linguistics.'[25] Chapman's encouraging response to the proposed revision of the Concise took Henry rather by surprise: 'Really, Mr Chapman, this is so very sudden! I must have time to think & ask Mamma.'[26] He did agree, however, to prepare a plan for the revision of the Concise, to be undertaken when his current commitments had been finished.

Months later, in the winter of 1925–6, when the Fowlers had moved to Somerset and the Concise proposal was awaiting a decision, Kenneth Sisam put forward another idea. He approached Henry with the suggestion that, instead of the proposed revision, he should consider producing a great new dictionary of current English; this would be much bigger than the Concise with 1500 quarto pages and, unlike other big dictionaries, would be 'brave enough to discard inherited obsolete matter'.[27] This proposed book was later to be called the Oxford Dictionary of Modern English, abbreviated to ODME, but is most easily referred to by its first and shortest title, the Quarto, although for a time it was known at Oxford as the Unconcise Quarto. Flattery was used in the battle to persuade Henry to undertake the work; Oxford had, as a result of the great public demand for his dictionaries, developed a taste for them which approached mania, Sisam explained. Henry began eventually to succumb to this approach, admitting the attractions of the proposed work and clearly pleased by references to his successes; but he felt that, if the Press wanted the dictionary regardless of the author, they should not wait for him to finish the Shorter and find the collaborator needed for such a big project.

'He is beginning to nibble,' Kenneth Sisam reported to Humphrey Milford, the head of the London office, after this cautious response; the new dictionary had been proposed by Milford and he was to be involved in the discussions about its future. Robert Chapman, on the other hand, thought that it might be prepared by the dictionary staff in Oxford; but they were still involved in revising the Shorter material and finishing the *OED*, with a supplement to prepare for it when the main work was complete. Sisam believed this area to be Henry's 'special and peculiar province', paying a handsome tribute to the elderly author in his memo to Milford: 'his work has freshness which the trained historical lexicographer seems to miss.'[28] On hearing that the Oxford people would get together to discuss exactly what was wanted in the Quarto, Henry was quite happy to leave the matter, although he did make it clear that, if approached when he had finished his current projects, he might accept. He protected himself against the possibility of a collaborator proposed by Oxford with a firm statement of his position: 'I am a rank individualist, no good at team-work.'[29] He had been able to work with Frank and would be able to cooperate with Arthur, who shared his opinions, but with a stranger this would not be very likely.

Meanwhile discussions continued about the Concise, and Henry was forced to accept that what was required was not the complete revision he had planned but a supplement, as he called it, taking in the old Addenda which had been prepared some years before. At first it seemed that he was required to make these additions hastily for a reprinting in early 1926, but after examining what was required he was forced to admit that he could not possibly manage the work in the ten days allowed and must leave it. After this it was agreed that the new *COD* Addenda should be prepared at a far more leisurely pace during the following year, and it was this work which Henry was beginning when he set aside his struggle with the Un- words in the Shorter.

Henry welcomed the change to searching for words to bring the Concise up to date and was pleased to find a recently arrived neighbour (whose name, unfortunately, remains unknown) who was ready to join in the task and collaborate in this enjoyable word-hunting. Henry wrote to Oxford to ask for Sisam's approval of his plan, which was to produce sixty-six pages of new material, both corrections and additions, to be placed at the end of the text, and to enquire also about the etymologies in the final, S–Z, section of the book; Henry had always been unhappy about these and had revised them earlier for the American Concise project, keeping a copy of his work, which he intended to use to make the same changes in the new Addenda. In reply Sisam communicated a change of heart which delighted Henry: the Concise printing plates were worn out and would need to be replaced, so the new material could be incorporated into the text as it had to be reset, rather than being kept at the end of the book. This would not be the complete recasting for which Henry had hoped, for there were to be no changes in method, only as he later put it 'filling of gaps, correction of mistakes, & scrapping of lumber';[30] he was nevertheless very pleased with this prospect of a new revised edition.

There were unfortunately delays in the work, and Henry was forced to admit this to Oxford, and to ask for more time. He and his collaborator began on too lavish a scale and fell behind their promised date; they were supplying material also for the American Concise, still at that time in preparation, and this must have caused an additional difficulty. The whole business had been far more involved than Henry expected, and, as he told Sisam, 'a new edition is a teasing business unless you have a private Einstein to provide you with a time-space continuum'.[31]

Henry's health too interfered with his work for the first time when he had to miss a few days while an eye was removed. He wrote to Kenneth Sisam to inform him of the impending operation, beginning his letter with the sinister quip, 'Moriturus oculus te salutat'[32] ('the eye about to die salutes you'), echoing the gladiators' greeting to the Roman emperor, 'Morituri te salutant' ('those about to die salute you'). Henry had lost the sight in this eye some time before and had hoped to have it removed, but had not dared to mention it for fear of upsetting Jessie. When the eye specialist informed them that it must be removed as it was interfering with the sight of the other eye, Jessie was discovered in fact to be quite prepared for it. Henry expected the operation to be simple and hoped to be back to work very quickly. Sisam nevertheless wrote kindly to Jessie offering financial help if necessary; but within four days Henry was home writing to thank him and reassuring him that he was about to begin work again. He had meanwhile lost his anonymous collaborator who had only agreed to a fixed term and after an additional six weeks was unable to continue; he too was about 70 and had a weak heart, so was perhaps glad to escape from his colleague's demanding regime.

Henry continued with the work alone, but after another three months had to report that he was still not finished with the revision. He explained to Sisam that neither laziness nor eye problems had caused this, but his own 'incurably sanguine temper',[33] which made him plan to achieve in a day what would in fact take a week and also induced him to delude himself about the delays which complications might cause. He was by then also wondering whether an increase in the agreed length of the book might be acceptable, suspecting that when he sorted out his material he might find that he had greatly exceeded his limit of sixty-six extra pages. All the changes were written out on slips of paper, cut and supplied by Oxford for the purpose; some were corrections and would make no difference to the length and there were also some items to be removed, but it was the remaining pile of additions which Henry felt might be much larger than he had intended when he came finally to sorting out his work and estimating the length.

This project had taken much longer than originally planned, nearly the whole of 1927 in fact, but by Christmas Henry was able to report that it was nearly ready, reassuring Sisam, 'If I were motorcuted today, my decease would be of no importance, the slips being ready to send.' The second edition of the Concise was published in April 1929 and there was delight at Oxford in its success; Humphrey Milford of the London office approved too, describing it to Henry as 'certainly a peach!'[34] Sales were immediately good, with 19,000 copies sold by mid-June. Henry had been through a very difficult year, working extremely hard despite his sight problems, and must have been very pleased to have produced an improved version of his first dictionary. A gift of books from the Press catalogue was offered by his grateful employers in Oxford, but he took nothing, replying, 'my spare reading time is precisely nil, & I am the most unliterary person that ever posed as an expert on how to write.'[35]

With the Concise finished Henry turned again to the Shorter and resumed his work; the dictionary staff at Oxford were preparing W. He spent six months finishing the abridgement of U and in June 1928 was able to send the completed work to Oxford. Sisam was very pleased with Henry's section, thinking it exceptionally good, and was anxious that the work should not be given to a junior in the OED office for lengthy checking. He believed that

Onions should look briefly through it himself, but feared that, always suspicious of Henry, Onions had 'designs of long researches in the hope of catching him out'.[36] The Shorter was not finally published until 1933, delayed by the struggles of the Dictionary staff to complete the *OED* itself and then its Supplement, published in the same year as the Shorter. With this the Dictionary room in the Old Ashmolean Museum in Broad Street was abandoned and the team scattered; only Charles Onions remained in Oxford as Reader in English Philology and later Librarian of Magdalen College, collecting corrections and additions for the Shorter and the *OED* itself until the project was revived twenty-five years later when work began on a further Supplement.

Henry was invited to join the celebrations for the publication of the *OED*, a dinner at Goldsmiths' Hall in London in the summer of 1928 with the Prime Minister, Stanley Baldwin, as the main speaker. Naturally Henry refused the invitation, declaring that he was not likely to hazard himself 'among all the big-wigs of the Clarendon Press & the OED'.[37] At that time Humphrey Milford was the only Press contact Henry had met when he called in to the office occasionally during visits to London. His refusal was not accepted, and he was compelled to make it much clearer, writing to Robert Chapman, the Secretary at Oxford, 'it is the nature of the beast to avoid public functions, &, even if I were to accept in a rash mood, I should funk it at the last moment & send an indisposition to make my excuses'.[38]

⚜ ⚜ ⚜

Ill health, not feigned in the least, was by then a most important factor in the Fowlers' lives. Jessie, whose cancer had only recently been diagnosed when they moved to Somerset, was steadily declining and in the autumn of 1928 was in hospital in London for an operation, while Henry, after taking her up to town and settling her in, returned to Somerset to work. The anniversary verses had already been dropped, perhaps too great a flippancy for Henry when matters had become so serious and life so difficult. As well as his heavy dictionary workload he was caring for Jessie and taking a hand in the household duties, something which he had never shirked in the past and would always willingly turn to when necessary.

The Oxford people had recognized the need for help long before when the Fowlers had moved into their new home. In urging Henry to consider the proposed new Quarto dictionary Sisam had jokingly suggested that they should send an elderly man from the *OED* staff, nominally as Henry's assistant but in reality to help with the housework. By recounting this jest Chapman softened a serious suggestion that Oxford should pay the wages of a household servant for the years it would take to produce the dictionary. Perhaps Henry had brought on this offer by a little bragging earlier about his situation when explaining the delay in getting back to work after the move; 'my wife & I (average age 67) do all—well, very nearly all—our household work, cookery, & gardening, ourselves'.[39] Nevertheless he was very annoyed to be considered feeble and in need of help, replying furiously to Chapman with details of his morning running and swimming to prove his fitness, and refusing the offer of a servant with the foolish assertion that household help would be 'the means of slow suicide and quick lexicography'.

Henry continued without assistance, caring for his wife and home and undertaking still more work. 'I must go my slow way',[40] he had told Sisam, and so he continued determinedly independent to the end.

14

A New Manner of Life

W ith the Shorter safely dispatched, Henry turned to the collections of essays published long ago at his own expense when he first arrived in Guernsey. He was keen to have them reissued and began to send them on the rounds of publishers. *More Popular Fallacies*, the least successful of his collections, and *Between Boy and Man*, his lectures for schoolboys, were not taken, but the autobiographical *Si Mihi!* quickly found a publisher. It was published under a new title, *If Wishes Were Horses*, by George Allen & Unwin in 1929 and the reason for its acceptance was made quite clear by the printing on the dust jacket of the words 'By the Author of "A Dictionary of Modern English Usage"'. In a brief preface Henry explained that it had been written when he was 'a sensitive young thing of under fifty' and hoped that as such 'the views of the callow youth' would be read 'with an indulgent smile'.

Henry sent out also an unpublished collection which he had submitted to publishers before when his earlier books came out, hoping at that time to use for it the pseudonym 'Plummet'. His preface, the only new part of the book, recorded that he had quickly given up his first attempts to find a publisher, but in 1929 he was successful; the book was published by Basil Blackwell at Oxford under the title *Some Comparative Values*. To modern eyes this seems an even more unattractive collection than his first, *More Popular Fallacies*, but the two new books received at least one favourable review, in the *Times Literary Supplement*. Henry suspected that the author might have been Robert Chapman from the Oxford office, who sent a copy of the review down to Somerset. The piece ended with a reference to one of Henry's quirks, mentioning him as 'an exponent, far beyond current wont, of the place in the sentence of the semicolon'.[1] This particular stylistic feature had been mentioned by a friend, a great lover of statistics, who had been compiling data about paragraph lengths, use of punctuation, and other features in different writers; Henry carried off the prize for semicolon use.

✤ ✤ ✤

With all his other work finished Henry turned his thoughts to the Quarto, the large dictionary of current English which had been proposed to him first in 1925, but never finally settled. He had to decide, as he told a friend, 'whether such an undertaking is for a unocular septuagenarian or whether he would rather put himself on the shelf'.[2] Milford, Chapman, and Sisam had decided after their first approach to Henry that it was best to wait until he was ready to do the work rather than look for another editor; although they badly wanted a dictionary of this type, no one else would do it better. There were nevertheless frequent hints in their letters about the Quarto project so that Henry should not forget their eagerness to begin it; an offer, for instance, of a collection of newspaper cuttings which might be useful for the new book was calmly repulsed by Henry, who suggested that they would be best kept in the office until a decision was made. He was not to be hustled into agreement, but he could be tempted.

Henry had been thinking about the Quarto as he finished off his other work, writing to Oxford occasionally with ideas. The question of a collaborator occupied him mostly, for he knew that he could not possibly attempt the work without help, particularly with scientific and technical terms. His first thoughts had been of Arthur, whose wife, Ada, had died in September 1925; but Arthur refused when approached only three months after her death. He told Henry that he felt good for nothing but the carpentry which he had undertaken to help a friend; he would consider the matter again when he had recovered. After some time, however, he refused finally, as did another possible assistant approached by Henry whose name he never revealed to Sisam. He spotted other possibilities among his correspondents, a South African, for instance, who sent in contributions and might have been useful had he lived in England and not been 'busy with some other importunate unimportant occupation',[3] as Henry put it.

The arrival in Hinton St George of a new book provided a possible solution to Henry's problems. This was *Webster's New International Dictionary*, sent down by Kenneth Sisam, always generous with offers of books; it had pages divided by a line with words considered important and meriting fuller treatment above and other more minor words below, foreign words and phrases and abbreviations for example. To Henry this was immediately appealing for he saw it as an answer to his problems. Words requiring more detailed treatment would be put above the line in the Quarto and words requiring merely definitions below; Henry planned that he would take responsibility for the literary words at the top and an expert, produced by the Oxford people, would deal with the technical words below the line. Sisam also had difficulty finding help with technical words and had some other reservations about the plan, feeling that the two alphabets might confuse readers. On the other hand he was intrigued by the idea that the technical lower half of the page might be enlivened with diagrams which would make some difficult definitions easier to understand, although he admitted that the page arranged in this way might look 'like a cake with all the plums at the bottom'.[4] The idea was left for discussion later, but Henry had taken a step towards committing himself to the book.

Sisam brought up the Quarto again when Henry was still struggling with the revision of the Concise; the manager of the New York branch was visiting London and had been enquiring about the introduction of American words into the proposed dictionary. This had prompted Sisam to write to Henry and introduce the topic of changing attitudes to Americanisms which he believed to be 'gaining ground in English-speaking countries';[5] to all this he received a quick and decisive response. Although Henry had 'no horror of Americanisms', he knew nothing about them and would not deal with them; the Quarto was, he reminded Sisam 'still quite in the clouds',[6] and in the decision about who should write the book, this would be a matter to consider. This was a blow to Sisam's plans, but he was able to recover his position in his reply by suggesting that Henry might use the work of the surviving *OED* editor, with whom Henry had had no contact in the past.

Sir William Craigie[7] had worked for the *OED* from 1897, at first in James Murray's Scriptorium as an assistant but from 1901 as an independent editor. He was small and irascible but extremely able; memories still linger at Oxford of his tiny figure topped by an enormous hat. Craigie had held an Oxford professorship but was by that time Professor of English at Chicago, returning at frequent intervals to Oxford and his work on the *OED*. He was editing a dictionary of American English and supplying Americanisms for the *OED* Supplement on which work was just beginning. This source would be just what Henry needed for the Quarto and Sisam was able to write triumphantly to him, 'we have successfully stopped that hole by which you might slip out of the editorship.'[8]

It was late in 1929 before Henry was able to seriously consider the Quarto again. Apart from preparing his two books of essays for publication, the year had been fraught with domestic problems. Henry had been nursing Jessie after her operation in the previous autumn and dealing with housework, while also involved with Charles, who had become ill some time before. Arthur had moved to Wimborne in March to care for him and remained there until Charles died in September, leaving Arthur and Henry as the only survivors of the family. After Charles died Henry wrote to Kenneth Sisam to explain his silence during this confused time and received in reply a letter begging him to take on the Quarto; 'the young heroes show no courage for the task,'[9] Sisam wrote. Despite a favourable report from Henry's doctor and eye specialist and much encouragement from Oxford he appeared to be unable to decide about the book; but in fact he was quietly working out his plans.

It must have been a surprise, then, for Sisam to receive in January 1930 a lengthy letter from Henry beginning with the announcement that it was time for the Quarto 'to come down from the clouds to brass tacks'. He began with a long list of questions designed to discover from Sisam the type of book Oxford wanted; Henry's own feeling was that the Quarto should have more information than the Concise, but that this should be much easier to find. He asked too about the number of words the new book should have and the time limit for its production, and wondered whether he would be allowed to abandon the work 'for reasons short of utter inability' or, more plainly, if he found 'the job too trying'.[10] There were other questions too about typography, dividing the page with a line as discussed before, and differences between the proposed book and the old Concise. Then he moved on to a list of twelve proposals for the Quarto, all made with the presumption that he would be using the Concise as a base; these points included the recasting of all the areas of the old book which had dissatisfied him, pronunciations for each word, and the addition of technical words, some diagrams, and Americanisms.

In response Henry received from Sisam four pages of typescript setting out answers to his questions and the Oxford view of the Quarto. They were hoping for a book which expanded and improved the Concise, not just a longer version of it, intending that it should comprise about two and half million words. It was to be a dictionary of current English 'with enough obsolete material to carry a reader through the great writers back to Shakespeare', and the addition of literary words omitted from the Concise was felt necessary. Of course the Oxford people accepted that if the work became too much for Henry he would give it up and they would make arrangements for its continuation; they did not intend to make a burden for their ageing author. There was also to be no time limit; they presumed that Henry would draw up a programme for the work himself but would not consider it binding, and would devise a financial arrangement to fit his plans. About all the technical matters Sisam reported complete agreement, although with a few suggestions in some areas. He did think, for instance, that Henry might in a bigger book give more alternative pronunciations and some explanation of more difficult cases, perhaps hoping to avoid their problems in the past with his more unusual decisions in this field. A good beginning had been made to plans for the Quarto and Henry could settle down to more detailed discussions of particular points, after a brief delay while he dealt with corrections for a reprinting of *Modern English Usage*.

Henry hoped to be allowed to prepare the letter A before making final decisions about the details of style, but some matters could be discussed. There was some debate, for example, about changing the way a main word was indicated when repeated within an entry in the dictionary; in the Concise this had been done by putting the first letter of the word followed by a full stop rather than writing out the whole word several times in the entry, but in the new book Sisam suggested that a swung dash ~ should be used for repetitions of the main word and Henry was happy to agree. Both men were nervous about the line across the page and the use of two alphabets in the book, but felt that it should be tried and a decision made when a sample page of the text could be printed. There was disagreement, on the other hand, about pronunciations: Henry would rather not give alternatives 'by way of encouraging uniformity',[11] but promised not to be obstinate about it. As he had always been impossible to move when challenged about pronunciations in the past, this undertaking must have surprised Sisam, but he persisted with his plan to include alternatives; it would have been particularly foolish to give American words and not include pronunciations for them where they were different.

With all these and other matters settled Henry set to work on the first two or three pages of A to produce a small trial showing his proposed arrangement. This he quickly did and sent a copy to Sisam, whose response was very positive. His only real problem was with the line across the page; he was surprised by the allocation of different words to their places and wondered whether it might be better to keep unusual words below the line, finding it strange to find familiar English words banished to sit below it. Sisam intended to discuss this trial piece with Chapman and write to Henry in more detail about it, but before he could do this they received a lengthy letter from Somerset.

Henry had broken a rib and was prevented by it from working, for he could lift nothing heavy and found writing uncomfortable; but the quiet spell had given him time to think and he wrote to Oxford offering to give up the Quarto. There were two reasons for his offer, the first being his age: the book would probably take ten years to complete and for a man to take on such a piece of work at the age of 72 seemed to him to be 'flying in the face of the actuaries', but this was a matter for Oxford to decide and they appeared to be happy about it. The second and main reason for his unhappiness was a strong feeling that he was not the man to edit the proposed book. He told Sisam, as he had before, 'I am no true lexicographer; the only parts of the science I care about . . . are grammar & idiom.'

Henry's main difficulty was with Sisam's proposed inclusion of American words, spellings, and pronunciations which he felt would make the dictionary as much American as English. Henry had on previous occasions refused to deal with American material and again expressed his unhappiness about it telling Sisam, 'I am neither hostile to nor scornful of

American, but am utterly ignorant of it.' Henry recognized the value of its inclusion in the Quarto, but realized that his lack of knowledge would mean that he was always working with second-hand material. The offer of Craigie's Supplement collection, with its liberal inclusion of American terms, had been intended to help him, but it was no comfort, as he hated working at second-hand, as he regarded it. The technical terms would present the same problem, as he had failed to find a collaborator and would need to work on this area himself. The decision about the inclusion of multiple pronunciations made him anxious too, for he believed that, although readers might pronounce any word in any way they chose, they should be able to use the dictionary to find a pronunciation which they could trust rather than a set of variants. This inclusion of several different pronunciations would suggest that any other omitted was incorrect, which was not necessarily true, and it would also encourage the use of less usual versions, so hindering 'the natural progress to a desirable uniformity'.[12]

All these difficulties led Henry to feel that his Quarto and the book hoped for by Oxford were very different and so he suggested abandoning the enterprise; later he told a friend, 'I had a half-hearted try to wriggle out of it.'[13] At Oxford the disastrous prospect of losing the new dictionary prompted instant action and Robert Chapman, the Secretary, dealt with business himself. His letters to Henry have not survived, but a note to Sisam reveals the attitude adopted: Chapman had written, he said, 'with all the eloquence I command. We must do anything, agree to anything, ignore anything, to keep him in his admirable rut!'[14] Whatever Chapman wrote Henry was clearly pleased, and his answer reveals the extent of his capitulation: 'After that, what can I say but that you have given me a grand send-off? & what can I do but get to sea . . . without more ado?'[15]

With all this settled things seemed to improve and Henry found a collaborator, writing to Sisam to warn him that the stranger would be in touch. Major Lyne had been a correspondent for many years, offering suggestions for the Concise, but the two men had lost touch when they both moved house. They were again in contact and Lyne, a retired Indian Army doctor, was living in St Ives in Cornwall. He seemed the perfect collaborator and was enthusiastic about the proposal when Henry put it to him, but matters were not finally arranged when Henry was forced to set aside his work and the Quarto was for a time abandoned.

In August 1930 Henry wrote to Chapman at Oxford to explain that, after struggling for six years against cancer, Jessie had been declared incurable; he had been told that she would die within weeks or perhaps months, and he would work no more at the Quarto while she lived. Writing to an old friend with the same message, he added, 'Better not answer; such letters are the devil to deal with but I wanted you to know.'[16] Henry had by then nearly reached breaking point himself, but the arrival of Florence Shayer, Jessie's assistant long ago in the nursing home in Guernsey, was to save him from serious illness. Nurse Shayer had left her own work to take over the nursing which Henry had been doing himself for many months.

On her arrival she found Henry in an exhausted state after a very difficult year. He had help only with the heavy work in the house, doing all the rest himself. His old friend Gordon Coulton, described a demanding regime for anyone, let alone an elderly man, beginning at 4 or 5 in the morning with housework and the preparation of breakfast for the invalid, while dictionary work was fitted in during quiet spells; Henry did explain, when revealing the situation to Oxford, that he had been managing very little work. There had also been frequent trips to London—six stays in hospital during the last year of Jessie's life. All this had exhausted Henry and, as Jessie grew worse, he had very little sleep at all. Nurse Shayer was able to take over the nursing and encourage him to rest.

Jessie's condition quickly deteriorated, for the cancer had spread to her lungs; Henry described later the last two months spent in dreadful watching, 'looking helplessly on at incessant discomfort & utter weariness'. In mid-September he wrote to Chapman in Oxford, who had offered financial help should he need it, 'My invalid has ups & downs, but the tendency is downwards.'[17] Jessie died on 1 October 1930; she and Henry had never discussed her coming death and she had never questioned the doctors about her state, but as a nurse she would have known perfectly well what was happening. Henry believed that she had made a great effort to live until a very dear friend who had visited her daily for many weeks had left the village; just a few hours later Jessie died and, Henry told Chapman, left him 'in the end without farewells'.

Jessie was buried in the churchyard at Hinton St George, her grave marked by a stone cross with a lead plaque giving the simplest details of her life. Henry had a horror of the excesses of funerals and even her friends were not told the time of her burial; similarly, he never allowed them to put flowers on her grave. She had always attended the village church which Henry never entered, according to Gordon Coulton, although he was on friendly terms with both vicars during their time in the village; he would escort Jessie to the porch for services and collect her again afterwards. She had loved the view across to the church from their cottage and the sound of the bells particularly, but had been saddened when problems with the hanging meant that they became too dangerous to use. In her memory Henry arranged for the repair of the bells, and a memorial tablet was attached at the base of the tower inside the church to record this. Henry was always careful to give nothing himself which might be used for church business, but this gift came from Jessie and so was acceptable. The bells were dedicated in a ceremony the following February and were rung again for the first time that day; Henry would surely not have attended, but perhaps he might have been tempted to break his rule for the unveiling of this memorial.

In writing to Oxford after Jessie's death Henry had told Chapman that he would be in touch again when he had 'hammered out a new manner of life';[18] and this he began to do with the help of Florence Shayer, who had agreed to remain and keep house, so making his continued dictionary work possible. It was some weeks, however, before the Oxford people heard of him again, and this was on a matter far removed from his current project.

✤ ✤ ✤

In sorting out Jessie's papers Henry had discovered all the verses written for her during the twenty-two years of their marriage and had been arranging these and preparing them for publication. Naturally, perhaps, Henry offered this small book to Oxford before going elsewhere, although years before he had been told that his verses were not acceptable. He described them to Chapman as 'mostly playful, perhaps rather childish', but considered them worth publishing as 'a not unattractive picture of commonplace middle-aged matrimonial felicity'. 'Billets Doux of Darby to Joan',[19] he proposed to call them, and was pleased to send them off when Chapman asked to see them. The Oxford people were highly embarrassed by this situation, but they felt quite unable to publish the poems when they had seen them and particularly disliked the title; Humphrey Milford in the London office was eventually to reply, as the business came in his area, and he told Henry that they would 'gladly pay for the production of this little book'.[20] Despite age and grief Henry was not so foolish as to miss the implication of the offer, realizing that the Oxford people intended to print the verses in a private edition and would not publish them as their own book. He responded quickly to both Milford and Chapman, declining the offer and telling them that he wanted his verses published if they were of commercial value; if they would not pay their way he would send them round to friends in manuscript. He was sorry, he told Milford, 'to be looking so handsome a gift-horse in the mouth',[21] but he would try to find a publisher who might bring out the book as a commercial venture. Chapman explained that collections of verse very rarely sold enough to cover the cost of publication; many sold only a few dozen copies despite deserving a better sale. Henry was nevertheless still determined; 'let me be adamant rather than be a sponge', he told Chapman, admitting that he nearly took the offer, being a 'conceited old thing, & uxorious old thing'.[22] Months later he wrote again to Milford with the news that the book was to be published; many had refused even to inspect his manuscript, so he was forced to admit the truth of the gloomy picture given to him by Chapman and Milford of 'an unknown versifier's chance'.[23]

Rhymes of Darby to Joan was published by J. M. Dent and Sons in 1931; Chapman at Oxford admitted some doubts to his colleagues about the motives of the publisher, but all felt that Henry was 'too old and faithful to be seduced'.[24] The little book was dedicated to Lillian Henderson, the friend who had visited Jessie each day during her illness, and there was a photograph of Henry and Jessie in the garden at Moulin de Haut as a frontispiece. Henry had written an Epilogue, cataloguing in verse Jessie's final illness from the fall which he believed began it.

> And Joan is dead!—and buried, near
> The bells she loved and does not hear.[25]

✤ ✤ ✤

'He has had a sad life, and I should think would have gone off his head if it hadn't been for C.O.D. P.O.D. and the rest,'[26] Milford had written to a colleague after hearing of Jessie's death, ascribing Henry's ability to cope with his difficulties to his dictionary work rather than to his naturally stoical personality and his secure home life during his later years. Nevertheless Henry did turn quickly back to work, and by February of the next year was picking up the threads again. He had visited a doctor and an eye specialist and was able to report to Kenneth Sisam that his prospects were good; 'both eye & I have rather better than the ordinary expectation of life at 73.' He had also contacted Major Lyne, who was still ready to collaborate, and the two men had agreed the arrangements for their work together. Lyne would read technical textbooks and produce lists of words with rough definitions which Henry would then shape into dictionary entries. He hoped that Lyne would eventually be able to do this himself, but at first, 'being lexicographically timid', he was only to produce this 'raw material'. Henry would have to pay him, and so he needed to discuss the financial arrangements. He approached Sisam apologetically, explaining that for himself, progressing at a 'snail's pace',[27] he would be quite happy to wait a year or two and then discuss money, and suggesting that perhaps the Press should make a separate agreement with Lyne.

Sisam appears to have been the most sympathetic Press representative in financial dealings with Henry, paying him fairly for his work even when the older man protested that he was being overpaid, and offering to provide the books needed by Henry at the Press's expense; in the past he had paid for many books himself, although Oxford had supplied the most important. When approached about payment for the collaborator, Sisam's response was that he would not make a separate arrangement with him, but he suggested that Henry should be paid £200 a year, quarterly or whenever he preferred, from which he could pay Lyne himself. This arrangement would continue for five years, which was the time Sisam thought the work would take, and on handing over the manuscript Henry would be paid a bonus of £1,000; if he died before completion the work would go to Oxford and they would arrange for it to be finished, if enough had been done to make it worthwhile. Sisam presented this as a suggestion and asked Henry to say if he needed more money, but he said nothing at first, replying instead, 'you seem to be offering me the chance of a subsidized sojourn in lotusland for several years.'[28]

After thinking more carefully Henry began to feel that £200 was far too much if the Press were to continue the bonuses which it paid to him each

Christmas. If this 'incalculable Christmas rain', as he called it, were to be paid as before, he suggested halving the annual payment to £100 for ten years, which he felt to be a more appropriate projected time for finishing the book. Sisam in reply explained the situation plainly but firmly; the Christmas payments were given to thank Henry, when the publisher had a good year, for the books which belonged contractually to the Press and for which he received no royalty but had been paid lump sums as he would be for the Quarto. These sums could not be discussed, as they varied from time to time and might not be paid at all in a bad year. Sisam did accept the point that ten years seemed a more likely time span for completing the book, and suggested that if the work took longer than five years the annual payments would continue just as before but the amount of the final bonus would be smaller if the work continued for a longer time. All this Henry finally accepted with a characteristic quip: 'if you insist on making a millionaire of me, do so.'[29]

Meanwhile Major Lyne had been out to Hinton St George to stay with Henry and the two had planned their work. Henry found him 'a diffident sort of person (for a budding lexicographer)',[30] but it quickly turned out that his enthusiasm for dictionary-making had disappeared after an interview with the master. He had taken fright and, safely back home, wrote to Henry with the news that he felt unable to continue with the undertaking, mentioning that 'life would be one long headache' caused by this 'slavery to *OED*'. Henry was nevertheless quite cheerful about this seeming reverse, telling Sisam, 'I am already sanguinely crying vive le roi.'[31] Henry had succeeded in persuading an old friend to step into Lyne's vacant place and, knowing that the newcomer was far more suitable for the task, was delighted.

✤ ✤ ✤

Herbert Le Mesurier[32] was a retired lieutenant-colonel in the Royal Engineers who had served during his long military career in India and, after his retirement, had settled in Exmouth in Devon with his wife and daughter. He had first corresponded with Henry many years before when stationed in Simla and the two had become firm friends. Le Mesurier had read and commented on *Modern English Usage* before publication and had drawn up for Henry a method of reducing it, not adopted because the Oxford people were prepared to publish it despite its length; all this work Henry had acknowledged in the book. Le Mesurier had advised too on the revision of the Concise, sending at least one long detailed letter about the inclusion of technical words involved with work or hobbies. For the Quarto he would be a most useful collaborator; as an engineer all the technical words would come easily to him and American vocabulary was no problem too, for he had had an American mother and was a devoted film fan. Henry wrote to Sisam of his great hopes for the partnership, describing how Le Mesurier approached the work 'in a very coming-on spirit' and declaring boldly, 'I am now off with the old love, & on with the new.'[33]

The two old friends set to work then on the new enterprise, although Le Mesurier had to postpone his start for a few weeks to settle some other business. It seemed sensible to Henry to ask Oxford to print a page of his text as a specimen to show any problems with his plans for the book and help Le Mesurier to see exactly what was required. There were many points to be settled—the double-decker arrangement, for instance, with a line across the page, the inclusion of Americanisms, and many lesser matters. It was clear to all that there would have to be several attempts before a final form could be hammered out for the book.

Before sending the small section of A already prepared to the printer, Sisam commented to Henry on the absence of signs to indicate which words were Americanisms, wondering if he had decided not to include them. William Craigie of the *OED*, then the expert on American language, confirmed that the amount of American material would vary from letter to letter and A was not considered a good example. With this Henry later agreed, confirming that A was 'the happy hunting ground not of Americanisms, but of scientific verbiage' and declaring it to be for them 'the rottenest letter in the alphabet'. In an ideal dictionary Sisam suggested that words or particular uses of words which were only English should be marked with 'E.' and those only American with 'U.S.'; there would of course be very many words, common to both, which had no marking. Henry still felt this all rather a problem, 'that difficult matter of holding the scales even between English & American',[34] as he called it. As he had Le Mesurier to help, this particular business should be easier to settle, but they left it aside to be discussed at a more suitable time.

When the page arrived from the printer there were many small items, details of arrangement and typography, to be discussed, but Sisam, sending on the page to Henry, declared the actual dictionary material itself to be 'entrancing'. He sent copies of the page to the London office for the comments of Humphrey Milford and three members of his staff, Hubert Foss the head of the Music Department, Charles Williams the poet and novelist, who spent his working life with the University Press, and Frederick Page, who worked for many years as an editor, sharing an office with Williams. These four were united in disliking the line across the page and the two alphabets; Hubert Foss suggested that words in the smaller lower sequence should be mentioned in the main alphabet, with a reference to the reader to look for them below, while his colleague Charles Williams argued that if the system were really necessary to save space then it would have to be accepted but, if not, then one alphabet would be best.

Before the page arrived Henry had been careful to prepare Sisam by explaining the new system in a letter, trying, he said, 'to create a favourable atmosphere for the two-decker arrangement'. Henry was anxious that the lower section of the page should not be regarded as 'a dustbin or a cemetery or a glory-hole', but that it should be seen as 'a place where . . . words of modest pretension may find good enough company, though not luxurious accommodation'.[35] The words above the line were those which needed illustrative phrases with their definitions, while those below were words which could be dealt with more simply with just a definition. By printing words in the smaller type used at the lower level much space would be saved, and collaboration would be made easier because only Henry would work on the more complex vocabulary above the line.

All this sounded fine, but there were considerable problems when the page arrived. The text above the line was arranged in three columns because of the size of type and the page size, but below the line, as the type was smaller, it was arranged in four; as a result the words in the bottom section did not match alphabetically those in the top, which would cause difficulties for readers in finding their way around the book. Casting about for a solution Sisam suggested a system of small arrows under words in the top section to indicate that the following word would be found in the section below. Le Mesurier, on the other hand, came up with what Henry called a 'topsy turvy, subsuperversive proposal';[36] he suggested transposing the sections, putting the section with the words which required briefer treatment at the top and those requiring longer treatment at the bottom; these words would be listed at the top of the page or in the margin so that they could be more easily spotted, and the position of the line would be varied so that the alphabetical sequences kept pace with each other. Sisam was prepared to print another page from this suggestion if Henry wished, but pointed out that readers were used to finding small type at the bottom of a page and their habits had to be considered; it would be, he thought, like printing footnotes at the top of a page. Henry could see the way things were heading, of course: his 'pet eccentricity' would be rejected and the 'monalphabetistae',[37] as he called those who favoured one alphabetical sequence, would have their way.

All were by then waiting for the opinion of Charles Onions of the *OED*, who had originally put into Henry's mind the possibility of using the two-decker system by praising the technical superiority of the new Webster. When his report arrived it surprised both Kenneth Sisam and Henry, for he was absolutely opposed to the system, describing the division of Webster's page as 'exasperating' and stating firmly, 'the horizontal division of the page would be a fundamental blunder.'[38] There was nothing to be done but accept that the experiment was over and the divided page must be abandoned. Henry wondered briefly whether the two sizes of type could be kept for the different alphabets when they were combined, but he quickly accepted that a uniform size would be best and a new trial page was ordered.

The printer tried the page again with the alphabets run together and various other changes, and there were later experiments to adjust margins and make small typographical alterations. Within the text of the dictionary changes were suggested too; Sisam, for instance, put forward the idea of double pronunciations, suggesting that each word should be pronounced by the system already used with the pronunciation in phonetic notation next to it; this he believed would be best for foreign buyers. Henry disliked phonetics and was scornful about this idea, believing that the Quarto would have little sale overseas, apart of course from America and Commonwealth countries. The Concise, however, did sell well overseas, and Sisam was able to tell Henry that, leaving the USA aside, half its sales were for export, Japan and Germany being the best customers. This led Sisam to expect that the Quarto would also sell well to teachers and advanced students overseas who would value phonetic pronunciations. Henry was persuaded by this that the best plan would be to put the two sets of symbols in columns in the preface so that readers might sort out the pronunciations themselves. To Le Mesurier, always practical, this seemed an inconvenient arrangement; he suggested a sheet folded into the back of the book with both sets of symbols printed on it to be unfolded for use when required. Although Sisam was clearly impressed by Le Mesurier's innovation, he did point out that the paper would have to be very strong to withstand constant use, and this matter was dropped to be finally decided at a later date.

Through the autumn of 1931 into the winter the work went on; Henry in Hinton St George and Le Mesurier in Exmouth prepared their different sections of the Quarto, while in Oxford new versions of the page were produced for Sisam, anxious to get the style settled finally. Examining them, Le Mesurier began to suspect that their book would be much longer than the 1,500 pages allocated for the Quarto, and Henry, when informed, felt it wise to tell Sisam with the warning, 'Le Mesurier has been trying to make my flesh creep.'[39] Sisam regarded the message as worrying too for a one-volume book could be little bigger than the agreed length for purely physical reasons; the pages used, for instance, would have to be too thin to be easily turned and the book would sag in its binding. A two-volume work would compete with the Shorter and not take the place planned for it in the Oxford stable of dictionaries. For Henry the problem would be which part to cut, his own more detailed work or Le Mesurier's technical section. All parties were agreed that this should be left until an estimate could be made from a much larger sample, and it was decided that further discussion should be delayed for six months.

Here and there in his letters Henry was by then apologizing for his slowness; 'Le Mesurier is keeping up his end splendidly, but I am far behind with mine',[40] he told Sisam in one letter. Before the six-month review came round there were great changes in Hinton St George.

15

Deaths and Other Such Inconveniences

❧

Cony and chick and such small deer
Have been Tom's food for this half year

In the autumn of 1932, with this quotation from *King Lear* playfully adjusted, Henry informed Kenneth Sisam of a breakdown in his health which he had been keeping from him for some time; he had carefully concealed his decline from his friends while he could, but inevitably it was spotted by the ever-vigilant Nurse Shayer. Gordon Coulton had been down to stay with his old friend in the spring of 1932 and found him working steadily; his great experience enabled him to keep on despite his failing physical abilities. He had nevertheless been suffering from spells of giddiness, almost fainting at times and needing to sit down quickly to avoid falling if he felt an attack beginning. All this he managed to hide from his visitor, but after Coulton left, Miss Shayer persuaded him to visit the doctor again. When last examined Henry had been considered fit to begin work on the Quarto, but after a year the doctor found many changes, among which high blood pressure was perhaps the most important. He set out a new regime and ordered alterations in Henry's behaviour, reported months later to Kenneth Sisam; 'He cut off my running, cold bath, lawn-mowing, all weight-lifting or other exertion, & any food more meaty than chicken.'[1] Henry was to report back for a further examination in six months' time.

He decided to wait until after the next check before telling Sisam at Oxford about this change in his health, but he did mention this 'disquieting overhaul' to Le Mesurier, describing himself as reduced 'to a semi-invalid, with strict diet and all sorts of prohibitions'.[2] Within a few weeks, however, Henry was reporting that the new regime was producing good results, and when he returned to the doctor this all-round improvement was confirmed. A visit to the eye specialist also seemed wise and the sight in the remaining eye was said to be as good as ever, although later events showed this reassurance to have been misleading. It was at this stage that Henry decided to tell Sisam about the business and offer him the chance of withdrawing from the arrangement if it seemed best. Of course, with the situation under control and Henry's health improving, Oxford was prepared to go on with the Quarto.

This confidence in the project must have been increased by the news, received some months earlier, that Arthur Fowler had agreed to join Henry and Le Mesurier as a third collaborator taking on part of Henry's work; Le Mesurier was able to cope with his section without help. Arthur had just finished collecting new words for the Supplement to the *OED* and his skill at the work had impressed Sisam. When writing about his health problems Henry revealed that the change of heart on Arthur's part was, as he put it, 'in compassion for my newly discovered senility'. By then Arthur had been working for some time and the three collaborators had 'all learnt the rudiments of co-operation',[3] so Henry was able to promise some acceleration in the rate of work.

The new arrangement was in fact very successful and the two recruits were eventually to become good friends, although, as Le Mesurier actually only met Henry on five occasions, he probably saw little of Arthur before his brother's death. Le Mesurier was himself a delightful man, and gave in his charming, gossipy letters a picture of the surviving Fowlers for the benefit of the Oxford office. Henry, short and sturdy, with his luxuriant moustache and a barely lingering fringe of hair, was likened to the great field marshal whom Le Mesurier had seen during his service in India: 'In appearance he was the living spit of Lord Roberts . . . an astonishing likeness, in face, figure, and suggestion of alertness.' Le Mesurier felt that he had never seen two brothers less alike in appearance, for Arthur was 'tall, grey, vandyke bearded, and very "distinguished" looking . . . the type Hollywood tries to find for an ambassador'.[4]

Henry had long hoped for help from Arthur, and the decision was quickly taken that he should move to Hinton St George when a house could be found for him. He eventually lived in the thatched cottage next door to Henry, known as End Cottage, but changed its name to Elsham in memory of his home in Poole, which was let until he could return to it. Henry clearly needed support, but managed to continue with his work.

✤ ✤ ✤

Letters still came for Henry as the author of *Modern English Usage* and editor of the two dictionaries, some arriving in the offices at Oxford or in London, others finding their way to Somerset. Henry kept up a regular correspondence with a circle of advisers and also answered enquiries which came directly to him, while checking and keeping note of corrections and suggestions which were sent in for his books. There were also responses to published letters; one, for instance, discussed whether 'cocksure' began with a reference to cocks of hay and corn, as suggested by an earlier correspondent. Henry replied representing all the 'men in the street who instinctively associate the word with the bird', suggesting that, as the cock was such 'a confident, loud, challenging, self-conscious creature',[5] it was only natural that people with the same qualities should have been called 'cocksure' after him.

More tricky enquiries were sent on to Oxford; a visiting lecturer from China, for instance, enquired about translating the Pocket dictionary into Chinese, a project which came to nothing but had been discussed many years before. Letters which arrived in Oxford were answered there, and in the London office Frederick Page, described by Humphrey Milford as Henry's disciple, would draft replies, often sent to Henry for approval. There were still light-hearted exchanges and Henry never lost his touch; his old friend from Sedbergh days, Bernard Tower, had brought to his attention a notice about the 'Spectator edition' of the Concise; 'Are we being, like other showy but useless articles, given away with a pound of tea?', Henry asked Kenneth Sisam, receiving a reply assuring him of the respectability of the arrangement.

As Henry worked through the proofs of the forthcoming Supplement which he was using for the Quarto he was still noticing corrections and additions; the phrase 'go phut', for instance, he suggested should be mentioned as possibly Indian in origin. He remembered years before being pleased with himself for deciding 'that it had nothing to do with "foot" mispronounced, but was a perfect echo of a toy balloon collapsing';[6] in more recent times he had received many comments about its Indian roots. There were continual discussions about these suggestions put forward by correspondents. A New Zealander, for example, provoked a debate on 'kiwi' by objecting to the use of 'apteryx' [wingless] in the definition, feeling it to be far too scientific. Henry, discovering that Kenneth Sisam was a New Zealander, could not resist a small jest: 'you N.Z.ers . . . must not let your N.Z.ery run away with you (or me).' When the business was settled Henry promised to 'be of good behaviour' in the Quarto, but it was agreed that the plates of the Concise would not be altered in 'retrospective penitence'. He had yet another little piece of fun by pointing out to Sisam that by that time 'kiwi' also meant a 'non-flying or apterygoidal member of the R.A.F.'.[7]

Newspaper letters, unprompted by the suggestions of others, also took some time; to *The Times*, for instance, on converting the War Loan, Henry wrote:

> I am horrified to find myself-unmitigated grammarian that I am-in possession of a surely most ungrammatical piece of property called 'Assented War Loan.' I never assented any War Loan, I feel sure. Did, or can, anyone ever assent War Loan? And, if no War Loan has been assented, can assented War Loan exist? And, if my supposed property is in fact a non-existent unthinkable entity, what becomes of my little dividend?[8]

In a postscript he did admit that this use of 'assent' would once have been possible, but by then it was classified as obsolete.

✿ ✿ ✿

In addition to all these sidelines there was work on the Quarto; Henry had promised a longer trial piece of text to help with assessing the scale of the proposed book and with discussions about length, postponed for six months after the earlier scare when the first piece was submitted. The arrival of this new section was a little delayed, and when it appeared it also turned out to be much too long. Henry, anxious not to begin drastic reductions too hastily, suggested another trial piece of similar length but from a different part of the alphabet, perhaps L with part of M. This, he explained, was a complete contrast to A, which was full of technical words and classical derivatives, while L comprised mostly general and literary words. The only other suitable letter was W but, as they had no Supplement proofs yet to help with that, it was best to use L. The section chosen was in fact L–Mammy; when the estimate on its length was finally made it proved to be just right, and the worries about cutting down could be laid aside.

Henry was quick to take offence when Kenneth Sisam reported that the attitude among those who had examined the new section was that it was too much like the Shorter. Sisam pointed out that the Quarto was proving, in the first sections shown to Oxford, rather more generous with early quotations than intended, and suggested gently that no quotations before 1500 should be included except for sayings still in use; this would make the Quarto appear more modern, which had been the intention when work began. Henry, on the other hand, felt that he should be able to choose the best quotations rather than being limited by date, and hoped for 'more flesh & blood, but less dry bone'[9] by using them to illustrate the definition rather than merely to establish the date of a word. The discussion with Sisam was finished when he indicated that, if the work had to be cut, he would rather give up some very early quotations to keep modern technical material.

Robert Chapman, the Secretary, also joined in the debate, writing to Henry about the differentiation of the Quarto and pointing out that for commercial reasons it must not appear like the Shorter. To all this Henry was forced to submit, grudgingly agreeing that the proportion of new material to old should be higher in the new book, but still insistent upon clinging to the old: 'we don't want to be cut off from Chaucer, nor even from obsolete senses that throw light.'[10] 'The great thing is to hack your way through,'[11] Chapman told Henry, and this he continued to do.

Batches of slips and suggestions still came in from regular correspondents and Robert Chapman contributed a large collection of his own material, although Henry might have been doubtful about its value when he read the description: 'it is mostly muck, and I am a muckraker,' Chapman said, adding that he could not watch 'the barbarians making the language look silly without wanting to take notes'.[12] All these slips were in his dreadful handwriting on odd-sized scraps of paper and were not alphabetically arranged, so Henry wrote for permission to cut them up and sort them, declaring them to be 'naturally unhandy for use at present'. With a little mythological wordplay on Aesculapius, the Roman god of healing, he added that 'a touch of Procrustes & ABCsculapius would put them in the way of functioning properly';[13] Procrustes was, of course, the wily character on the road between Eleusis and Athens who lured in passing travellers and adjusted them to fit his bed by shortening the tall and stretching the short, until he was trimmed to fit his own bed by a passer-by, Theseus, who chopped off his head.

The collaboration was going well, the two younger men were enabling Henry to continue with his work, while he was himself very generous with his praise for both of them. Le Mesurier was the first to be singled out by Henry. The matter of supplementing both the Concise and Pocket dictionaries with lists of new words to be added when they were reprinted came up in 1933; when this was put to Henry he could not agree to undertake the work without seriously holding back the Quarto. He admitted that his own progress was extremely slow and suggested Le Mesurier for the work, as he was already well ahead with his part and so could spare the time. Henry praised Le Mesurier's quickness and accuracy and mentioned his knowledge of Anglo-Indian and American vocabulary, suggesting that, as long as his natural temptation to excess was controlled by a strict limit to the number of additions, he would be an excellent choice for the work. He asked that Sisam should deal directly with Le Mesurier and this was done. New editions of the Pocket and Concise came out in 1934, with Addenda prepared by Le Mesurier, and a further edition of the Pocket in 1939 for which he was also responsible.

Henry was very grateful for Arthur's presence and assistance and was quickly impressed by his younger brother's skill. In November 1933 he wrote to Chapman about progress with the Quarto, explaining that Arthur had the 'family word-consciousness' and how well the three of them were working 'in triple harness'. He estimated that the work would take six more years, 'barring deaths & other such inconveniences'; in other words the Quarto would be finished at the end of 1939. Having mentioned death Henry went on to tell Chapman that Arthur would be perfectly capable of carrying on the work alone, being, Henry said, 'in full possession of any notions of mine that might make for a readable dictionary'. The word 'splendid!'[14] written across the bottom of the first page of this letter suggests how well received it was at Oxford. Robert Chapman sent a copy to Humphrey Milford in the London office indicating that, although no one could be as good as Henry, he believed Arthur would have been sitting at his brother's 'feet long enough to be competent to finish without palpable inferiority'.[15] Henry was told that his 'view of the possible succession'[16] had been noted, but it was hoped that it would not be necessary to act upon it.

✤ ✤ ✤

Despite all this effort Henry was in reality achieving much less work. He was rapidly losing his sight, and although he joked about revolutionizing Braille, it seemed that complete blindness was not far away. He was still up and about early in the morning, but struggled to achieve his usual tasks and his friend Coulton recounted the difficulties; Henry needed two candles, for instance, to be able to see when lighting the fire, and struggled with other household jobs because of his restricted sight. When the fire was lit, he always heated milk to drink before his breakfast, but Miss Shayer reported that he was often reheating it or sitting gazing into the fire when she came down to begin her duties. Although he disappeared into his room, she believed he did little work. He felt the cold far more than before, wrapping himself up to keep warm in the house, and when electricity came to the village bought himself an electric fire to keep his feet warm. Miss Shayer considered the house in Hinton St George uncomfortable and inconvenient and had commented to her new friend Mrs Le Mesurier on the lack of normal amenities—not even a tea-cosy, for instance, to keep Henry's tea hot as he liked it.

In August 1933 Bernard Tower, Henry's old friend and colleague at Sedbergh, died; despite his great sadness, Henry must have been pleased to be asked to compose an epitaph for the proposed memorial in the school chapel at Sedbergh. This model of Latin composition, Henry's last work, was much admired by all and a fitting tribute to his greatest friend. He was able also to do Tower another service by offering comfort to his niece, Daisy Tower, who had cared for her uncle for many years. In 1933 Daisy was invited to spend Christmas with Henry and accepted the invitation. He had been alone the previous year, when Miss Shayer went home to Guernsey to visit her family, but, with Arthur living next door to add to the party, he was pleased to have company and made great preparations for his guests; Coulton described enthusiastic shopping for gifts, chocolates, and other frivolities. Although Henry disliked Christmas festivities he was determined to make the occasion agreeable for Daisy Tower.

About ten days before the holiday Henry became unwell but managed a final workaday letter to Oxford, asking for proofs of the Supplement to use for the Quarto. He wrote also to Le Mesurier in a very cheerful frame of mind, sending him a specimen from some limericks he had been writing; in response Le Mesurier had told him that 'he evidently loved a frolic as much as Dr Johnson'.[17] Henry continued with his work until too ill to do more, but finally Nurse Shayer was able to summon a doctor and influenza was diagnosed. A night nurse was engaged and a specialist summoned from Bath, but Henry quickly developed pneumonia. On Christmas Day Arthur wrote to Oxford with the news that his brother was seriously ill and the doctor had 'practically given up hope'.[18] Henry eventually became unconscious and on the following day, 26 December 1933, at 1.00 p.m., he died peacefully in his sleep. He had himself arranged long before for his body to be cremated at Bristol and this was done on 29 December, with only Arthur and Miss Shayer present, as he would have wished. There were no flowers; Henry hated all these funeral traditions. Presumably his ashes were interred in Jessie's grave or scattered there; it seems hard to believe that he would not have wanted this, but there is nothing to confirm it.

Arthur informed Oxford by telegram of his brother's death and Le Mesurier wrote too. Both emphasized the terrible threat of blindness: Arthur felt that his brother had been 'spared a great deal' by dying before his loss of sight became complete and before he realized that he was losing his 'power of work'.[19] He had become dreadfully slow during the last year and Arthur had feared that he would become miserable when faced with his declining health. Perhaps, however, he knew more than Arthur suspected, and his letter suggesting his brother as a successor reflected his recognition of his rapidly fading strength.

Both Robert Chapman and Kenneth Sisam wrote from Oxford to express their sorrow to Arthur. Chapman revealed that he had been trying to arrange an honorary degree for Henry; he had made the attempt on several occasions but been prevented by some problem with the regulations. He had begun to try again because of a recent rule change and all was in the process of being discussed, although nothing had been arranged, and for this Chapman reproached himself. Arthur felt that Henry might have been pleased despite his modesty; he had been seen, Arthur told Chapman 'purring quietly over an intelligent appreciation of some bit of his work'. The Delegates of the Press, meanwhile, at a meeting in January issued the usual printed order recording 'their sense of loss', praising Henry's work which, although consisting 'largely of compilation', 'exhibited not only great learning and sound judgement, but also a rare originality'. As well as the dictionaries his other work was mentioned; *Modern English Usage* was singled out as 'a model of sound learning, good taste and good feeling' which had done much 'to maintain the purity of the English language'.[20]

✤ ✤ ✤

'I am quite alone now,'[21] Arthur had written to Chapman soon after his brother's death, and so he was, the last of the Fowlers. He also had three houses, two rented in Hinton St George and one which he owned in Poole but had let when he reluctantly left it to live near his brother. He had made a great financial sacrifice in giving up the home he loved, but he remained wisely where he was for the time being and was eventually persuaded by the Oxford people to continue his collaboration with Le Mesurier, as Henry had hoped he would. The Quarto was still regarded by the Press as a viable enterprise; Kenneth Sisam had reported to Chapman just before Henry's death that it was 'a knock-out book of the usual Fowler kind' and was going to be 'a huge success'.[22] The letters A and L had been finished and F was practically done, while M was partly complete and B had just been begun; with the lines laid down by Henry it seemed that these two much younger men might well bring the work to a successful conclusion.

Arthur Fowler and Herbert Le Mesurier became firm friends, visiting Oxford together to discuss plans for the Quarto. They were a great success at the University Press, and were later entertained to dinner and sent out to see a Gilbert and Sullivan performance. Afterwards Chapman described them in a letter to Milford in the London office; Arthur was taller than Henry, with white hair and beard, slight in build and deaf ('no bad thing for a lexicographer', Chapman thought) and had inherited his brother's sense of humour and to some degree his instinct for the work; Le Mesurier, on the other hand, was talkative, although 'modest and tractable',[23] but suffered with high blood pressure; his poor health meant that he could work for only six hours a day and spent Sundays in bed.

Eventually Arthur moved to Exmouth to live near Le Mesurier and the two were able to continue their work and friendship, even making trips to the cinema, 'that vast field of lexicographical study', as it was described in the Press magazine.[24] The partnership was, however, short-lived, for Arthur soon began to suffer from chest problems which were quickly diagnosed as lung cancer. He was nursed through his long illness, as Jessie and Henry had been, by Florence Shayer, who remained with him as housekeeper after Henry's death. The Oxford people, despite their brief official relationship with Arthur, were happy to support this last Fowler, providing Nurse Shayer with money to pay for specialists and various delicacies for the invalid. After dreadful suffering, Arthur died in October 1939. Miss Shayer returned home to Guernsey, where Henry had left her the two small cottages which he and Frank had built so long before and where they had begun their work together. She lived on through the German occupation and died in 1956 in a Guernsey nursing home, presumably rather like Sunnycroft, where her career had begun years before.

During Arthur's long illness another collaborator was found for Le Mesurier, Ernest McIntosh, a former headmaster who was prepared to move to Exmouth to work on the Quarto. These two also got on well, sharing a passion for the cinema, but Le Mesurier too was in poor health and after a massive heart attack he died in February 1940. McIntosh continued with the work through the war, but the Quarto was eventually dropped and Henry's last dictionary was never published.

✧ ✧ ✧

Reactions to Henry's death came in from all round the world. After much discussion it was agreed that a memoir should be prepared and published among the Society for Pure English Tracts which had seen the pre-publication issue of entries from *Modern English Usage*. An author was sought and eventually Henry's old friend Gordon Coulton was appointed and went down with his wife and daughters to Hinton St George to stay with Arthur, who had known him since his brief spell at Sedbergh as a young schoolmaster. Coulton very wisely consulted the landlady of the *George*, who would naturally have known all that went on locally. She spoke to him of Henry's friendliness to all and commented, 'For he was a great man, wasn't he?'[25] His generosity to the village children, whose games he enjoyed watching, had been particularly noted; for them he ordered from Mr Horsey at the village shop Christmas presents which were given to them anonymously, and treats in the form of brightly coloured drinks. In the village Henry and Jessie are still remembered; the daughter of Mr and Mrs Haines, who worked in the house and garden, still recalls her nervousness when, as a small girl, she was summoned by Nurse Shayer from her play at a parent's side to talk to 'HW' sitting at his desk.

In the wider world praises came from every quarter, in verse in *Punch* and prose elsewhere. *The Times*, heading its obituary 'A lexicographical genius', declared that Henry 'had a crispness, a facility, and an unexpectedness which have not been equalled'.[26] In the *Sunday Times* 'Atticus' described how 'obscure people in quiet country districts suddenly reveal a genius for the study of words', spending their remaining days in this pursuit, drawn to dictionaries which have the power of attracting 'the most diverse helpers'.[27] Henry's death was described in varying terms, in one journal depriving 'British scholarship of one of its brightest ornaments',[28] while elsewhere 'students of English' were said to 'have lost their best philosopher and friend'.[29] In Arthur's opinion it was really 'Atticus' who wrote the best piece, describing Henry as having 'overflowing humour and a most delicate wit, and a perfect genius for precise and memorable statement'.

The remarks of the professional commentators brought out the memories of Henry's friends and colleagues in pieces submitted to local or national newspapers. Pupils remembered him; Sir Alexander Lawrence, for example, perhaps assisted a little by hindsight, recorded how as a boy he had believed that the young man teaching him 'was wasted as a schoolmaster'. Another recalled his running, swimming, and rather uninspired teaching, but had kept up his friendship through the years, visiting Henry in Hinton St George months before his death. Coulton too drew attention to his friend's private life, more remarkable, he believed, than his public career had been, noting particularly his 'zest for all good things . . . and very deep and unostentatious affection for all human beings'. He had 'lived the perfect philosophic life . . . a most English life of quiet balance, with reserve of wonderful strength for any emergency'.[30]

Henry's dictionaries had found their way to countless bookshelves and school satchels, and those who used them came to feel that they knew him, writing to offer suggestions long after his death. *Modern English Usage* had slipped into the life of the nation, capturing the imagination of its public in an area where the professionals found it hard to rouse interest and creeping into twentieth-century life. In Elinor Glyn's novel *Sooner or Later*, for instance, the young heroine anxiously studied 'Genteelisms' in Henry's book, while, as the century moved on, in the midst of another world war, Churchill, planning the invasion of Normandy, snapped at an aide to check a word in 'Fowler'.[31] The young man on the Oxford train, going home to his dying father and his desolate mother and her children, had grown, through his natural sturdy stoicism and gentle good humour and with the unfailing support of his cheerful wife, into a man whose quiet, painstaking work had brought him into homes, schools, and offices throughout the English-speaking world.

❧ Notes ❧

❧ Chapter One ❧

1. These physical details are taken from Henry's army discharge papers.
2. Buckfastleigh, a large village in the valley of the river Dart with at that time about 2,500 inhabitants, was a centre of the local woollen industry, with four blanket and serge mills.
3. This rambling building had also at times been known as the Plymouth Inn, suggesting perhaps its importance for passing traffic. By the end of the eighteenth century it was already a private house, or perhaps two. Information about this property was gleaned from deeds in the possession of Mary Maguire of Buckfastleigh, which were read by the author in the charming surroundings of the inn yard, still known as Fowler's Yard.
4. John Townsend Fowler. From 1851 to 1855 tutor to student teachers at the York and Ripon Training College, then principal of the Government Normal School in Madras. Held various posts in the education department in Madras during more than 30 years' distinguished service. Retired in 1888 and moved to New Zealand. Died in 1912 aged 83 at Napier.
5. The name was changed to St Luke's College in 1930. It became part of the University of Exeter School of Education in 1978.
6. Details of Robert's early career from Reports of the Exeter Diocesan Board of Education; Devon Record Office 4085E/1–3.
7. Now the Duke of York's Royal Military School, Dover.
8. Deacon at Chester in 1853 and priest at Ely two years later, becoming briefly curate at West Lavington, Wiltshire.
9. The 1851 census shows him farming 330 acres and employing 15 men.
10. The farm buildings and all of the church but its tower were destroyed in the redevelopment of Dartington, but the Watson family tomb, where Caroline's parents and earlier family members were buried, survives under a great yew in the remains of the churchyard.

11. *Examples in the Elementary Rules of Algebra for the Use of National Schools* (1857) and *Fowler's Elements of Algebra* with key (1861).
12. 1871 census information.
13. OEDA, Additional Letters, 28 Dec. 1933.
14. OEDA, ODME/9/472, 28 Oct. 1939.
15. Ibid. 6/105, 20 Apr. 1934.
16. A small town with about 1,000 inhabitants about 65 miles north of Melbourne on the road to Castlemaine.
17. Then temporarily renamed Sandhurst.
18. Alexander's name was inscribed on the family tomb in the Old Cemetery at Tunbridge Wells, which provided the key to unravelling the stories of all Henry's siblings who died overseas.
19. GGC, p. 101.
20. *MPF*, p. 35.
21. OEDA, MISC/370/36, 11 Mar. 1906.
22. *SM*, p. 17
23. *Midland Times and Gazette*, 1 July 1876
24. Robert Whitelaw (1843–1917). Educated at Lancaster Grammar School and Trinity College, Cambridge. Taught at Rugby, 1868–1913.
25. OEDA, Additional Letters, 28 Dec. 1933.
26. Another son of John Fowler (see n. 4 above) was educated in England: Robert Clive Fowler at Exeter College, Oxford. Both Harry and Robert moved with their father to New Zealand. Robert became a sheep farmer and Harry, at first a schoolmaster in Madras, was later a headmaster at Invercargill in New Zealand and for many years at Nelson College.
27. GGC, p. 101.
28. Ibid. 102.
29. Benjamin Jowett (1817–93) had been a student at Balliol and was later Master and Regius Professor of Greek. Published translations of Plato, Thucydides, and Aristotle with the University Press. Later Vice-Chancellor of the University.
30. GGC, p. 101.
31. Percy Ewing Matheson (1859–1946) became a fellow of New College. Also published many books with Oxford University Press.

❧ Chapter Two ❧

1. Henry George Hart (1843–1921). Born in India and educated at Rugby and St John's College, Cambridge. Taught first at Haileybury and Harrow.
2. Sedbergh School, Governors' Minutes, Head Master's Report, 17 Apr. 1882.
3. *Yorkshire Post*, 2 Jan. 1934, p. 4.
4. Wilson's house was later renamed Sedgwick House, when the old system of naming houses after their current housemaster was abandoned.
5. *BBM*, p. 57.
6. GGC, p. 104.
7. Probably W. Snow, the son of a clergyman from Milnthorpe.
8. *Yorkshire Post*, 2 Jan. 1934, p. 4.
9. GGC, pp. 104–5.
10. Ibid. 106.
11. *BBM*, p. 97.
12. GGC, p. 106.
13. Ibid. 108.
14. *Yorkshire Post*, 2 Jan. 1934, p. 4.
15. GGC, p. 107.
16. *Sedberghian*, 55(1) (Mar. 1934).
17. Ibid. 12(5) (Oct. 1891), p. 156.
18. At the top of this slope the school cloisters now commemorate the dead of two world wars, a fitting memorial to boys who revelled in the wintry weather.
19. *Sedberghian*, 13(6) (Dec. 1892), pp. 161–3.
20. GGC, pp. 108–9.
21. Ibid. 107.
22. Ibid. 109.
23. Frederick Payne Lemarchand (1862–1933). Educated at Queen's College, Oxford.
24. Bernard Henry Tower (1858–1933). Educated at Lancing and Pembroke College, Oxford. Left Sedbergh for headmastership of Lancing, from which he retired after seven years due to ill health.
25. GGC, p. 103.
26. *Sedberghian*, 54(5) (Nov. 1933).
27. George Gordon Coulton (1858–1947). Born in King's Lynn, Norfolk, and educated at Felsted and St Catharine's College, Cambridge. Fellow of St John's College, Cambridge, and University Lecturer in English.
28. GGC, p. 106.
29. Ibid. 127.
30. Ibid. 108.
31. Ibid. 128.

32. *Ceylon Government Gazette*, 11 Dec. 1885, 22 Jan. 1886; PRO.
33. PRO, Colonial Office Papers, CO337/15.
34. OEDA, ODME/9/472, 28 Oct. 1939.
35. *SM*, p. 19.
36. SL, undated draft.
37. *SM*, p. 100.
38. Ibid. 102.
39. *DNB*, 'H. W. Fowler'.
40. *SM*, pp. 95–109.
41. SL, 2 June 1898.
42. Ibid., undated draft.
43. GGC, p. 111.
44. *SL*, undated draft.
45. OUPA, LB2048, 17 June 1906.
46. Hart retired in 1900 and worked as an inspector of schools for London University until the war.
47. *Sedberghian*, 55(1) (Mar. 1934).

❧ Chapter Three ❧

1. TAG, BL Add. MS 63559, 19 Apr. 1902.
2. Edmund Howe, b. 1866, Priors Hardwick, Warwickshire. Joined Metropolitan Police on 3 May 1886. Married Rosa Ann White, 7 Jan. 1890. Information about Howe's career from Records Management Branch, Metropolitan Police Service, and PRO, MEPO 21/33 and 34.
3. OEDA, QOD/1931/5, 2 Mar. 1931.
4. Ibid. 7, 4 Mar. 1931.
5. *BBM*, p. 131.
6. GGC, p. 119.
7. *Spectator*, 20 Jan. 1900.
8. John St Loe Strachey (1860–1927). Editor of the *Spectator* 1898–1925.
9. GGC, p. 119.
10. Begun by Lady Randolph Churchill in 1899; only 12 quarterly issues were published.
11. *Anglo-Saxon Review*, June 1901, pp. 165–70.
12. BLib. MS Eng. lett. c762, fos. 175–6, 18 Dec. 1919.
13. *DtoJ*, p. 21.
14. GGC, p. 119.
15. Rose Dorothy Ilbert, an orphan, working as a governess for a particularly difficult aunt.
16. CL, 3 Apr. 1903.
17. Ibid. 5 Feb. 1903.
18. GGC, p. 118.
19. John Dickson Batten (1860–1932). His Dante illustrations were shown in an exhibition at Leighton House, London, in 1900 but not

published until used in an edition in 1933 by Oxford University Press.

20. CL, 5 Feb. 1903.
21. GGC, p. 118.
22. Ibid. 126.
23. Thomas Anstey Guthrie (1856–1934). Educated at King's College School and Trinity Hall, Cambridge. Called to the Bar but never practised. Wrote fantastical novels later produced as plays. A distinguished contributor to *Punch*.
24. TAG, BL Add. MS 63558, 29 Oct. 1900.
25. *Westminster Gazette*, 30 Oct. 1900, p. 5.
26. GGC, p. 120.
27. TAG, BL Add. MS 63559, 15 June 1902.
28. Ibid. 16 June 1902.
29. Ibid. Add. MS 63560, 9 Apr. 1903.
30. Guy Pollock (1878–1957). Wrote verse for *Punch* and the *Westminster Gazette* and worked as a journalist for the *Evening Standard* and the *Daily Express*. After war service returned to newspaper journalism.
31. TAG, BL Add. MS 63559, 28 Mar. 1902.
32. Ibid. Add. MS 63557, 13 Apr. 1900.
33. William Archer (1856–1924). Educated at Edinburgh University. Theatre critic for several newspapers, and editor of Ibsen. Proposed abolition of censorship and the establishment of a national theatre.
34. TAG, BL Add. MS 63560, 20 Nov. 1902.
35. At Greenbank School, Liverpool.
36. TAG, BL Add. MS 63560, 5 Feb. 1903.
37. *Punch*, 26 Aug. 1903.
38. Ainslie died in 1908, aged only 47.
39. GGC, p. 120.

❧ Chapter Four ❧

1. St Paul's school reports.
2. James Wilson, b. 25 Oct. 1871 at Gateshead.
3. Henry Rule Wetherall (1869–1939). From Kettering, Northants.
4. OEDA, ODME/9/472, 28 Oct. 1939.
5. St Paul's school reports.
6. Wilson married Mabel Jane Marchant on 8 Sept. 1897 at Dartford, Kent.
7. *SCV*, pp. 105–6.
8. *SM*, p. 164.
9. Ibid. 161.
10. GGC, p. 121.
11. *SM*, p. 113.
12. Ibid. 164.
13. GGC, p. 122.
14. *SM*, p. 41.
15. Ibid.
16. Charles Lamb (1775–1834), *Popular Fallacies*.
17. *MPF*, p. 44.
18. Ibid. 18.
19. Ibid. 21.
20. OEDA, MISC/369/13, 6 Aug. 1905.
21. *Lucian*, intro., p. xix.
22. OUPA, unlisted letter.
23. *The Times*, 14 Oct. 1897.
24. Henry Frowde (1841–1927). B. Southsea. Became manager of the London office in 1874 and Publisher in 1883; retired in 1913.
25. Charles Cannan (1858–1919). Educated at Clifton College and Corpus Christi College, Oxford. Classical tutor and Dean, Trinity College. Delegate of the Press, 1895, and Secretary, 1898, a position which he still held at his death.
26. *DNB*, 'Charles Cannan'.
27. Humphrey Sumner Milford (1877–1952), b. Wiltshire. Educated Winchester and New College, Oxford. Then assistant to Cannan. Moved to London to assist Frowde and in 1913 succeeded him. Retired 1945.
28. James Augustus Henry Murray (1837–1915), b. Denholm, Hawick. Schoolmaster at Mill Hill School, 1870–85. Became editor of Dictionary in 1879 and moved to Oxford in 1885. Died before work was completed. Knighted in 1908.
29. OUPA, Secretary's Letterbook, vol. 87.
30. Ibid. vol. 88.
31. OEDA, PP/1903/6.
32. OUPA, Secretary's Letterbook 88, fo. 365, 13 July 1903.
33. OEDA, MISC/369/2.
34. GGC, p. 123.
35. OEDA, MISC/369/5, 30 May 1904.
36. Lucian, intro. p. xxiii.
37. William Walter Merry (1835–1918), Fellow and classical tutor, Lincoln College, 1859–84, and Rector, 1884–1918.
38. OEDA, MISC/369/9, 31 Jan. 1905.
39. OEDA, Additional Letters, 28 May 1905.
40. OEDA, MISC/369/10.
41. *TLS*, 25 Aug. 1905.
42. *New York Times*, quoted in Peter Sutcliffe, *The Oxford University Press: An Informal History* (Oxford University Press, 1978), p. 151.
43. OEDA, MISC/370/25, 7 Sept. 1905.
44. *New Age*, 3 Nov. 1921.

❧ Chapter Five ❧

1. OEDA, MISC/369/6, 29 Nov. 1904.
2. *MPF*, p. 173.
3. OEDA, MISC/370/25, 7 Sept. 1905.
4. Ibid., 3, 19 Dec. 1904.
5. Ibid. 10, 31 Jan. 1905.
6. Ibid. 4, 22 Dec. 1904.
7. Ibid. 5, 23 Dec. 1904.
8. Ibid. 7, 8 Jan. 1905.
9. Ibid. 10, 31 Jan. 1905.
10. Ibid. 9, 16 Jan. 1905.
11. Ibid. 14/1, 23 June 1905.
12. Ibid. 13, 5 May 1905.
13. Ibid. 14/1, 23 June 1905.
14. Ibid. 13, 18 Sept. 1905.
15. Henry Bradley (1845–1923). Appointed editor of Dictionary, 1889, and chief editor, 1915.
16. OEDA, MISC/370/20, 10 July 1905.
17. Ibid. 22, 31 July 1905.
18. Ibid. 35, 15 Feb. 1906.
19. Ibid. 37, 21 Mar. 1906.
20. Ibid. 39, 22 Mar. 1906.
21. Ibid. 30, 1 Nov. 1905.
22. Ibid. 20, 10 July 1905.
23. Ibid.
24. Ibid. 34, 14 Feb. 1906.
25. Ibid. 31, 1 Nov. 1905.
26. Ibid. 32.
27. Ibid. 36, 11 Mar. 1906.
28. Ibid. 33, 9 Feb. 1906.
29. *Timon of Athens*. I. i. 48.
30. OEDA, MISC/370/45, 22 May 1906.
31. GGC, p. 123.
32. Quoted in OEDA, PBED015141, 11 Jan. 1908.
33. OEDA, MISC/370/44, 20 May 1906.
34. OUPA, LB1996, 5 July 1906.
35. *Guernsey Evening Press*, 30 June 1906, p. 1.
36. See Ch. 3 above, n. 34.
37. *Daily Leader*, 2 June 1906.
38. *KE*, p. 23.
39. Ibid. 24.
40. BL Add. MS 45291, fos. 130–2, 3 June 1906.
41. Ibid. fo. 134, 7 June 1906.
42. Ibid. fos. 135–6, 10 June 1906.
43. Ibid. fo. 137.
44. OUPA, LB1996, 3 July 1906.
45. OEDA, MISC/370/48, 3 July 1906.
46. *The Times*, quoted in OEDA, MISC/210/111, 18 June 1906.
47. Ibid.
48. Ibid.
49. OUPA, LB2048, 8 July 1906.
50. OUPA, LB1996, 5 July 1906.
51. OEDA, MISC/370/54, 8 Aug. 1906.
52. Ibid. 56, 9 Aug. 1906.
53. *KE*, 2nd edn., p. iv.
54. OEDA, MISC/369/24, 5 Jan. 1926.
55. *Englishman*, 9 Mar. 1905.
56. *SA*, Preface.
57. F. P. Lemarchand, OUPA, LB2048, 22 May 1906.
58. Cyril Gooch, OUPA, LB2048.
59. OEDA, MISC/370/44, 20 May 1906.
60. OUPA, LB 2048, report received 22 June 1906.
61. Ibid. 17 June 1906.
62. Edwin Abbott Abbott, *How to Tell the Parts of Speech* (London, 1874).
63. *SA*, Preface.
64. OUPA, HSM Letterbook 4, 3 June 1907.
65. *Glasgow Herald*, quoted on jacket of *SM*, 2nd edn.
66. BLib. MS Eng. lett. c762, fos. 175–6, 18 Dec. 1919.
67. *SM*, p. 170.
68. *Bristol Mercury*, quoted on jacket of *SM*, 2nd edn.
69. *Yorkshire Observer*, quoted on jacket of *SM*, 2nd edn.
70. *Pall Mall Gazette*, quoted on jacket of *SM*, 2nd edn.
71. *WWH*, jacket.
72. *BBM*, Preface, p. v.
73. Ibid. 119–20.
74. Ibid. 62–7.
75. GGC, p. 123.
76. James Surtees Phillpotts (d. 1930). Educated at Winchester and New College, Oxford. Taught at Rugby, 1862–74. Headmaster of Bedford Grammar School, 1874–1903.
77. OUPA, 29 Mar. 1928. Letter inside copy of *MEU*.

❧ Chapter Six ❧

1. OUPA, HSM Letterbook 1, fo. 202, 13 Oct. 1906.
2. Ibid. fos. 225–6, 17 Oct. 1906.
3. William Little (1848–1922), b. Manchester. Educated at Manchester Grammar School and Corpus Christi College, Oxford. Lecturer and tutor, Corpus Christi, 1870–83. Called to the Bar, Lincoln's Inn, 1884. Retired to Cornwall 1887.

4. OUPA, HSM Letterbook 1, fos. 225–6, 17 Oct. 1906.
5. Ibid. fos. 412–13, 4 Nov. 1906.
6. Ibid. 2, fo. 90, 4 Dec. 1906.
7. Ibid. fo. 206, 20 Dec. 1906.
8. Ibid. fo. 298, 8 Jan. 1907.
9. Ibid. fo. 400.
10. Ibid. fo. 442.
11. Ibid. fo. 443, 4 Feb. 1907.
12. Ibid. 1, fo. 293, 20 Oct. 1906.
13. For further information on pronunciation in the *OED* see L. Mugglestone (ed); *Lexicography and the OED*. OUP, 1999, p. 172.
14. OUPA, HSM Letterbook 3, fo. 120, 26 Feb. 1907.
15. Ibid. 3, fo. 79.
16. Ibid. 2, fos. 299–301, 6 Jan. 1907.
17. Ibid. 3, fo. 120, 26 Feb. 1907.
18. Ibid. fo. 121, 26 Feb. 1907.
19. Ibid. fo. 194, 7 Mar. 1907.
20. Ibid. 4, fo. 202, 13 May 1907.
21. Ibid. fo. 203, 10 May 1907.
22. *OED*.
23. *COD* 1911.
24. OUPA, HSM Letterbook 4, fo. 203, 10 May 1907.
25. Ibid. 5, fo. 106, 1 July 1907.
26. Ibid. fo. 158, 5 July 1907.
27. Ibid. fo. 311, 23 July 1907.
28. Ibid. fo. 167, 6 July 1907.
29. Ibid. fos. 211–12, 9 July 1907.
30. Ibid. 8, fo. 259, 12 Dec. 1907.
31. Ibid. 10, fo. 259, 11 Mar. 1907.
32. *SM*, pp. 121–2.
33. Ibid. 132.
34. Ibid. 134.
35. Ibid. 140.
36. On 4 Aug. 1903 at All Saints, Margaret Street, in Marylebone, London.
37. GGC, p. 126.
38. After leaving St Peter Port Flanagan wandered on, and eventually died in 1914 at Funchal, Madeira.
39. GGC, pp. 125–6.
40. *DtoJ*, p. 28.
41. Ibid. p. 13.
42. WL, 29 Feb. 1916.
43. *DtoJ*, p. 30.
44. OUPA, HSM Letterbook 113, 3 July 1923.
45. *DtoJ*, p. 13.
46. *MPF*, p. 47.
47. GGC, p. 146.
48. Mabel died in South Africa in 1922.
49. *DtoJ*, p. 32.
50. Ibid. p. 34.
51. BLib. MS Eng. lett. c762, fos. 175–6, 18 Dec. 1919.

✛ Chapter Seven ✛

1. OUPA, HSM Letterbook 11, fo. 17.
2. OUPA, PBED015141, 11 Jan. 1908.
3. Robert William Chapman (1881–1960), b. near Dalkeith. Educated at High School Dundee, St Andrews, and Oriel College, Oxford. Assistant Secretary, 1906. 1914–18, served in Salonica, Royal Garrison Artillery. Secretary to the Delegates, 1920. Retired, 1942.
4. OUPA, PBED015141, 15 Apr. 1908.
5. OUPA, HSM Letterbook 11, fo. 474.
6. OUPA, PBED015141, 13 May 1908.
7. Ibid. 28 June 1908.
8. OUPA, HSM Letterbook 8, fo. 256.
9. OEDA, COD/M/1/3, 11 Aug. 1908.
10. OUPA, HSM Letterbook 12, fo. 250.
11. OEDA, COD/M/1/4, 13 Aug. 1908.
12. OEDA, MEU/1/1, 20 June 1909.
13. *COD*, Preface, p. iv.
14. OEDA, COD/M/1/15, 15 Feb. 1911.
15. *COD*, Preface, p. iii.
16. *TLS*, 20 July 1911.
17. *COD*, Preface, p. iii.
18. *Athenaeum*, 1911.
19. *COD*, Preface, p. iii.
20. *COD* 2nd edn. (1929), Preface.
21. *Modern Language Notes*, Dec. 1911, p. 264.
22. *COD*, Preface, p. iv.
23. *New York Sun*, 1911.
24. *Periodical*, July 1912, p. 67.
25. Daniel Jones, *An English Pronouncing Dictionary*, 1917. J. M. Dent and Sons.
26. OEDA, COD/M/1/2.
27. OEDA, MEU/1/40, proposed preface to *MEU*.
28. *COD* 2nd edn., Preface, p. iv.
29. *Scotsman*, 1911.
30. *TLS*, 20 July 1911.
31. *Boston Herald*, 1911.
32. *Western Morning News*, 1911.
33. OEDA, COD/M/1/23, 14 Aug. 1911.
34. Ibid. 22, 10 Aug. 1911.
35. Ibid. 23, 14 Aug. 1911.
36. Ibid. 24, 16 Aug. 1911.
37. *Scotsman*, 1911.
38. OUPA, HSM Letterbook 40, fo. 263, 21 Oct. 1911.

39. *Modern Language Notes,* Dec. 1911, p. 264.
40. *Assistant Masters Association,* 1911.
41. OEDA, POD/1/7, 17 June 1913.
42. OEDA, COD/M/1/8, 28 July 1910.
43. Ibid. 14, 3 Oct. 1910.
44. William Douglas Lowe (1879–1922), b. Manchester. Educated at Pembroke College, Cambridge. Classical lecturer at Durham.
45. OEDA, COD/M/1/12, 6 Oct. 1910.
46. OEDA, POD/1/1, 11 Oct. 1910.
47. Una Jane Mary Maud Godfrey (1889–1936), b. Twickenham.
48. John Roger Rush Godfrey, d. Torredembarra, Spain, 1931; m. Maud Matson. Educated at Merton College, Oxford. Barrister, Inner Temple.
49. OUPA, HSM Letterbook 38, fo. 443.
50. *DtoJ,* p. 36.
51. OEDA, MEU/1/3, 6 Jan. 1911.
52. OUPA, HSM Letterbook 35, fo. 286.
53. OEDA, MEU/1/3, 6 Jan. 1911.
54. OEDA, MEU/1/5, 11 Jan. 1911.

❧ Chapter Eight ❧

1. OUPA, HSM Letterbook 54, 25 Nov. 1913.
2. OEDA, MEU/1/4, 10 Jan. 1911.
3. Ibid. 6, 17 Jan. 1911.
4. OUPA, HSM Letterbook 38, fo. 423, 17 July 1911.
5. *POD* (1924), Preface.
6. Charles Talbut Onions (1873–1965). Educated at Mason College, Birmingham. Appointed to staff of *OED,* 1895. Independent editor from 1913. Reader in English Philology, University of Oxford, 1927–49.
7. OEDA, COD/M/1/1, 15 July 1912.
8. *POD* (1924), Preface.
9. OUPA, HSM Letterbook 3, fo. 193, 7 Mar. 1907.
10. OEDA, MEU/1/4, 10 Jan. 1911.
11. Ibid. 5, 11 Jan. 1911.
12. Ibid. 6, 17 Jan. 1911.
13. Ibid. 8.
14. Ibid. 5, 11 Jan. 1911.
15. Ibid. 7, 5 Apr. 1911.
16. Ibid. 8.
17. Ibid. 9, 13 May 1911.
18. Ibid. 10, 26 May 1911.
19. Ibid. 7, 5 Apr. 1911.
20. Ibid. 9, 13 May 1911.
21. Ibid. 10, 26 May 1911.
22. Ibid. 12, 11 June 1911.
23. Ibid. 13, 21 Sept. 1911.
24. *MEU,* p. 74.
25. OEDA, MEU/1/16, 25 Sept. 1911.
26. Ibid. 18.
27. Ibid. 20, 15 Oct. 1911.
28. Ibid. 19, 10 Oct. 1911.
29. Ibid. 20, 15 Oct. 1911.
30. *DtoJ,* p. 41.
31. Ibid. p. 42.
32. George Jones, b. 1857 at Dover. Educated at St John's College, Cambridge; m. 1889 Ethel Leathes Metcalfe; d. 1932 at Torquay.
33. Sidney Faithorne Green (1841–1916), b. Eltham, Kent. Educated at Tonbridge and Trinity College, Cambridge; d. Sydenham, Kent.
34. Mary Theodora Hesketh Jones (1902–1983), b. Sandford St Martin, Oxon; d. Worthing.
35. *DtoJ,* p. 42.
36. GGC, p. 126.
37. Fred W. Ward, *The 23rd (Service) Battalion Royal Fusiliers (First Sportsman's)* (London: Sidgwick & Jackson, 1920), p. 22.
38. *Westminster Gazette,* 2 Dec. 1914, p. 7, c. 4.
39. OUPA, HSM Letterbook 62, fo. 153.
40. WL, 12 Oct. 1915.
41. Ibid. 27 Aug. 1915.
42. GGC, p. 127.

❧ Chapter Nine ❧

1. WL, 25 Dec. 1915.
2. Ibid. 26 Dec. 1915.
3. Ibid. 27 Dec. 1915.
4. Ibid. 24 Dec. 1915.
5. Ibid. 2 Jan. 1916.
6. Ibid. 18 Jan. 1916.
7. Ibid. 11 Apr. 1916.
8. GGC, p. 127.
9. WL, 28 Dec. 1915.
10. Ibid. 1 Jan. 1916.
11. Ibid. 7 Jan. 1916.
12. Ibid. 27 Dec. 1915.
13. Ibid. 31 Dec. 1915.
14. Ibid. 29 Dec. 1915.
15. Ibid. 31 Dec. 1915.
16. Many details of the Battalion movements are taken from the trench diaries kept at the Public Record Office, Kew.
17. Ibid. 6 Jan. 1916.

18. Ibid. 9 Jan. 1916.
19. Ibid. 10 Jan. 1916.
20. Ibid. 28 Dec. 1915.
21. Ibid. 19 Jan. 1916.
22. Ibid. 25 Jan. 1916.
23. Ibid. 19 Jan. 1916.
24. Ibid. 21 Jan. 1916.
25. Ibid. 23 Jan. 1916.
26. Ibid. 30 Jan. 1916.
27. Ibid. 31 Jan. 1916.
28. Ibid. 2 Feb. 1916.
29. Ibid. 1 Feb. 1916.
30. Ibid. 2 Feb. 1916.
31. Ibid. 16 Feb. 1916.
32. Ibid. 3 Feb. 1916.
33. Ibid. 13 Feb. 1916.
34. Ibid. 17 Feb. 1916.
35. Ibid. 15 Feb. 1916.
36. Ibid. 4 Feb. 1916.
37. Ibid. 6 Feb. 1916.
38. Ibid. 7 Feb. 1916.
39. Ibid. 17 Feb. 1916.
40. Ibid. 18 Feb. 1916.
41. Ibid. 19 Feb. 1916.
42. Ibid. 12 Jan. 1916.
43. Ibid. 21 Feb. 1916.
44. Ibid. 22 Feb. 1916.
45. Ibid. 28 Feb. 1916.
46. *MEU*, p. 441.
47. GGC, p. 135.
48. WL, 25 Feb. 1916.
49. Ibid. 31 Dec. 1915.
50. Ibid. 29 Jan. 1916.
51. Ibid. 26 Feb. 1916.
52. Ibid. 28 Feb. 1916.
53. Ibid. 27 Feb. 1916.
54. Ibid.
55. Ibid. 29 Feb. 1916.
56. Ibid. 3 Mar. 1916.
57. Ibid. 20 Feb. 1916.
58. Ibid. 5 Mar. 1916.
59. Ibid. 6 Mar. 1916.
60. Ibid. 24 Feb. 1916.
61. Ibid. 29 Feb. 1916.
62. Ibid. 6 Mar. 1916.
63. Ibid. 16 Mar. 1916.
64. Ibid. 22 Mar. 1916.
65. Ibid. 23 Mar. 1916.
66. Ibid. 26 Mar. 1916.
67. Ibid. 27 Mar. 1916.
68. Ibid. 28 Mar. 1916.
69. Ibid. 2 Apr. 1916.
70. Ibid. 30 Mar. 1916.
71. Ibid. 7 Apr. 1916.

72. Ibid. 4 Apr. 1916.
73. Ibid. 1 Apr. 1916.
74. Ibid. 7 Apr. 1916.
75. Ibid. 5 Apr. 1916.
76. Ibid. 8 Apr. 1916.
77. Ibid. 12 Apr. 1916.
78. Ibid. 22 Apr. 1916.
79. Ibid. 18 Apr. 1916.
80. Ibid. 16 Apr. 1916.
81. Ibid. 26 Apr. 1916.
82. Ibid. 27 Apr. 1916.
83. Ibid. 28 Apr. 1916.
84. Ibid. 30 Apr. 1916.
85. Ibid. 3 May 1916.
86. Ibid. 4 May 1916.
87. Ibid. [6] May 1916.
88. Ibid. 5 May 1916.

✄ Chapter Ten ✄

1. Florence Ethel Shayer (1873–1956), b. Vauvert, St Peter Port, the daughter of a smith, Charles Shayer, and his wife, Laura.
2. WL, 14 Feb. 1916.
3. Ibid. 4 May 1916.
4. Ibid. 6 Apr. 1916.
5. Ibid. 21 Apr. 1916.
6. Ibid. 7 May 1916.
7. Ibid. 16 May 1916.
8. Ibid. 11 May 1916.
9. Ibid. 18 May 1916.
10. Ibid. 13 May 1916.
11. Ibid. 12 May 1916.
12. Ibid. 9 June 1916.
13. Ibid. 14 June 1916.
14. Ibid. 16 June 1916.
15. Ibid. 5 June 1916.
16. Ibid. 18 June 1916.
17. Ibid. 16 June 1916.
18. Ibid. 20 June 1916.
19. Ibid. 23 June 1916.
20. This was a two-year course beginning in July 1917.
21. *Westminster Gazette*, 25 June 1918.
22. OEDA, MISC/369/14, 6 Nov. 1918.
23. George John Clement Dent (1878–1959). Educated at Sedbergh and Peterhouse, Cambridge.
24. WL, 16 May 1916.
25. PRO, Register of Lunatics, MH94/110, Admission nos. 65911 and 69692.
26. *DtoJ*, p. 47.

27. Ibid. p. 51.
28. GGC, p. 145.
29. *DtoJ*, p. 57.
30. GGC, p. 145.
31. BLib., Dep. Bridges 109, fos. 59–60, 11 Mar. 1921.
32. Told to the author by Marie de Garis of Les Reveaux.

❧ Chapter Eleven ❧

1. OEDA, POD/1/11, 14 Feb. 1919.
2. WL, 31 Mar. 1916.
3. OEDA, POD/1/14, 4 Apr. 1919.
4. Ibid. 16, 10 Apr. 1919.
5. Ibid. 19, 16 Apr. 1919.
6. Ibid. 17, 11 Apr. 1919.
7. Ibid. 9, 10 Jan. 1919.
8. Ibid. 11, 14 Feb. 1919.
9. Ibid. 9, 10 Jan. 1919.
10. Ibid. 12, 21 Feb. 1919.
11. Ibid. 33, 13 Sept. 1919.
12. Ibid. 35, 22 Sept. 1919.
13. Ibid. 46, 4 Nov. 1920.
14. Ibid. 48, 15 Nov. 1919.
15. Ibid. 53, 26 Feb. 1921.
16. Ibid. 52, 3 Mar. 1921.
17. Ibid. 29, 14 July 1919.
18. Ibid. 44, 3 Nov. 1920.
19. Ibid. 54, 27 May 1921.
20. OEDA, COD/M/1/50, 22 Dec. 1919.
21. Ibid. 78, 18 Dec. 1922.
22. Ibid. 79, 20 Dec. 1922.
23. Ibid. 81, 31 Dec. 1919.
24. This correspondence was published in the *Jewish Chronicle* in Sept. 1924.
25. OEDA, Additional OED126, 1 Oct. 1924.
26. Ibid. 27 Sept. 1924. See also R. W. Burchfield, *Unlocking the English Language* (1989).
27. OUPA, Oxford Pkt, 138.12.
28. George van Santvoord, b. 1891. Oxford-educated and a master at Winchester.
29. OUPA, CPED001257, 30 Apr. 1922.
30. Ibid. 001259, 18 May 1927.
31. Ibid. 9 July 1930.
32. *TLS*, 25 Sept. 1925.
33. *New Statesman*, 1925.
34. *Notes and Queries*, 1925.
35. OEDA, PP/1922/23, 14 Sept. 1922.
36. Ibid. 25, 28 Sept. 1922.
37. Ibid. 30, 26 Oct. 1922.
38. Ibid. 1923/135, 19 Nov. 1923.
39. WL, 19 May 1916.
40. G. G. Coulton, *Fourscore Years*, p. 111
41. A. R. H. Moncrieff, *Black's Guide to Dorsetshire* (London: A & C Black, 1921).
42. *The Residential Attractions of Parkstone, Dorset* (Bristol: Clifton Publicity, 1934).
43. GGC, p. 146.
44. *DtoJ*, p. 61.
45. Ibid. p. 17.
46. Story told to author by Alfred Lainé, son of D'Arcy.
47. *SM*, p. 65.
48. OEDA, SOED/1923/2.
49. *DtoJ*, p. 65.

❧ Chapter Twelve ❧

1. OEDA, MEU/1/22, 25 Mar. 1919.
2. Ibid. 27, 2 Apr. 1919.
3. Ibid. 29, 16 Apr. 1919.
4. Ibid. 30, 15 Apr. 1919.
5. Ibid. 29, 16 Apr. 1919.
6. OUPA, CPED001257, 30 Apr. 1922.
7. *TLS*, 19 Feb. 1920.
8. SPE Tract 1, 16 Oct. 1919.
9. *The Times*, 20 Jan. 1923.
10. Robert Seymour Bridges (1844–1930). Educated at Eton and Corpus Christi College, Oxford. Began work as a doctor; published first volume of poetry in 1873.
11. BLib., Dep. Bridges 109, fos. 59, 60, 11 Mar. 1921.
12. Ibid. fos. 61, 62, 28 Nov. 1923.
13. SPE Tract 15, 8 Nov. 1923.
14. *Journal of Education*, 5 Jan. 1924.
15. *Manchester Guardian Weekly*, 30 Nov. 1923.
16. Otto Jespersen (1860–1943). Originally proposed the International Phonetic Alphabet. Author of *Modern English Grammar* in four volumes.
17. For further information see R. W. Burchfield, *The New Fowler's Modern English Usage*. 1998; Clarendon Press, Oxford. p. 608, possessive with gerund.
18. SPE Tract 22, 26 Nov. 1925.
19. SPE Tract 25, 'Jespersen, *Disputed Points in English Grammar*', 2 Dec. 1926.
20. GGC, p. 124.
21. SPE Tract 26, 24 Mar. 1927.

22. BLib., Dep. Bridges 109, fos. 63, 64, 15 Dec. 1925.
23. Ibid. 109, fos. 59, 60, 11 Mar. 1921.
24. Ibid. 13/2, fos. 113–15, 31 Dec. 1929.
25. Ibid. fo. 116, 4 Jan. 1930.
26. OEDA, MEU/1/36, 4 July 1924.
27. Ibid. 37, 10 July 1924.
28. Kenneth Sisam (1887–1971), b. New Zealand. Educated at Merton College, Oxford. Rhodes Scholar. Assistant to Henry Bradley on *OED*. After illness, worked at Ministry of Food from 1917 until he joined the Press in 1923. Assistant Secretary, 1925. Secretary to the Delegates, 1942.
29. OEDA, MEU/1/39, 8 Nov. 1924.
30. *Glasgow Herald*, 20 Sept. 1924.
31. OEDA, MEU/1/39, 8 Nov. 1924.
32. Ibid. 40.
33. Ibid. 42, 14 Nov. 1924.
34. Ibid. 30, 15 Apr. 1919.
35. Ibid. 2/5, 20 Aug. 1925.
36. Ibid. 1/49, 7 June 1925.
37. Ibid. 52, 17 June 1925.
38. OEDA, SOED/1923/2, 20 July 1923.
39. Ibid. 1924/2, 12 Jan. 1924.
40. Ibid. 3, 14 Jan. 1924.
41. Ibid. 4, 18 Jan. 1924.
42. Ibid. 6, 11 Feb. 1924.
43. *DtoJ*, p. 94.
44. Ibid. p. 84.

16. BL Add. MS 60666, fo. 184, 8 Apr. 1926.
17. OEDA, MEU/2/16, 1 July 1926.
18. OEDA, MEU/2/20, 5 July 1926.
19. OEDA, COD/M/2/6, 16 Jan. 1928.
20. Ibid. 9, 27 Jan. 1928.
21. Ibid. 6, 16 Jan. 1928.
22. Alan Alexander Milne (1882–1956). Educated at Westminster and Trinity College, Cambridge. Worked as assistant editor for *Punch*. Playwright and children's writer.
23. OEDA, MISC/21/13, 6 Oct. 1926.
24. Ibid. 16, 31 Jan. 1927.
25. OEDA, MEU/1/45, 7 Feb. 1925.
26. Ibid. 46, 11 Feb. 1925.
27. OEDA, SOED/1925/2, 27 Nov. 1925.
28. Ibid. 5, 15 Dec. 1925.
29. Ibid. 7, 16 Dec. 1925.
30. OUPA, CPED001259, 13 Dec. 1927.
31. Ibid. 22 May 1927.
32. Ibid. 15 Aug. 1927.
33. Ibid. 15 Nov. 1927.
34. OUPA, HSM Letterbook 133, fo. 167.
35. OUPA, CPED001259, 13 Dec. 1927.
36. OEDA, SOED/1928/12, 19 Sept. 1928.
37. OEDA, PP/1927/291, 27 Dec. 1927.
38. OEDA, PP/1928/16, 13 Jan. 1928.
39. OEDA, SOED/1926/10, 30 July 1926.
40. This letter of 6 Nov. 1926 is reproduced as an illustration in GGC. The original is lost.

✑ Chapter Thirteen ✑

1. OEDA, SOED/1926/10, 30 July 1926.
2. BLib., Dep. Bridges, fos. 63, 64, 15 Dec. 1925.
3. OUPA, HSM Letterbook 123, 25 June 1926.
4. GGC, p. 124.
5. *The Times*, 19 Oct. 1926.
6. *Periodical*, June 1926, p. 123.
7. *TLS*, 10 June 1926.
8. *Review of English Studies*, 2(8), Oct. 1926.
9. *Modern Language Notes*, Mar. 1927, pp. 201–2.
10. *John o' London's Weekly*, 13 Jan. 1934, p. 582.
11. All quoted in the *Periodical*, Feb. 1927.
12. *Methodist Recorder*, quoted in OEDA, MEU/2/29, 28 July 1926.
13. *Periodical*, June 1926, p. 123.
14. GGC, p. 151.
15. Giles Lytton Strachey (1880–1932). Educated at Trinity College, Cambridge. Critic and biographer.

✑ Chapter Fourteen ✑

1. *TLS*, 19 Dec. 1929.
2. GGC, p. 150.
3. OEDA, QOD/1929/8, 27 Dec. 1929.
4. Ibid. 1927/3, 2 May 1927.
5. Ibid. 1928/1, 21 June 1928.
6. Ibid. 2, 3 July 1928.
7. William Alexander Craigie (1867–1957). Educated at St Andrews and Oriel College, Oxford. Began work on *OED* as assistant to James Murray, 1897. Independent editor, 1901–33. Rawlinson and Bosworth Professor of Anglo-Saxon at Oxford, 1916–25. Professor of English, Chicago, 1925–36. Also editor of *Dictionary of American English* and *Dictionary of the Older Scottish Tongue*.
8. OEDA, QOD/1928/3, 5 July 1928.
9. Ibid. 1929/2, 1 Oct. 1929.

10. Ibid. 1, 19 Jan. 1930.
11. Ibid. 4, 21 Feb. 1930.
12. Ibid. 14, 1 May 1930.
13. GGC, p. 150.
14. OEDA, QOD/1930/14, 2 May 1930.
15. Ibid. 13, 9 May 1930.
16. GGC, p. 149.
17. OEDA, QOD/1930/20, 17 Sept. 1930.
18. Ibid. 21, 6 Oct. 1930.
19. OUPA, CPED000015, 20 Nov. 1930.
20. OUPA, HSM Letterbook 137, fo. 752.
21. OUPA, CPED000015, 8 Dec. 1930.
22. Ibid. 12 Dec. 1930.
23. OUPA, HSM Letterbook 138, fo. 770, 23 Mar. 1931.
24. OUPA, CPED000015, 24 Mar. 1931.
25. *DtoJ*, p. 94.
26. OEDA, QOD/1930/19, 13 Aug. 1930.
27. Ibid. 1931/2, 10 Feb. 1931.
28. Ibid. 1, 22 Feb. 1931.
29. Ibid. 7, 4 Mar. 1931.
30. Ibid. 5, 2 Mar. 1931.
31. Ibid. 8, 13 Mar. 1931.
32. Herbert Grenville Le Mesurier (1873–1940). Educated at Wellington and Woolwich. Served in India until retirement in 1922.
33. OEDA, QOD/1931/11, 19 Mar. 1931.
34. Ibid. 30, 22 Aug. 1931.
35. Ibid. 20, 23 July 1931.
36. Ibid. 47, 21 Sept. 1931.
37. Ibid. 57, 27 Sept. 1931.
38. Ibid. 58, 28 Sept. 1931.
39. Ibid. 1932/11, 1 Feb. 1932.
40. Ibid. 1932/13, 26 Mar. 1932.

⚛ Chapter Fifteen ⚛

1. OEDA, QOD/1932/30, 20 Sept. 1932.
2. GGC, p. 153.
3. OEDA, QOD/1932/30, 20 Sept. 1932.
4. OEDA, Additional Letters, 28 Dec. 1933.
5. *TLS*, 19 Jan. 1932.
6. OEDA, EP/FOWLE/8/1, 7 Jan. 1933.
7. OEDA, COD/1932/3/1–5, 11–18 May 1932.
8. *The Times*, 19 July 1932.
9. OEDA, QOD/1932/33, 12 Oct. 1932.
10. Ibid. 1933/4, 14 Mar. 1933.
11. Ibid. 1, 8 Mar. 1933.
12. Ibid. 8, 5 July 1933.
13. OEDA, QOD/1933/9, 4 July 1933.
14. OEDA, QOD/1933/14, 4 Nov. 1933.
15. Ibid. 15, 6 Nov. 1933.
16. Ibid. 16, 6 Nov. 1933.
17. OEDA, ODME/6/18, 27 Dec. 1933.
18. Ibid. 15, 25 Dec. 1933.
19. Ibid. 19, 28 Dec. 1933.
20. OEDA, QOD/1933/21, 14 Jan. 1934.
21. OEDA, ODME/6/19, 28 Dec. 1933.
22. Ibid. 8, 19 Dec. 1933.
23. Ibid. 58, 8 Feb. 1934.
24. *Periodical*, Dec. 1939, p. 97.
25. GGC, p. 157.
26. *The Times*, 28 Dec. 1933.
27. *Sunday Times*, 31 Dec. 1933, p. 11.
28. *Saturday Review of Literature*, 6 Jan. 1934.
29. *John o' London's Weekly*, 13 Jan. 1934, p. 582.
30. *The Times*, 30 Dec. 1933.
31. W. L. S. Churchill. *The Second World War*, v (Cassell, 1951, London), p. 16.

Bibliography

Fowler, H. W.:

More Popular Fallacies (London: Elliot Stock, 1904).

Sentence Analysis (Oxford: Clarendon Press, 1906).

Si Mihi! (London: Brown, Langham, 1907); reissued as *If Wishes were Horses* (London: George Allen & Unwin, 1929).

Between Boy and Man (London: Watts, 1908).

A Dictionary of Modern English Usage (Oxford: Clarendon Press, 1926).

Some Comparative Values (Oxford: Blackwell, 1929).

Rhymes of Darby to Joan (London: J. M. Dent & Sons, 1931).

Shorter works:

'Books We Think We have Read' in *The Spectator*, 20 Jan. 1900.

'Outdoor London' in *The Anglo–Saxon Review*, June 1901.

'Irony and Some Synonyms' in *Gentleman's Magazine*, vol. 291, p.378, Oct. 1901.

'Quotation' in *Longman's Magazine*, vol.37, p.241, Jan. 1901.

'On Hyphens, 'Shall' & 'Will', 'Should' 'Would' in the Newspapers of Today', in Society for Pure English Tract 6 (Oxford: Clarendon Press, 1921).

'Note on "*as to*" ', in SPE Tract 8 (1922).

'Grammatical Inversions', in SPE Tract 10 (1922).

'Metaphor', in SPE Tract 11 (1923).

'Preposition at End', in SPE Tract 14 (1923).

'Split Infinitive, &c.', in SPE Tract 15 (1923).

'Subjunctives', in SPE Tract 18 (1924).

'Notes on *fasci, fascisti, broadcast(ed)*', in SPE Tract 19 (1925).

'Italic, Fused Participles, &c.', in SPE Tract 22 (1925).

'*Ing*', in SPE Tract 26 (1927).

'*Comprise*', in SPE Tract 36 (1932).

Fowler, H. W. and F. G.:

The King's English (Oxford: Clarendon Press, 1906).

The King's English, abridged edn. (Oxford: Clarendon Press, 1908).

Concise Oxford Dictionary (Oxford: Clarendon Press, 1911; 2nd edn., 1929).

Pocket Oxford Dictionary (Oxford: Clarendon Press, 1924).

(trans.), *The Works of Lucian* (Oxford: Clarendon Press, 1905).

Little, W., Fowler, H. W., and Coulson, J., *The Shorter Oxford English Dictionary* (Oxford: Clarendon Press, 1933).

Further Reading:

The Cyclopedia of New Zealand (Wellington: Cyclopedia Co., 1897–1908).

The Residential Attractions of Parkstone, Dorset (Bristol: Clifton, 1934).

Round Tunbridge Wells (London: Marshall Japp & Co., 1881).

Campion, S., *Father* (London: Michael Joseph, 1948).

Churchill, P. and Mitchell, J., *Jennie, Lady Randolph Churchill* (London: Collins, 1974).

Clarke, H. L. and Weech, W. N., *A History of Sedbergh School*, 1525–1925 (Sedbergh: Jackson & Son, 1925).

Bibliography

Coulton, G. G., *Fourscore Years* (Cambridge: Cambridge University Press, 1943).

Elliott, Sir Ivo (ed.), *The Balliol College Register* 1833–1933 (Oxford: 1934).

Ensor, R. C. K., *England* 1870–1914 (Oxford History of England; Oxford: Clarendon Press, 1936).

Fuller, F. W. T., *The History of St Luke's College, Exeter* (Exeter: St Luke's College, Exeter, 1970).

Gardiner, R. Barlow, *The Admission Registers of St Paul's School*, 1876–1905 (London: G Bell, 1906)

James, L. Warwick (ed.), *Marlborough College Register* 1843–1952 (Marlborough: 1952).

Jamieson, A. G. (ed), *A People of the Sea: The Maritime History of the Channel Islands* (London: Methuen, 1986).

Le Huray, C. P. (ed. Uttley, J. C. T.), *The Bailiwick of Guernsey* (London: Hodder & Stoughton, 1969).

Lempriere, R., *The Channel Islands* (London: Hale, 1990).

Liddell Hart, B. H., *History of the First World War* (London: Faber & Faber, 1934).

Lucking, J., *The Great Western at Weymouth* (Newton Abbot: David & Charles, 1971).

Mason, P., *A Shaft of Sunlight* (New Delhi: Vikas Publishing House, c.1978).

Mathieson, *Tunbridge Wells and Tunbridge Directory for* 1867–68 (Tunbridge Wells: R Pelton, 1868).

Michell, A. T., and Higginbottom, G. (eds.), *Rugby School Register* (Rugby: 1901–29).

Moncrieff, A. R. Hope, *Black's Guide to Dorsetshire* (London: A & C Black Ltd., 1921).

Murray, K. M. E., *Caught in the Web of Words* (New Haven, London: Yale University Press, 1977).

Peile, J., *Biographical register of Christ's College* 1505–1905 (Cambridge: Cambridge University Press, 1910, 1913).

Price, R. G. G, *A History of Punch* (London: Collins, 1957).

Rouse, W. H., *A History of Sedbergh School* (London: Duckworth & Co., 1898).

The Sedberghian, the Sedbergh School magazine.

Selfe, S., *Chapters from the History of Rugby School* (Rugby: A J Lawrence, 1910).

Simpson, J. B. Hope, *Rugby Since Arnold* (London: Macmillan, 1967).

Sutcliffe, P., *The Oxford University Press: An Informal History* (Oxford: Clarendon Press, 1978).

Thomson, J Radford, *Pelton's Illustrated Guide to Tunbridge Wells* (Tunbridge Wells: 7th edn., 1876).

Varley, G. H., *Radium: Its Therapeutic Uses in General Practice* (Oxford: Oxford University Press, 1924).

Walker, T. A., *Admissions to Peterhouse* 1615–1911 (Cambridge: Cambridge University Press, 1912).

Ward, F. W., *The 23rd (Service) Battalion Royal Fusiliers (First Sportsman's)* (London: Sidgwick & Jackson, 1920).

Yates, N., *Anglican Ritualism in Victorian Britain* 1830–1910 (Oxford: Clarendon Press, 1999).

Chronology

1856   Robert Fowler and Caroline Watson married
1858   Henry Watson Fowler born
1859   Charles Robert Fowler born

1861   Alexander Wilson Fowler and Jessie Marian Wills born
1864   Edward Seymour Fowler born
1865   Edith Caroline Fowler born
1868   Arthur John Fowler born
        Death of Henry Fowler senior

1870   Francis George Fowler born
1871   Henry begins school at Rugby
1873   Herbert Samuel Fowler born
1877   Henry leaves school and goes up to Balliol College, Oxford
1879   Deaths of Robert Fowler and Alexander Wilson Fowler

1881   Henry leaves Oxford and begins his first teaching post at Fettes
1882   Henry leaves Fettes for his first permanent teaching post at Sedbergh School
1886   Death of Edward Seymour Fowler in Colombo

1892   Gordon Coulton arrives to join the staff at Sedbergh
1895   Death of Caroline Fowler
1899   Henry leaves Sedbergh and moves to London
        Frank Fowler moves to Guernsey
        Beginning of the Boer War

1900   Henry joins Inns of Court Volunteers
1901   Death of Queen Victoria
1902   End of the Boer War
1903   Henry leaves London and settles in Guernsey
        Competition in *The Times* to celebrate the tenth edition of the *Encyclopaedia Britannica*
        Marriage of Arthur John Fowler and Ada Lemarchand
1904   Publication of *More Popular Fallacies*
        Henry and Frank make their first approach to the University Press at Oxford about their
            translation of Lucian
1905   Translation of the Dialogues of Lucian published
        Death of Herbert Samuel Fowler
1906   *The King's English* and *Sentence Analysis* published
        Henry and Frank begin work on their first Oxford dictionaries
1907   *Si Mihi!* published
1908   Publication of *Between Boy and Man* and the abridged version of *The King's English*
        Marriage of Henry Watson Fowler and Jessie Marian Wills

1911   Publication of the *Concise Oxford Dictionary*
        Marriage of Francis George Fowler and Una Jane Mary Maud Godfrey
1914   Death of Edith Caroline Fowler
        Beginning of First World War
1915   Henry and Frank Fowler enlist in the 23rd Battalion Royal Fusiliers and in December are sent
            to France
1916   Henry discharged from army after being sent back to England suffering from gout
1918   Death of Francis George Fowler from tuberculosis
        End of First World War
1919   Henry and Jessie move to Le Moulin de Haut

Chronology

1921 First publication of Henry's work in the Tracts of the Society for Pure English
1924 Publication of the *Pocket Oxford Dictionary*
1925 Henry and Jessie Fowler leave Guernsey and move to Hinton St George, Somerset
       Death of Arthur Fowler's wife, Ada
1926 Publication of *A Dictionary of Modern English Usage*
1928 Completion of *Oxford English Dictionary*
1929 *Si Mihi!* reissued as *If Wishes Were Horses*
       Publication of 2nd edition of the *Concise Oxford Dictionary* and *Some Comparative Values*
       Death of Charles Robert Fowler

1930 Henry begins work on the proposed *Oxford Dictionary of Modern English*
       Death of Jessie Fowler
1931 Publication of *Rhymes of Darby to Joan*
       H.G. Le Mesurier joins Henry as a collaborator
1932 Arthur Fowler agrees to assist his brother and moves to Hinton St George
1933 Publication of the *Shorter Oxford English Dictionary*
       Death of Henry Watson Fowler
1934 Publication of Gordon Coulton's memoir of Henry as a Society for Pure English Tract
1939 Death of Arthur John Fowler

Index

1. Sub-entries are in alphabetical order, except where **chronological** order is significant. 2. The following abbreviations are used: **AF** = Arthur Fowler; **FF** = Frank Fowler; **HF** = Henry Fowler; **JF** = Jessie Fowler.